3 QUESTIONS
for Today's Jazz Musicians

3 QUESTIONS
for Today's Jazz Musicians

Lilian Dericq

THE CRICKET PUBLISHER OF AURORA
AURORA, NEW YORK

Copyright © 2020 Lilian Dericq

All rights reserved. No part of this publication may be reproduced, stored in a retrieval system, or transmitted, in any form or by any means electronic, chemical, optical, photocopying, recording, or otherwise without prior permission in writing from the publisher.

Published by
The Cricket Publisher of Aurora
261 Main Street, Aurora, NY 13026

ISBN-10: 1-7923-2393-X
ISBN 13: 978-1-7923-2393-5

Pudlach, it's Tuesday morning and I am going to knock at your door . . .

PREFACE

Three Questions for Today's Jazz Musicians

The idea for *Three Questions* is directly related to my discovery, ten years ago, of the book by Pannonica de Koenigswarter, *Three Wishes: An Intimate Look at Jazz Greats*. At the origin of this book is a simple question that the author, a friend and benefactor of numerous jazz musicians, put to Thelonious Monk: "If you were given three wishes to be granted immediately, what would they be?" Monk answered: "First, that my music be successful. Second, that my family be happy. And third, that I'd have a fantastic friend like you." When Pannonica pointed out to him that he already had all three, Thelonious just smiled.

But the story did not end there. Indeed, between 1961 and 1966 many other musicians answered Pannonica these three questions. However, it was not until 2008, thanks to the hard work and remarkable perseverance of her granddaughter, Nadine de Koenigswarter, that their contributions were assembled in a book. Throughout these responses, as I read and reflected my way through them, sometimes at random, sometimes looking for specific musicians, I discovered a special pleasure. Then the idea came to me to contact the great jazz musicians of the 21st century, throughout the world, in order to prolong the adventure. Fifty years after Pannonica, I went to work.

The verb "to work" may be defined differently depending on the context. Should one say work on instrument, or practice one's instrument? It is the same for the verb "to play." Can one work while playing, or rather play while working? I wanted to "play" through this book, and I thank all the musicians who allowed me to work at it with so much pleasure.

As I followed in the footsteps of Pannonica, I chose not to adopt the concept of the three wishes, but to develop my own questions. The first question, potentially utopian, was to ask which musicians, not necessarily contemporaries of each other, the participants would have selected if they had been able to create their own "dream band." The second question was based on their own past, more precisely to recall a memorable moment from their career that they would like to share. The third question asks them to express a wish relating to the future; leaving them complete freedom to choose whatever theme they desired. Some spoke to me of music, some of politics, the environment or health. No restrictions were placed on the length of responses; some musicians were brief, others more eloquent, but from the whole of their answers springs a lovely music, good vibrations, benevolence, all that which makes the world of jazz so engaging.

I started by writing to musicians that I had met or knew personally, all of whom responded. This allowed me to gain the confidence of musicians whom I knew only by reputation, and to convince them to participate. All had read or heard of Pannonica's book, and were aware of the importance this extraordinary woman had in the careers of their illustrious predecessors. This is how the 334 testimonies in this book come from musicians ranging in age from 28 to 100 years, coming from 42 countries, and playing 28 different instruments. Thanks to the existence of email and social media, it was very easy to contact all the musicians, no matter what their countries of residence, without having to meet them. I am especially pleased to mention the names of musicians who participated in Pannonica's book and are also present in this one: Benny Golson, Charles McPherson, Jimmy Heath, Lou

Donalson, Louis Hayes, Ramsey Lewis, Richard Davis, Ron Carter, Roy McCurdy and Terry Gibbs.

Since the era when Pannonica de Koenigswarter compiled her book, the world of jazz has changed enormously: musicians devoted to jazz are found all over the world, giving their music a new and impressive quality and dynamism. I hope that you, the reader, will appreciate the responses contained in this book, and, perhaps, in reading certain among them, you will feel the desire to discover the musical universe of many new musicians.

Many thanks to all the musicians and agents who so generously gave of their time to participate in this project for our great pleasure.

The three questions asked of the musicians:

1. What musicians, from 1900 onwards, would have made up your "dream band?" You would be one of the musicians in this "dream band."

2. What is one of the most memorable musical events of your career so far?

3. What is your wish for the twenty-first century?

Aaron Parks piano, 1983 USA

1 Dream band is so tough! Okay, I'll try. This would be a large and perhaps somewhat unwieldy band but I'd love to hear it! Charlie Haden: bass; Elvin Jones: drums; Bill Frisell: guitar; Alice Coltrane: organ; Joe Zawinul: synthesizer; Miles Davis: trumpet and keys; Ornette Coleman: alto saxophone; Warne Marsh: tenor saxophone; Stevie Wonder: vocals and any other instruments he wants to play; Hermeto Pascoal: whatever he wants.

2 My most memorable musical experience? Well, I have a notoriously terrible memory, so I'd probably have to say that it's the last gig I played. There were definitely some experiences that were either beautiful or hilarious (or some combination of the two), but right now I couldn't pick one out. Or perhaps I could but just won't. You'll never know.

3 I wish that we would undergo a collective evolution of consciousness to truly realize that we are all here together on this tiny rock surrounded by infinite space, that separation based on 'nation' and 'race' is illusory, and that we have the resources and the technology to make it possible for many more human beings to explore their innate potential in creative, fun and fulfilling ways. I wish we could find ways to organize the affairs of this planet in a way that actually makes sense for more of us here. Or, less idealistically, a donut that doesn't make you fat.

Adam Cruz drums, 1970 USA

1 Dream bands:
- Thelonious Monk, John Coltrane, Bobby Hutcherson, Paul Chambers;
- Ornette Coleman, Wayne Shorter, Charlie Haden;
- Miles Davis, Jimi Hendrix, Jaco Pastorius, Giovanni Hidalgo, Orestes Vilató.

2 Hearing (and playing) my own compositions for the first time as a band leader, realized with a fantastic group of musicians at the Jazz Gallery in NYC.

3 Less violence. More Love.

Adam Holzman keyboards, 1958 USA

1 It was too hard to decide, so I created a fantasy big band! :-)
 Chaka Khan and Peter Gabriel: vocals; Miles Davis: trumpet; Wayne Shorter: tenor sax; Brecker Brothers: horn section; Clara Rockmore: theremin; John Scofield: guitar; Allan Holdsworth: guitar; Jeff Beck: guitar; Darryl Jones: bass; Jaco Pastorius: bass; Steve Gadd: drums; Dennis Chambers: drums; Mino Cinelu: percussion; + me on keyboards!

2 I played an outdoor concert with Miles Davis near the walls of the old city of Jerusalem, in 1987. I remember looking across the stage and seeing Miles bent over in his classic 'question mark' position, with the moon right above him. I thought to myself, "Oh man, I'll remember this for my whole life." Amazing moment.

3 Here are three wishes:
- I hope that the Internet stops taking advantage of musicians and starts paying them (I'm talking about free streaming services like YouTube, Spotify, etc., etc.).
- On the political front, it is my sincere wish that Trump be impeached and taken to jail.
- And . . . personally, to keep playing!

Adam Nussbaum drums, 1955 USA

1 Very challenging question . . . I have been very fortunate to play with many of my heroes. If I could jump into a time machine, I would've loved the chance to have played with some of the past masters (Louis Armstrong, Lester Young, Charlie Parker, Monk, Bud Powell, John Coltrane, Jimi Hendrix a.o.) who helped to define this art form. That would be a very big list. :-)

2 It's hard to pick just ONE. There have been so many wonderful events! . . . Some beautiful moments with John Abercrombie, Jay Anderson, Richie Beirach, Bob Berg, Jerry Bergonzi, Seamus Blake, the Breckers, Bob Brookmeyer, Joey Calderazzo, Steve Cardenas, Don Cherry, Todd Coolman, Albert Dailey, Eliane Elias, Gil Evans, Carol Fredette, Jimmy Garrison, Stan Getz, Dizzy Gillespie, Benny Golson, Eddie Gomez, Joe Henderson, Terumasa

Hino, Marc Johnson, Vic Juris, Kenny Kirkland, Dave Liebman, Joe Lovano, Sheila Jordan, Ron McClure, Jim McNeely, James Moody, Oz Noy, Gene Perla, Nate Radley, Sonny Rollins, Renee Rosnes, John Scofield, Steve Swallow, Ohad Talmor, "Toots" Thielemans, TIG, McCoy Tyner, Gary Versace, Kenny Wheeler, Phil Woods. I've learned so much from ALL my experiences. I'm looking forward to more.

3 I pray for peace, compassion and understanding. This goes for humanity in general. I really hope that this music will be given the respect that it deserves and warrants.

Airto Moreira   percussions, 1941 Brazil

1 Hermeto Pascoal: keyboards; Ron Carter: bass; Joe Farrel: sax and flute; Vinnie Colaiuta: drums; Flora Purim: vocal.

2 Miles Davis at the Isle of Wight.

3 To continue my evolution as a human being and to play for people around the world.

Alan Broadbent   piano, 1947 New Zealand

1 Do you mean a big band? Let's see ...

Trumpets: Louis Armstrong, Freddie Hubbard, Dizzy, Chet Baker; trombones: J.J. Johnson, Bill Watrous, Bob Brookmeyer, Curtis Fowlkes; alto sax: Bird, Lee Konitz; tenor sax: Lester Young, Coltrane, Bari; sax: Harry Carney; piano: I guess me, but Bud Powell best; guitar: Wes Montgomery; bass: Charlie Haden; drums: Philly Joe Jones.

2 Recording my piece Developing Story for Trio and Large Orchestra at Abbey Road, produced by Ralf Kemper, conducted by me.

3 World peace and respect for each other, the end of poverty and deprivation, the end of Donald Trump.

Alan Pasqua   piano, 1952 USA

1 Dave Holland, Paul Motian, Larry Young, Roy Eldridge, Paul Gonsalves, Gary Bartz and Sheila Jordan.

2 Three events actually. First, playing George Russell's incredible piece, *Living Time*, at Carnegie Hall, 1974. George was conducting, and that is where he introduced me to Tony Williams who subsequently asked me to join the Lifetime.

   The second was a recent guest performance with the WDR big band and Vince Mendoza, who arranged a lot of my compositions. An amazing band with Vince's touch made it a memorable evening. Lastly, composing and playing the solo piano underpinnings for Bob Dylan's Nobel Prize acceptance speech.

3 More peace, kindness and compassion throughout the world. Less building, pollution, traffic impatience, selfishness and ugliness. More beauty. Let nature do its thing.

Aldo Romano drums, 1941 Italy

1 Playing in duo with Joe Lovano.

2 Played with Keith Jarrett.

3 To be able to play more.

Alex Acuña percussions, 1944 Peru

1 Coltrane Quartet with Elvin, McCoy and Jimmy would have been my favorite dream band to play with.

2 Weather Report, of course, was my memorable musical experience. With Manolo and Jaco in it.

3 Yes, my blessings have been accomplished already in this 21st century:
- Playing with all great composers on major movie sound tracks in Hollywood.
- Also playing sometimes with the L.A. Philharmonic with conductor Gustavo Dudamel.

Ali Jackson   drums, 1976 USA

1 I will make it a big band. There are too many great musicians in Jazz, unlike other genres of music. The genres that are very popular and economically viable lack the density of high quality musicianship and artistry. The most prolific composer and band leader of our music, Edward Kennedy "Duke Ellington; piano: Marcus Roberts or Mary Lou Williams; bass: Paul Chambers; guitar: Wes Montgomery; trumpet: Clark Terry, Louis Armstrong, Kenny Dorham, Ryan Kisor; trombone: Tricky Sam Nanton, J.J. Johnson, Curtis Fuller, Vincent Gardner; tenor sax: Lester Young, James Carter; alto sax: Charlie Parker, Ted Nash; bass sax: Pepper Adams; vocalist Sarah Vaughan or Jon Hendricks; tap dancer: Sandman Sims or Gregory Hines.

2 Twelve years with Jazz at Lincoln Center Orchestra, learning and sharing the essence of the traditions of the music we call Jazz. Having a daily connection with 14 other dedicated, talented and optimistic musicians that believe in music traditions and who utilize them. Having the platform to share that collectivity with the world.

3 People relearn how to listen to music. People relearn how to connect to humanity. People relearn how to absorb a feeling.

Anat Fort piano, 1970 Israel

1. I have no one "dream band." I have, and have always had, many musicians I'd like to play with. Some of them I played with, some I still do. Many are gone, some I still hope to collaborate with one day.
    Some examples would be: Bill Frisell, Brian Blade, Jim Black, Pat Metheny, Louis Sclavis, Anouar Brahem, Jean-Louis Matinier, Sting, and the list goes on and on . . .

2. I was very blessed and honored to play with my idol, drummer Paul Motian, the last gig he played in his life. I only played with Paul on my record, and twice more in live settings. It was amazing and special every time. I didn't know he was ill when I played with him for the last time. It was an evening I will never forget: Paul was very happy and sounded wonderful as always. A couple of months later he passed away — and that's when I found out that he canceled all gigs after that last one we played together. That thought still brings chills up my spine!

3. The 21st century moves very fast. It would be nice to not forget that there are other speeds to go with in life. Other ways to look at things not just in a linear fashion. I wish that for myself, everybody around me and certainly for everyone who listens to music deeply,

to remember to take our time and space with everything we do, not get distracted by the ever-growing noise around us and not to take anything, ever, for granted.

Anders Jormin   bass, 1957 Sweden

1. A very hypothetical question and, of course, something I have never thought of . . . ! With a smile and not thinking of how the musicians would actually go together, I would say: Elis Regina, John Coltrane, Joe Zawinul, Esperanza Spalding and Jack DeJohnette. With Bix Beiderbecke as guest soloist and composer, together with Maria Schneider. I would be the promoter . . . :-)

2. The warm tension and expectations in the room playing improvised solo bass in front of curious students at Kim Won Guyn Music Academy in Pyongyang, North Korea. The very first time improvised music was ever heard at this school.

3. That music itself — an absolutely positive force that by its nature opens for the truth and reflective meeting between people, a meeting where also listening is essential — regain its position as an important humanistic subject for all students in schools and in general education. All over the world. Including my own country.

André Ceccarelli drums, 1946 France

1 Throughout my career and to this day, I have had the chance to make music with hundreds of wonderful musicians. "My dream band" would be made up of all those friends who are on earth or very high in the sky.

2 I have thousands of beautiful memories, but since I have to choose, I would say the concerts we gave, with my father Jean, my brother Jean-Paul, my son Regis and myself. Four perfectly synchronized drums, and with friends. It was magical.

3 That all religions vanish.

Andreas Schaerer vocal, 1976 Switzerland

1 I am in the convenient situation of being surrounded by many "dream bands", nowadays. All these various projects I am playing right now are so enriching! Jazz is happening here and now, so I am more than happy to play with all these fantastic, contemporary musicians. But of course, I would have loved to have met Igor Stravinsky! Having a chat about music, watching him rehearse and conduct one of his pieces. It would have been great to have played in one of Miles Davis' bands or to have been on tour with Frank Zappa. That's the beautiful thing about Jazz and music in general, it is influenced by the past with all its masters, mentors and heroes, and echoes these influences through a contemporary perspective.

2 There are some moments I will never forget! Like the fully improvised concert I played together with Bobby McFerrin. Or when my first symphony was performed at the newly opened — and sold out — Elbphilharmonie, with a full orchestra on stage. Another memorable moment was in France, when we played in a grand, old Amphitheater. After our last encore, the audience started softly humming one of our pieces and did not stop until we came back on stage. All these experiences and many more fill me with a great inner peace.

3 There are no simple answers to complex global and political problems! But there is an answer, that can make a huge difference in our daily lives: do not let fear control our being! Stay open for the unknown, the new, the strange. In Jazz, musicians understood from the very beginning that other cultures, different behaviors or foreign languages are no reason to be afraid, but a rich source of inspiration!

Andrew Cyrille   drums, 1939 USA

1 Duke Ellington: piano; Charlie Parker: alto saxophone; John Coltrane: tenor saxophone; Sonny Rollins: tenor saxophone; Dizzy Gillespie: trumpet; Oscar Pettiford: bass and Andrew Cyrille: drums.

2 The Great Concert of Cecil Taylor: *Nuits de la Foundation Maeght*, in St. Paul De Vence, July 29, 1969, featuring Cecil Taylor (piano), Jimmy Lyons (alto saxophone), Sam Rivers (tenor saxophone, and Andrew Cyrille on drums. (Shandar Records, Vol. 1, France).

3 As long as possible, for me to continue growing in music, and peace and love in the world — music and musicians being one of the resources helping to bring it among people and nations.

Andy Laverne   piano, 1947 USA

1. My dream band would consist of Woody Shaw, Joe Henderson, Bobby Hutcherson, Dave Holland, Jack DeJohnette, and lucky me on piano!
2. One of the most memorable musical events of my career, so far, is when I played at the Lionel Hampton Jazz Festival with my trio — consisting of myself, Brian Bromberg and Elvin Jones!
3. Humanity's continued progress and evolution to a peaceful, healthy world filled with music (jazz of course).

Anna Maria Jopek   vocal, 1970 Poland

1. I feel like I've reached my lifelong limits by singing with the most Absolute Artists of our Time . . . now it's rather a wish to be able to create by inspiration of all. They gave to me, my real Masters . . . but well . . . there is one surreal wish I do sometimes have. I dream that I'm allowed to sit a few minutes and have a coffee with John Coltrane. No talk. Just be for a moment around Him . . .

2   It was far away from any studio or stage. Far away from any "career" in fact, but being in Real Creation . . . The moment of labor when my Child was born. In unbearable pain I heard my own cry. Stronger than any sound I've ever heard . . . That minute I knew who I was and for what the Sound was given to me.

3   I love to read antic thinkers, so I'd gladly follow those wiser than me — I care for the value of my wish. I repeat after Plato: please stay in the state of TRUTH, BEAUTY and GOOD. (These three were from Plato, one in fact, same value. That beauty must be real and will always make You strong.)

The Human in Truth, Beauty and Good is unbreakable. I wish we would keep those values . . . Especially in the Mission of Music.

Antonio Farao   piano, 1965 Italy

1 Like so many musicians, I love Debussy, Stravinsky, Bartók, etc., in short, all that period that has greatly characterized the music we play. I could add other geniuses such as M. Davis, J. Coltrane, B. Evans, M. Tyner, C. Corea, W. Shorter, B. Golson, C. Parker, T. Monk, H. Hancock, T. Williams, J. Williams, etc., that have influenced my way of playing, assimilating their styles. My dream team would actually be the quintet of Miles Davis with Tony Williams, Ron Carter, Herbie Hancock, Wayne Shorter. A band that revolutionized the way of playing in the sixties, especially through its interplay.

2 In fact I could mention several . . . But the one that marked, in a sense, my destiny to choose this path, was certainly the first concert I attended at the Teatro Lirico, in Milan, with Ella Fitzgerald accompanied by the Big Band of Count Basie; I was just 6 years old, the spectators were incredulous: how could a child of that age understand this music? . . . I still remember perfectly that incredible sound that I had never heard before . . .

I would also mention the Martial Solal Award, won in 1998. It was a nice moment that I shared with my colleagues and friends.

3 The desire to enhance and spread more and more, in the world, this music that unites different cultures and breaks down every boundary. I think it's a fact to be taken seriously, even as an example of peace and respect in human relationships.

Antonio Hart saxophone, 1968 USA

1 (a) Woody Shaw, me, Gary Thomas, Roy Haynes, Rodney Whitaker, Mulgrew Miller.

(b) Miles Davis, me, Branford Marsalis, Marcus Miller, Dennis Chamber, Herbie Hancock.

2 Playing with Dizzy Gillespie at the Blue Note in the early 90s. I was terrified because I realized Charlie Parker stood right where I was, next to the Master. There was nothing I would play to impress him because he created the language. I think Master Gillespie saw I was scared, so he started drinking this huge bottle of water. He drank the entire bottle while the audience started to laugh. After, he looked at me and smiled, and without words told me to relax and enjoy the experience. This was weeks before he passed, and one of the most important moments for me. I'm so happy that this has been documented.

3 I have so many wishes for the future, but first I really pray for people to be mentally, physically, and SPIRITUALLY healthy. I'd love for future musicians to LOVE what they do. It's not about the recordings, gigs, travel, etc. It's about trying to add your story to this great legacy. Also, it's a gift to bring positive energy to people that might not feel that way. Always show your joy for this blessing, and this will bring people to you and your music. Music should express your beliefs, desires, and dreams. Study the entire history, and then add your God-given voice to it.

Antonio Sanchez   drums, 1971 Mexico

1 Miles Davis on trumpet and as a band leader, Wayne Shorter and Chris Potter on saxophone, Herbie Hancock and Chick Corea on piano, Pat Metheny and John Scofield on guitars, Scott Colley and Matt Brewer on bass. Me on drums. I know, just a little greedy . . .

2 Having collaborated with Alejandro González Iñarritu in creating the soundtrack for his Oscar-winning film *Birdman*. I've worked with incredible musicians throughout my life, but collaborating with somebody at such a highly creative level, in a completely different art form, was truly inspiring. The whole experience was highly influential and life changing for me.

3 First of all, taking money out of politics. It's a cancer that has grown into a deadly tumor. Then, to have smart, kind and empathetic people running the world. Politicians that truly want the best for the majority of the people and not just for the privileged ones. There are too many mean-spirited and divisive demagogues out there who are eroding our society as we know it, and they're stealing it blind in the process. I would love to see some truth and substantive change in my lifetime.

Ari Hoenig   drums, 1973 USA

1 Anything with, Tigran Hamasyan, Gilad Hekselman, Matt Penman, Jean-Michel Pilc, Jacques Schwartz-Bart, Tivon Pennicott, Orlando le Fleming, Nitai Hershkovits, Eden Ladin, Johannes Weidenmüller, François Moutin.

2 Recording my album *The Pauper and the Magician*, playing at Carnegie Hall with Herbie Hancock.

3 To continue to perform and record my own music with such magical players. Also, to record and tour with my nonet.

Three Questions

Arild Andersen bass, 1945 Norway

1 What about a sextet with Miles Davis: trumpet; Lester Young: tenor sax; Bill Frisell: guitar; Bill Evans: piano; Brian Blade, Philly Jo Jones or Jack DeJohnette: drums; Arild Andersen: bass!

2 It is probably a concert in 1981, at the Norwegian Molde Festival. Actually I was asked to put a "dream band" together for the festival, and the line-up was Bill Frisell on guitar, John Taylor on piano, Alphonse Mouzon on drums, and Arild Andersen on bass. The concert was released on ECM. Then again, I've just played two concerts with a 12-string from Trondheimsolistene as soloist . . . It was something I will remember. It is interesting to notice, as a friend said: "Now you are over 70 and one of your most memorable concerts was only 14 days ago!!"

3 Of course, there are very important wishes for the world, but if we keep this to music ; I hope interplay, improvisation and communication between musicians on stage and with the audience will continue to be the most important thing.

Arturo Sandoval trumpet, 1949 Cuba

1. Piano: Oscar Peterson; bass: Niels-Henning Ørsted Pedersen; drums: Buddy Rich; percussion: Tata Güines; sax: Michael Brecker.
2. May 1977 – the first time I played with Dizzy Gillespie.
3. Complete World Peace.

Aydin Esen piano and keyboards, 1962 Turkey

1. Miroslav Vitous, Bob Moses, Dave Liebman, Woody Shaw, Mick Goodrick, Karajan, EIC (Ensemble Intercontemporain).
2. Concours International de Paris in 1989... There was a little secret mission going on about that week: it wasn't the winning for me, but how I was able to portray my new music swimming along in all the things we love in contemporary modern music and jazz, which is how I grew up. I was challenging the jury, in my own silly way, but, seriously, especially Mr. Hodeir whom I had great respect for. How fearlessly and rightfully too, I thought, he trashed some of 20th century's great composers and put Jean Barraqué on top, as I completely heard and felt and knew while I was reading it, years before... After my performance, I see someone running towards my room in the backstage: "that's Hodeir" I said to myself... He hugged me and leaned toward my ears gently and said in a somewhat

intense way: "It's impossible how and what you played. Oh my! Thank God, finally I heard it." That for me was the secret mission accomplished . . .

3 The most important thing would be quitting the standard approach of chord changes where almost everyone plays the same thing. Past masters did their best but times are different now . . . One must study even 100 times harder than Mozart did or Oscar Peterson or Henri Dutilleux or Brian Ferneyhough . . . and make it really accessible somehow. Regular people and, more importantly, the bookers of music must educate themselves even more . . . dig deeper, find youngsters who are killing themselves to get a chance to make a point . . . the maximal is not the answer . . . Where is the music? That is the question I will always ask . . . simplicity with silent surgical

operations, combined with great taste. The smart use of technology/ electronics must also be there as they have always been with us since the birth of them. Our new 21st century demands a lot . . . Going back to acoustic or bringing back Stevie Wonder or Earth, Wind and Fire simply won't do but may help and show up sometimes to make us smile and appreciate the past. In short, that one music has all the music in it, giving pleasures to everyone and kindly, also, educating them . . . Today's jazz is too smelly for my taste, missing lots of important elements. On the other hand, today's contemporary Classical/electronic music is sometimes too fastidious and advanced for most people. Also it may sound strange and almost primitive for such complex art . . . the missing sense is that it doesn't sound like ONE music . . . We must gather and become one body for our beloved planet in everything . . . That includes all art and sciences . . . We need some dazzling moves between harmonic changes with incredible taste and those magical echoes will resolve in new ways of single note playing powers . . . Learn more, hear and respond better, hopefully resonate sensitively and listen and work on trusting more in-harmony, and musical cosmos will ever extend.

All musicians famous or not will have to sit down, once again, and study harder for the sake of future generations . . . We must leave them real fresh stuff, instead of leftovers. Wishing these issues of our time will get results soon among all contemporary musicians and composers and agents; realizing there is still lots of room for improvement. The next century is here but the real next level may take some time . . .

Baptiste Trotignon   piano, 1974 France

1 Let's see now . . . You wouldn't necessarily have to come up with an unlikely configuration, so let's say: Miles Davis, etc.
2 My piano lessons when I was a child!
3 That it be less rich and turbulent than the twentieth century; that it SLOW DOWN.

Barre Phillips   bass, 1934 USA

1. A quartet — Urs Leimgruber: saxophone; Jacques Demierre: piano; Thomas Lehn: analogue synthesizer, and me on bass.
2. Playing for a week under Leonard Bernstein, with Don Ellis and Joe Cucuso as soloists, with the New York Philharmonic in 1964.

3 My deep wish is that, before this century is over, music making has gotten to the point where we are no longer asked the question: "Do you play by ear or read music?"

Barry Altschul   drums, 1943 USA

1 There is not one band that I would consider my dream band. Though there are a few bands, I would have liked to play with in different eras of the music:
- Earl Hines, Louis Armstrong, Coleman Hawkins, and Jimmy Blanton;
- Charlie Parker, Dizzy Gillespie, Bud Powell, Ray Brown, Jimmy Slyde (taps);
- Miles Davis, John Coltrane, Eric Dolphy, Thelonious Monk, Charles Mingus;
- Ornette Coleman, Sam Rivers, Albert Ayler, George Lewis, Muhal Richard Abrams, Dave Holland. These are some of my dream bands.

2 A concert in Berlin in 1965 or 1966 with Paul Bley and either Kent Carter or Mark Levinson playing bass. We were improvising in a way that could be called "stream of consciousness" style, and we were "in the zone" when I had an out-of-body experience where I was able to see and hear the band, as if I was in the audience while playing, or so it seemed.

3 Peace, understanding, and acceptance of all people, their culture and beliefs.

Béla Fleck   banjo, 1958 USA

1 That's a tough one, let's make it interesting! Benny Goodman with Stanley Clarke, Paul Desmond, Oscar Peterson, Terence Blanchard, and Carter Beaufort. This is a totally bizarre band. I can't wait to hear us.

2 I would have to say my trip to Africa is one of the big ones. I went for 6 weeks to interact with great acoustic musicians, and it was incredible. I would also say playing in a duo with Chick Corea is right up there too. I learn so much from experiences like these.

3 I hope great live music continues to be celebrated, and that instrumental ability is considered meaningful as time goes on. I also hope that the players who attain high artistic levels can find an audience and make a living at it, so they can pursue their ideals full time.

Ben Sidran   piano, 1943 USA

1 My dream would have been to sit in with Horace Silver's 1959 band with Blue Mitchell, Junior Cook, Gene Taylor and Roy Brooks.

2 Performing at the tribute concert to Eddie Jefferson that was held in 1980 in Carnegie Hall, New York, with myself along side of Dizzy Gillespie, James Moody, Richie Cole, The Manhattan Transfer, Bobby McFerrin, Jon Hendricks and more. It was the first time I ever sang without sitting behind the piano — it was a duet with Tim Hauser on "What's This."

3 Peace

Benjamin Koppel   saxophone, 1974 Denmark

1 Duke Ellington, Elvin Jones, Billie Holiday, John Coltrane, Earl Bostic, Langston Hughes, Marvin Gaye, Oscar Pettiford, Jimi Hendrix and Hazel Scott.

2 The continuous work with our trio Koppel/Colley/Blade Collective with Scott Colley, Brian Blade and myself, including our upcoming releases: a trio album and an album with a trio and symphony orchestra.

3 More tolerance, more care for the climate, less war, less selfishness, less focus on economic issues.

Benjamin Wendel   saxophone, 1976 Canada

1 Well, I'm not sure this would be a good band, but these are the musicians I would have loved to play and learn from: Django Reinhardt, Charlie Parker, Miles Davis, Thelonious Monk, Tony Williams, Jaco Pastorius.

2 Playing the Village Vanguard with my band for the first time. It changed me and I will always look back on that memory as one of the most joyful and powerful experiences of my musical life.

3 That somehow we find a way not to destroy all the resources of earth, including our natural habitat and all its creatures on land and sea. I think there is a battle going on between the best and worst qualities of humankind, and we will see the outcome in our lifetime. I believe art is one of the ways we reveal our better selves, and hope that it inspires people from all cultures and countries to work more together to solve these global issues.

Benny Golson   saxophone, 1929 USA

1 Not that these notables would all be in one band, but candidates for any band: Louis Armstrong, Art Tatum, Oscar Petiford, Sid Catlett, Coleman Hawkins, J.J. Johnson, Dizzy Gillespie, Miles Davis, Art Farmer, Stan Getz, Freddie Hubbard, Lee Morgan, Ron Carter, Elvin Jones, Roy Haynes, Bill Evans, Dexter Gordon, Gerry Mulligan, Bud Powell, Curtis Fuller, Duke Ellington, Count Basie, Thelonious Monk, Charlie Mingus, Philly Joe Jones, Charlie Parker, John Coltrane, Sonny Rollins, Milt Jackson, Lionel Hampton, Joe Pass, Kenny Burrell, Hank Mobley, Kenny Dorham, Ray Bryant, Horace Silver, Jimmy Heath, Kenny Baron, Rufus Reed, Mulgrew Miller, Oscar Peterson, Wynton Marsalis, Gene Krupa, Jon Faddis, Wayne Shorter, Bob Brookmeyer, Johnny Hodges.

2 Playing with Art Blakey every night as a member of The Jazz Messengers (Lee Morgan, Bobby Timmons, Jymie Merit, and Art Blakey) was heavenly. This man did not know how *NOT* to swing. He endlessly took the mind and the heart to another level at will — and yet he was completely non-academic with no formal training whatsoever. He couldn't even read the music we played! Yet he had the incredible ability to remember even the most complicated things inherent to the ongoing music. The memory of him still has a grip on my psyche. There was no other quite like Art Blakey. He was the greatest experience of my career.

Though not totally musical, coming to know both Steven Spielberg and Tom Hanks, and having them as personal friends is fantastic. In the end, they are just ordinary people. Steven created a film about ME — *The Terminal*. They both put together a video congratulating me as I was being honored at the Kennedy Center a few years ago. All of this happened because when Steven was a college student, unknown to me, he used to come to hear me perform. He told me that "I Remember Clifford" was his favorite composition from my pen.

Growing up in Philadelphia with John Coltrane, both as aspiring teenagers, was wonderful. We were as brothers; we did everything together — even preparing for our first frightful participation in a local jam session. "Suppose they call a tune we don't know," we thought.

Playing and knowing Dizzy Gillespie was completely enlightening.

3 My wish for the twenty-first century — and beyond — is that we, progenitors of the music we lovingly call jazz, never lose the curiosity of what lies behind that metaphoric door in our creative lives. Our discovery gives us authoritative entry into the embracing arms of the future where we find our names etched on its breast. Moving ahead and discovering is always essential.

Benny Green piano, 1963 USA

1 My dream band from the 20th century would be Lee Morgan, Dexter Gordon, Sonny Clark, Paul Chambers and Art Blakey — me on piano? Well, that would indeed be a dream!

2 One of the most memorable events for me was when Lewis Nash and I joined the original Oscar Peterson Trio (O.P., Herb Ellis and Ray Brown) onstage at Town Hall in NYC; not only for the unspeakable honor, but because this scenario, which for most anyone would be the most frightening thing to do, became some of the most fun I've ever had with my clothes on. Two pianos onstage, and Oscar showed so much real love to me that we were laughing, and it felt like he was literally carrying me in swing.

3 My wish for the 21st century is that the world finds a way to get rid of Donald Trump as soon as possible, that he be disempowered from hurting humanity any further, and that the young people of today, whose lives are already becoming dedicated to straight-ahead Jazz and bebop, carry the music ever onward to the following generations, with honor and heart. Jazz is forever!

Benoît Delbecq   piano, 1966 France

1. Ornette Coleman + James P. Johnson + Petter Eldh + Gerald Cleaver.
2. A solo piano concert at the Festival Bleu sur Seine, in 2004, on an extraordinary piano at the foyer of the Théâtre du Châtelet (Paris).
3. The disappearance of all fascism.

Bill Carrothers   piano, 1964 USA

1. There already was a dream band, the Miles Davis quintet of about 1965-1968. I guess I could fill in for Herbie. Not so sure if the other four guys would be happy about that.
2. My favorite musical thing that I've been a part of was the *Armistice 1918* project. If only one creative effort of mine could survive to be heard 100 years from now, this would be it.
3. I wish that mankind survive its technological adolescence long enough to see the twenty-second century.

Bill Evans saxophone, 1958 USA

1 Jimi Hendrix on guitar, Miles Davis on trumpet, Elvin Jones on drums, Bill Evans on piano (not me :-).

2 Playing with Miles Davis at Avery Fisher Hall, NYC, 1981 – our first big gig after playing the club "kix", our first gig in Boston, the previous week. It was rather surreal playing in front of a large audience for the first time, and doing it with Miles Davis. It was larger than life. Miles was my friend at that point and he made me feel very accepted. He said: "You belong here. Have fun!"

3 I have always been an advocate of "No Boundaries" music. I have always been inspired to combine different kinds of music and write what I hear in the process. For instance: jazz with Americana, folk with funk, things of that nature. All created with a "jazz influence" which is where I come from. It opens the door for so much innovation and freshness with the music. You hear things you never heard before. You play differently. You write different melodies. This is what gives so-called "jazz" the possibility of growth. Many open-minded jazz musicians are afraid of the concept, and this is astonishing to me. How was jazz created in the first place? Spending your life learning how to play jazz gives you the ability to say so much. So get up there and say it. There is no need to put on the brakes on innovation and stop with traditional jazz. We all love and play traditional jazz, but some of us would like to allow it to grow. Traditional jazz was created by musicians willing to take chances.

Bill Frisell guitar, 1951 USA

1 The most gigantic orchestra made up of all the wonderful musicians past and present. I love the way music is shared, passed along, and becomes a part of us. It's not a dream. It's real.

2 From the first notes I ever tried to play, it's been like one big long giant extraordinary gig. One song. Still going on.

3 A long time ago John Cage thought it would be a good idea if we stopped everything and listened to one another. I think that would be great. If we could all stop and LISTEN maybe we could begin to try figuring out what's going on.

Bill Mays piano, 1944 USA

1 Bassist Red Mitchell, drummer Lewis Nash, soprano/tenor sax and flute player Dick Oatts, trumpeter Clifford Brown, alto saxist Phil Woods, guitarist Peter Sprague, percussionist Duduka Da Fonseca, and second keyboardist (rhodes, synths, etc.) Lyle Mays.

2 The U.S. jazz community at Django d'Or in Paris in 1997 (where I played Horace Silver's "Summer in Central Park"), and, if I may add one more, the 2010 duo CD I made with alto saxophonist Phil Woods, *Phil & Bill,* and being in his band for several years.

3 An end to partisan in-fighting politics in the U.S., full cooperation between the U.S. and all countries to reverse global climate change, an end to world hunger, and total worldwide nuclear disarmament.

Billy Child piano, 1957 USA

1 In terms of my "dream band," there really is no "one" band that I prefer over another. It really depends on the music and who understands the vision of the music. I have to say that I have already played with this dream band, in one manifestation or another. Drums: Brian Blade, Eric Harland, Antonio Sanchez, Michael Baker, Vinnie Colaiuta, Smitty Smith. Bass: Scott Colley, Jimmy Johnson, John Pattitucci, Robert Hurst. Saxophone: Joe Henderson, George Coleman, Wayne Shorter, Steve Wilson, Bob Sheppard, Chris Potter

2 Probably my favorite musical experience was in 2005 at Disney Concert Hall. I wasn't a performer but my composition was being performed. It was a piece I wrote for the Los Angeles Master Chorale, called "The Voices of Angels." The text is made of six poems from children in the Terezen concentration camp, written around 1942. The poetry deals with the harrowing experience of being in the camp (most of the children died of typhus) and I found it incredibly moving and felt that I had to set it to music. So I composed a 45-minute

piece for chorus, orchestra, and two vocal soloists (Luciana Souza and Catherine Leech). The chorus and orchestra (led by Grant Gershon) rehearsed a lot of times and by the time the premiere night came, they were more than ready. Before the first note was played, you could hear a pin drop; the anticipation of the piece was really high (the concert was well publicized). The performance was profoundly moving, soulful, and note-perfect. After the last note rang out, the piece got a ten-minute standing ovation and four curtain calls! When I got to the stage to take a bow, the applause became deafening. Afterward, people came to me with tears in their eyes, shaking my hand so hard that it hurt. That was the most rewarding musical experience I've ever had.

3 My wish for the 21st century is that people resist the possibility of technology making us lose our humanity.

Billy Drummond   drums, 1959 USA

1 Very Difficult!!!!!!
Miles Davis, John Coltrane, Herbie Hancock, Bobby Hutcherson, Ron Carter or Paul Chambers. (I have played with a few of them so I know what that's like and want more!!)

2. Very difficult as there are many.

    I'd have to say that moving to New York was the most memorable, because that gave me the opportunity to be in a community where the world's greatest musicians lived and operated. With that I was able to participate in music-making with these people, and to grow as a musician in ways that I would never have imagined. Had I not done that, those opportunities would likely not have happened (at least not in that way). I'm very grateful for that and I get chills just thinking about what I've been able to accomplish because of this environment.

3. For humans to end racism and greed, and learn to love each other. Real love, compassion, and to have an understanding of what's really important in life for ALL HUMANS. Perhaps it will take beings from outside this planet to show us the way, since we can't seem to figure it out for ourselves. We ALL could have enough and live in a loving, caring, humane world if we understood and practiced love for each other and for our world. We all would prosper, the world would prosper and we could perhaps have Heaven on Earth for EVERYBODY with Love and Respect for our different cultures, nationalities, etc. It's the HUMAN RACE of PEOPLE.

Bob James   keyboards and arrangements, 1939 USA

1. Victor Borge: 2nd pianist and page turner; Sammy Davis: drums; Freddie Green: guitar; Steve Martin: banjo; Esperanza Spalding: bass and vocals; Elmo Tanner: whistler; Spike Jones: percussion; Joe Venuti: violin; Quincy Jones and Bill McElhiney: trumpets; Eric Dolphy: bass, clarinet and flute; Woody Allen: clarinet; Charlie Parker: alto sax; Ben Webster: tenor sax; Nick Brignola: baritone sax; Kai Winding and J.J. Johnson: trombones; Patti Lupone: tuba; Cary Grant: harp; Igor Stravinsky: arranger/conductor.

2. Montreux Jazz Festival, in 1985, with a supercharged band which included Gary King, Harvey Mason, Kirk Whalum and Dean Brown; or in 2010, Fourplay with the New Japan Philharmonic at Triphony Hall in Tokyo.

3. World peace, of course, and for the polarized camps of straight ahead and smooth jazz to merge and evolve as America's unique art form.

Bob Mintzer saxophone, 1953 USA

1 I have to say that I have been playing in my dream band(s) for the last 45 years: Tito Puente, Buddy Rich, Art Blakey, Thad Jones, Mel Lewis, Jaco Pastorius, Mike Manieri, Randy Brecker, Peter Erskine, Yellowjackets, and my various bands as a leader, and now chief conductor of the WDR big band in Cologne, Germany. I've recorded with many great artists, playing on over 1,000 recordings. This is all a dream come true. (Check the All Music Guide on line).

2 There have been so many. Playing the Berlin jazz festival with my big band, in 1985 and seeing Gil Evans and Chick Corea listening from the side of the stage. Playing North Sea festival in The Hague,

with Yellowjackets, for 15,000 people going crazy. Dave Sanborn had to follow us, and he came over to me and affectionately said: "Man, fuck you." Working with Herbie Hancock and Vince Mendoza with the Hollywood Bowl Orchestra, summers of 2014 and 2015. Getting to play with so many great musicians and travel the world for 4 1/2 decades. Playing in the Thad Jones/Mel Lewis band and having Thad conduct right in front of me. Sitting right to Mel's drums. Writing my first big band arrangements for Buddy Rich, and getting to play them every night, and learn from the experience. Getting to play every night for 2 1/2 years on the Buddy Rich band. Playing with a great band like the Yellowjackets for 28 years. Getting to record 30 of my own recordings with the greatest musicians in the world.

3 I hope that the United States and the rest of the world will come to their senses and return to democratic values where people can coexist and be free to live in peace, where everyone gets a fair shot at living a decent life. I pray that music, the arts and humanities are practiced and recognized as an important catalyst for bringing the world together.

Bob Moses (a.k.a. Ra-Kalam)   drums, 1948 USA

1 I can think of many, many dream bands, but in absolutely none of them would I choose myself as the drummer. Really, why would I choose myself when I could have Elvin Jones, Rashied Ali, Edgar Bateman, Roy Haynes, Pete La Roca, Billy Higgins, Jack DeJohnette, Jabali Billy Hart and on and on . . . So here it goes. My horn players would be John Coltrane, Pharoah Sanders. Eric Dolphy and Don Cherry on pocket trumpet (and his other instruments). On guitar, Bhapuji Tisziji Muñoz. On piano, Steve Kuhn. The bassists would be Scott La Faro and Charlie Haden, who played so beautifully together

on Ornette Coleman's recording *Free Jazz*. On drums, Elvin Jones and Rashied Ali. Their drumming on Coltrane's Meditations is, to my ears, the greatest example of two drummers playing together ever — simultaneously so free and so swinging. I was blessed to have heard that group play live at The Village Gate in New York, in the 60s and I've never forgotten it. And finally on congas and percussion, the great Don Alias. I would not want to play with this group. I would just want to be there to listen and be inspired.

2   I have been very fortunate to have played with quite a few excellent musicians in my life, but none have destroyed and healed me like the music of Bhapuji Tisziji Muñoz. To my ears, the trilogy of masterworks, *Alpha Nebula*, *Omega Nebula* and *Parasangate* by Spiritual Master, Guitar Genius, Bhapuji Tisziji Muñoz is the most majestic, potent expression to date, of what Tisziji calls Heart Fire Sound. I was deeply moved the first time I heard Tisziji play and, for close to forty years, have remained involved with his music both as a listener and a participant. I feel that the Nebula Trilogy is his most apocalyptic, cataclysmic work. For those with the heart to hear, it is simultaneously frightening, shattering, uplifting, inspiring and healing. One thing I love about the drumming on these recordings is that I can't recognize myself at all. Thanks to Tisziji, Bob Moses appears to disappear becoming Ra Kalam (the inaudible sound of the invisible sun) a no self no mind sky drummer just blending into the beautiful infinite cosmic mess of the universe.

3   My wish is that nationalism, tribalism and the illusion of separation recede, and humans experience a spiritual awakening resulting in loss of ego, selflessness and compassion for all living things, including Mother Earth itself.

Bob Sheppard   saxophone and woodwind, 1952 USA

1   I could imagine myself having drinks with my pals 30 years ago, posing this fun hypothetical question. This kind of speculation falls in the same category as imagining how I would spend a $10 million lottery win. If the answer doesn't change with age then something is seriously faulty. I've decided that this "dream band" question is impossible to answer. We are inspired and influenced by so many players

past and present, for infinite reasons. I've been very fortunate to perform in many great situations that I certainly considered a "dream band" at the time. It surely would have been a dream moment to get the chance to play with Elvin Jones, Thad and Mel, Clifford Brown, Nancy Wilson. I can go on and on thinking of all the genius figures who have inspired me to practice and pursue a musical life, some of whom I've actually had the opportunity to play with. The convergence of Coltrane's band with Elvin, Tyner and Garrison had great consequence on my musical journey; so, even the fantasy of including myself in that chemistry is frankly embarrassing. Living life long enough safely leads me to say that my "dream band" is hopefully right around the corner.

2 Most of my memories are tinged with a mixture of thrills and excitement, joy and humor and fear and panic. Again, this question is hardly possible to answer. The combined thrill and terror of sharing the stage with Freddie Hubbard has to be close to the top of the list. Carnegie Hall with Chick, the electrifying energy in Madison Square Garden with Steely Dan, as a Quindectet member, hearing the unrelenting power of Mike Brecker, the one on one with Joni Mitchell in the studio, feeling the energy of the crowd as Frank Sinatra hit the stage.

3 If I had a powerful magic wand to wave, there would be many wishes, some more obvious than others. From personal experience, I certainly would wish for people to talk and listen to each other. In our social media and electronic culture, I'm afraid society and children are not thinking for themselves. The double-edged sword of Facebook and the computers in general are creating isolation. In so many ways we are less connected and more anti-social than ever before. As in Howard Beale's rant in the movie Network, which I believe more relevant than ever "In God's name, you *people* are the real thing. *We* are the illusion. So turn off your television sets. Turn them off now. Turn them off right now. Turn them off and leave them off. Turn them off right in the middle of this sentence I am speaking to you, now. Turn them off — adding computers along with TV sets!

Bobby Broom guitar, 1961 USA

1 Oscar Pettiford, Billy Higgins, Kenny Kirkland, Joe Henderson, Terrence Blanchard.

2 Any opportunities I've had to perform with legends such as Stanley Turrentine, Sonny Rollins, Art Blakey, etc., as well as those leading my own groups.

3 Justice for all, retroactively and going forward.

Bobby Few piano, 1935 USA

1 I thought how great it would be to have all these musicians with different, almost opposite styles on the same bandstand, playing one of my compositions that might be totally free in structure, to see how each musician would respond with their own style! I think the result would be unexpected and maybe like a dream! Art Tatum, George Shearing, Cecil Taylor, Bobby Few, Bud Powell, Fats Waller, Jimmy Woode, Wayne Dockery, Ray Brown, James Lewis, Harry Swift, Jimmy Garrisson, Nat Adderley, Bill Hartman, Lee Morgan, Benny Bailey, Dexter Gordon, John Coltrane, Hank Mobley, Grachan Moncur, Roswell Rudd, Elvin Jones, Ichiro Onoe, Max Roach.

2 I recall one musical event I will never forget, with Albert Ayler on Impulse records. Albert and I played a lot in Cleveland, Ohio, where we both grew up, playing blues clubs and strip cabaret events. Albert left for New York City ten years before me, so we didn't see each other for years until I, too, moved to New York. One day, we met and Albert told me he wanted to record a piece, it would be called *music is the healing force of the universe*. I agreed and there was the drummer Muhammad Ali, and singer Mary Parks, and Stanford James on bass, and it happened, on that song, while I was playing, my body completely left the piano, but I was still playing! I had actually transcended for about 10 or 15 seconds. When I came out of it, there was just Albert starring at me like, "hey Bobby are you OK?" Wow this was the best free jazz recording of my life, one of the best musical events of my career, so far. There has been a lot but this one was exceptional.

3 Over the past 60 years of playing music, I have had the privilege to also compose many original songs, but never the real opportunity to record them using my voice. For the 21st century I would like to record and leave this world with some of these songs to enjoy, and

even dance to them! Maybe my wish will come true, and you can become a part of Bobby Few's 21st century musical world.

Bobby Shew   trumpet, 1941 USA

1 If you mean a combo, I'd go with a sextet: George Coleman or Larry McKenna: tenor sax; Carl Fontana: trombone; Wynton Kelly: piano; Paul Chambers: bass; Kenny Clarke: drums.

2 It's not easy to pick just one because there were many, but at different stages of my growth as a player. Here are a few: joining the Buddy Rich big band, in 1966, when it first was formed and being moved, by Buddy, to the lead chair from the jazz chair. Playing and recording with Horace Silver's band for a year and a half, following Tom Harrell — intimidating shoes to step into! Playing a quintet with Al Cohn, at the Otter Crest Festival, and with Phil Woods in a jazz fest, in Michigan. Playing with Toshiko Akiyoshi–Lew Tabackin big band for eight years.

3 A more peaceful, saner world to live in, and administrators who understand and encourage the value of creativity in our schools and in our lives. And an end to jobless, homeless, starving people.

Bobby Watson   saxophone, 1953 USA

1 This is my dream big band: Thad Jones: director; Freddie Hubbard, Woody Shaw, Lee Morgan, Dizzy Gillespie, and Clark Terry: trumpets; Slide Hampton, Curtis Fuller, J.J. Johnson, Dave Bargeron: trombones; Howard Johnson: tuba; John Coltrane, Joe Henderson, Me, Cannonball Adderley or Johnny Hodges, and Pepper Adams: saxophones; McCoy Tyner, Elvin Jones or Art Blakey, Paul Chambers, and Wes Montgomery: rhythm section.

2 Performing at the White House, and meeting President Barack Obama and the First Lady, Michelle Obama.

3 I hope that we don't destroy the environment, and that my children have the opportunity to realize their dreams, enjoy prosperity, stability, health and happiness, and live a better life than us. Find a cure for cancer, diabetes, and Alzheimer's.

Bugge Wesseltoft
piano, 1964 Norway

1 Jan Garbarek: saxophone; Charlie Haden: bass; Jon Christensen: drums; not sure about me in there, but, okay -:)

2 So many great memories! 1999, time in Montreux Jazz Festival; 2000, first time at Nice Jazz Festival; 2001, Paris Jazz Festival Live, in the Parc Floral, for almost 10.000 people.

3 Peace, freedom and equal opportunities for all people.

Carlos Lyra vocal, 1933 Brazil

1 My dream band: Carlos Lyra: voice; João Gilberto: acoustic guitar; Bill Evans: piano; Ron Carter: acoustic bass; Shelly Manne: drums; Dirceu Leite: flute, sax and clarinet; Chet Baker: trumpet.

2 One of the most memorable musical events of my career is my tour with Stan Getz all over the world in 1965 with Gary Burton, Steve Swallow, Roy Haynes and Chick Corea had a special moment in Washington when Benny Goodman came to the stage to play with us. One of the best moments of my musical career.

3 My wishes for the XXI Century is related to the authors' rights. Since digital platforms listeners have increased and CD buyers decreased, we have a new and easy way to listen to music but the authors are not receiving a proper share. I hope that new legislations are made to protect the copyright and related rights, in the Digital World.

Chano Dominguez piano, 1960 Spain

1 Kurt Rosenwinkel: guitar; Jack DeJohnette: drums; Carlos Enrique: bass; Diego Urcola: trumpet; and me on piano.

2 To be part of the Jazz at Lincoln Center family is for me such a wonderful blessing, we celebrated the 30th anniversary this last March, in the Appel room, sharing the stage with four generations of piano players, including the piano masters Dick Hyman, Sullivan Fortner and Joey Alexander.

3 Peace, love and music.

Charles McPherson   saxophone, 1939 USA

1 Dream band: Bud Powell: piano; Kenny Clark: drums; Oscar Pettiford: bass; Louis Armstrong: trumpet.
2 Seeing Bud Powell sit in with Mingus when I was in the band, in the late sixties.
3 Ending of all wars and world starvation.

Chico Freeman   saxophone, 1949 USA

1 My dream band would be — Chico Freeman: saxophone; Miles Davis: trumpet; Paul Chambers: bass; Elvin Jones: drums; McCoy Tyner: piano with Bobby Hutcherson on vibes.
2 That is nearly impossible to answer because I've had so many. Possibly, the most unique experience that I've had would be when I had just returned to New York from a 6-week tour in Europe with only one day off, and that day being a travel day with the Don Pullen Quartet that featured Don Pullen — piano, Fred Hopkins — bass, Bobby Battles — drums and myself on tenor saxophone. We opened for a week at Ali's Alley (Rashied Ali's club) in SoHo New York. On the last night, we had finished the last set, but the music was on such a high level and transcendent that we felt we weren't finished playing yet and wanted to continue! But it was after closing time, and Rasheid needed to close up the club, due to city regulations. However, Rasheid told the audience that he was going to lock the doors and turn off the outside lights, so that we could go on. Then he invited anyone who wanted to stay to do so, and those who wanted to leave should exit right then. No one left. He proceeded to lock the doors, etc. and we began to play. What happened next was nothing less than extraordinary. As we played I began to leave my body and witness myself on stage. I could see and hear myself playing. It was awesome, I had never experienced anything like this before. My playing was inspirational, not only to others but to myself, I could do no wrong and neither could any of the other members of the group. I witnessed the audience's reaction simultaneously with the group. It was as if I was inside the hearts and minds of everyone in

the room at the same time. After the music concluded, there was a pause, which seemed to go on forever, where we all needed time to feel and consider what had just happened. Then, the audience erupted in thunderous and frenzied applause and appreciation. It was indescribable. Later, I spoke with the guys in the band and they all said they had a similar experience, if not exactly the same one, that I had had. We were truly one voice that night both up, on and off the bandstand, the audience and us. It was enlightening and incredible.

3 I wish for a more complete understanding and acceptance of each other. I hope that we, as human beings, become as evolved as we should be, given our supposed higher intellect. It may be a cliché, but I would like to be a real force for good through my music. In real terms we humans need only to do really just one thing, "Treat each other as we would like to be treated." I think this is the key and the answer to so many of our problems; we need to be able to walk in others' shoes.

Chico Pinheiro   guitar, 1974 Brazil

1 That's a very tough question. I assume a JAZZ big band, is that right? I could think of at least six bands so, let me put together one BIG BAND (at least).

P.S.: Some of them I've already recorded with, but they're still my favorites (is that OK?):

Drums: Brian Blade; bass: Jaco Pastorius; piano: Brad Mehldau; percussion: Armando Marçal; tenor sax: John Coltrane and Michael Brecker; alto sax: Charlie Parker; trumpet 1: Dizzy Gillespie; trumpet 2: Clifford Brown; trumpet 3: Miles Davis; trumpet 4: Lee Morgan; trombone: Curtis Fuller.

2 Another difficult question, Lilian. Let me try to list a couple of them:
- When I first got into the studio to make my first album *Meia Noite Meio Dia*.
- The first time I played at the Original Carnegie Hall.
- Recording, with Placido Domingo, an album that includes *State*

and *Concierto de Aranjuez*, in Valencia, Spain. That was beautiful.
- Having been soloist with, and have some of my compositions arranged for, and played by the Orpheus Chamber Orchestra at the Lincoln Center Main Hall.
- Having recorded an album as a soloist with one of my main influences as a teenager, one of my biggest heroes, Bob Mintzer and his Big Band.

There are many memorable moments, but these are very dear to me.

3 My most sincere wishes are to live in a world with more humanity, less greed, more peace, more love, less war and hate and, of course, more music — good music.

Chris Minh Doky
bass, 1969 Denmark

1 I imagine a band that flows between improvisation and orchestral. Trumpet: Miles Davis; piano: Herbie Hancock; drums: Tony Williams; tenor sax: Wayne Shorter; alto sax: Jan Garbarek; guitar: Jimmy Hendrix; keyboards: Joe Zawinul; tablas: Zakir Hussain; with symphony orchestra arrangements by Vince Mendoza, conducted by Leonard Bernstein.

2 For sure when I played my first gig with Michael Brecker's quartet. I kept pinching my arm to make sure I wasn't dreaming. Musically it started a whole new adventure and expedition into music with this incredible musician and fellow band members.

3 I so hope the world will come to its senses. That we strive to be better, wiser, kinder, more awake. Those facts are not equal to opinions. Where a sense of community, civility, decency, being honorable, and having integrity is again a core quality and ambition. A place where we can agree to disagree without becoming mortal enemies. Basically living together in the same spirit as when you improvise together in music.

Chris Potter   saxophone, 1971 USA

1 Too many to list. The truth is I already get to play with my dream bands, on a regular basis! As far as people I never got the chance to play with, I'd say Elvin Jones, Jimmy Garrison, and Duke Ellington.

2 My very first paid performance, at age 10 or 11, performing with my elementary school music teacher, Miss Hall, at a private club in Columbia, South Carolina.

3 I wish for people in the world to understand how interconnected we are to each other and to the planet, and start acting accordingly.

Christian Escoudé   guitar, 1947 France

1 Wes Montgomery, John Coltrane, Oscar Peterson, Niels-Henning Ørsted Pedersen, Philly Joe Jones. My participation in this group? Carrying their suitcases. All kidding aside, as my work, for quite a while, has been composing and arranging, having them play my music.

2 One of my best memories is on the stage of The Village Vanguard when I performed with my quartet — Hank Jones: piano, Pierre Michelot: bass, Kenny Washington: drums.

3 An intelligent society.

Christian McBride   bass, 1972 USA

1 Am I playing in this band or just curating it? Anyway, it would be Freddie Hubbard on trumpet, Wayne Shorter on tenor sax, J.J. Johnson on trombone), McCoy Tyner on piano), Ron Carter on bass — only if I can't play in this band — and Tony Williams on drums.

   This band could change, however. Check back next week . . .

2 Getting to play with my childhood hero, James Brown.

3 That humans be nicer to each other.

Christian Scott   trumpet, 1983 USA

1 John Coltrane, Jimi Hendrix, McCoy Tyner, Max Roach, Charles Mingus, and me.

2 In 1998, playing NPR's *Toast of the Nation*, on New Year's Eve: a live global broadcast, with my uncle, sax great Donald Harrison, Jr.'s band from New Orleans. I was 15 years old and it is one of my earliest memories as a professional musician.

3 I have a lot of wishes, but musically my wish would be having lawmakers, around the globe, to reach legislation to protect artists' rights and resources from the highly exploitive business spaces. These exploitive spaces that continue to push modes of operating that walk artists out of the financial resources they are actually eligible for.

Christine Jensen   saxophone, 1970 Canada

1 Jack DeJohnette, Herbie Hancock and Dave Holland.

2 Memorable musical event: taking my jazz orchestra on tour across mighty Canada in 2015.

3 My wish for the 21st century is that we keep our earth clean. Let's try to reuse and recycle for future generations.

Chuck Israels   bass, 1936 USA

1 Pick a "dream band." How might I pick an ideal drummer? Kenny Clark, Max Roach, Roy Haynes, Larry Bunker (surely among my favorites) or the less well-known and perhaps the most wildly inventive, Donald Bailey. Then I would have omitted Billy Higgins and, who knows, who else I should include. There is no easy answer. If I must pick one, then my choice is Donald, but oh how I'd miss the others! Favorite pianist is easy, but Hank Jones and Tommy Flanagan are not far behind, and Miles Black (in Vancouver, BC) would be my choice for a band of living musicians I could form now. Maybe Kenny Washington would be a good drummer for that band. Aaron Diehl would be another good pianist, and Cécile McLorin Salvant would be my choice as a singer, though Joe Williams would be there too, were he alive to join. This gets a little crazy — picking favorites among the hundreds of people who have contributed to the richness of my musical life. Nobody outplayed Charlie Parker, but Phil Woods was superb. Lucky Thompson, Paul Gonsalves, Zoot Sims, Stan Getz, Sal Nistico and Hank Mobley are some favorites, in no particular order. Baritone sax is easier: Joe Temperley, unless you need a more chromatic player; then it's Ronnie Cuber. Do you prefer J.J. Johnson or Jimmy Knepper, Miles Davis or Clifford Brown? Charlie Porter satisfies my trumpet needs in my bands today, and I never think about anyone else when Charlie is playing. That's the litmus test: is there room during one performance to compare it with another? If the performance of the moment fills the attention space, it's the momentary ideal. The question of creating a personnel list for an ideal band is most often asked by people who don't play in bands. All-star teams don't beat a good working team. Art is created by working around limitations as well as abilities. My ideal band is the band I work with at any given moment, assuming everyone is sufficiently experienced and applying his or her full attention to realizing a consensual musical goal. Of course, some musicians are more closely attuned to my musical goals than others, and some exceed them. But my deepest musical pleasures come from teamwork and the sense that, for the moment, my life is connected with others

— not a lonely experience. Ellington's band was less an ideal band than he was an ideal composer/arranger/leader. In some ways, this question makes me feel lonely in that it demonstrates that people, who appreciate my music, may also be misunderstanding some of its fundamental values.

2. Pick one memorable musical event. I find this also not easy to answer. There's a list of several, for sure: a number of performances with Bill Evans — the *Town Hall Concert*; the recording with Monica Zetterlund; almost any night at the Gyllene Cirklen, in Stockholm, when the entire cast of the Gula Hund review (wonderful Swedish actors/singer/musicians) would show up for the last set, night after night, for two or three weeks in a row; the concert at the ORTF Hall in Paris with Bill; working with the Metropole Orchestra conducting my compositions and arrangements; many performances with the National Jazz Ensemble. It's a long list, and I would not choose to omit any of these, nor a number of others, I am simply not remembering at the moment.

3. Make America (and those in the rest of the world who seem to be following our political lead) sane again. I have hopes for musical changes as well, but I am not in control of much of any of this, so I am more concerned with making good choices  in circumstances I can control rather than hoping for others to make the choices I'd prefer. I grew up in a most unusual era, during which popular music was written by and supported by educated people. I thought this was normal. History proves otherwise.

Clarence Penn   drums, 1968 USA

1. Peter Gabriel, John Coltrane, Herbie Hancock and Charlie Haden.
2. When I played at the opening of the Louvre in Abu Dhabi, with Scott Colley: bass, Frank Woeste: piano, Rick Margitza: saxophone, Ibrahim Maalouf: trumpet.
3. More respect for each other.

Clark Tracey   drums, 1961 UK

1. Thelonious Monk, Paul Chambers, John Coltrane, Miles Davis.
2. Chicago Jazz Festival in 1989, with Stan Tracey Quintet.
3. My wish is that people appreciate jazz with their ears and not their eyes.

Claudio Roditi   trumpet, 1946 Brazil

1   My dream band would have Scott LaFaro on bass, Victor Feldman on piano, Art Blakey on drums, Booker Little on trumpet, John Coltrane on tenor sax, Charlie Parker on alto, and J.J. Johnson on trombone. I am not ready to be part of that band yet, even though that would be my dream band.

2   I had three experiences in my life that stand out: One was Dizzy Gillespie's United Nations Orchestra, primarily for the fact that, in 1959, I bought my first modern jazz LP and it was by Dizzy and Roy Eldridge. Thirty years later I was in the U.S.A. playing alongside Dizzy Gillespie in one of his bands. What a dream come true!

The band "To Diz with Love," led by Slide Hampton, was another musical highlight in my career. Among all the greats in that band were Freddie Hubbard and Red Rodney.

The third was Tito Puente's Golden Latin Jazz All Stars, with Paquito D'Rivera, Dave Valentin, Mario Rivera, Hilton Ruiz, Mongo Santamaria, Giovani Hidalgo, Andy Gonzalez, and Ignacio Berroa.

3   What I would like to see happening in the 21st century for jazz, and combinations of that style with music from around the world, is that it will be more respected, more well-known, and that musicians can better survive playing the music they love!!!

Courtney Pine   saxophone, 1964 UK

1   Drums: Dennis Chambers; bass: Stanley Clarke; acoustic piano: Thelonius Monk; keyboards: Herbie Hancock; beats: Rza; turntables: DJ premier; voice: Kendrick Lamar; vocals: Billie Holiday and Ella Fitzgerald; trombone: J.J. Johnson; alto saxophone: Maceo Parker; trumpet: Miles Davis.

2 Performing jazz at the free Nelson Mandela concert, at the old Wembley Stadium.

3 That all music will unify to show how we, as humanity, are better as a united voice using all our unique differences, or individuality, to create something positive and more than what we are.

Cyrus Chestnut   piano, 1963 USA

1 Paul Chambers, Art Blakey, and Hank Mobley. That would make me very happy!!
2 There are so many but, I guess, what comes to mind is playing at Aretha Franklin's birthday party and having her come on the bandstand to scat on rhythm changes.
3 My wish is peace, love, and respect for all humanity.

Dado Moroni   piano, 1962 Italy

1 It should be an easy question . . . but it's not. Because before being a pianist, I am a Jazz fan. Therefore I love this music with a passion, I love all facets of it, and so many musicians have conquered my heart and imagination, in every aspect of the language. I was lucky enough to have played with many of them, and each one gave me something that will forever stay with me . . . So here are two bands, one from my childhood years and one now:

Band one– Clark Terry: trumpet/flugelhorn; Zoot Sims: tenor sax; Ray Brown: bass; Buddy Rich: drums; plus special guest on vocals: Ella Fitzgerald.

Band two– Tom Harrell: trumpet/flugelhorn; Sonny Rollins: tenor sax; Gary Bartz: alto sax; Slide Hampton: trombone; Wes Montgomery: guitar; Bobby Hutcherson: vibraphone; Ron Carter: bass, Philly Joe Jones: drums.

2 In the mid 80s I had a chance to play a concert in Asti, a beautiful small town near Turin, with Dizzy Gillespie. I was attending law school at the time but also playing when I could. Master tenorist Gianni Basso (one of the first Italian musicians to make an international career with the likes of Chet Baker), Thad Jones, Johnny Griffin and many others, called me to be in the band and, with a mix of excitement and fear, I accepted. We played a lot of bebop classics, many written by Dizzy himself, and, on stage, he did everything he could to ease my palpable tension. Wonderful. After the gig he came to me while I was standing with my father, who had accompanied me to the concert, and said: "Man, that was great! You know all my tunes! Tell me your story. What do you do?" To which I replied that I was studying to be a lawyer and playing gigs here and there in my free time. He looked me in the eye, serious, and said: "Oh no! There are too

many f*****g lawyers out there and not enough good piano players. You've got to play! Play!" Well, if Dizzy says so . . . And that was the end of my career in law. He made me realize I could fulfill my dream, be a professional musician, and I don't regret it! Years later he had this pianoless band with Sam Rivers on tenor sax, Ed Cherry on guitar, John Lee on bass, and Ignacio Berroa on drums, and they played in Zürich. It was some kind of a jazz party at a small club called The Widder Bar, and I was sitting right in front of the stage, literally inches from the bandstand. Dizzy walks in and starts talking on the mike, then he looks down, sees me, recognizes me and says: "Man, whatcha you doin' sitting there? Your place is here!" and points to the empty piano seat. I ended up playing the whole set with him. Dizzy . . . !

3 Although, too often, Jazz is considered by many to be a type of music for elites only, hard to understand for the general public, I see that people always enjoy a good live performance.

All sorts of people, if given a good show played with heart, joy, intensity, creativity and passion, can appreciate it. I often invite childhood friends who don't normally listen to jazz, and there hasn't been a single time when they went home disappointed or, worse, bored. I think the main problem is that the media, mostly, ignore this music and bombard us with other things. Sometimes, very rarely I'd say, you manage to find a radio or TV channel with a bit of Jazz at terrifying hours . . . 2 or 3 am! My wish is that one day I'll turn on the TV at dinner time and, before the news, Count Basie and his big band will make us smile and swing our way to the table! But it would be crucial to start with swing music to capture people's attention. To broadcast Cecil Taylor at lunch time, as much as I love and respect him, could be dangerous. But Louis Armstrong, Ella, Duke, Erroll Garner, Dexter Gordon, Oscar Peterson, Nat King Cole, etc. . . . Starting with these giants, a whole lot of people would inevitably be drawn to jazz, and take it from there.

And good, dedicated, passionate teachers in the schools; teachers able to show the students that little burning flame. Playing music and playing with music!

Dan Tepfer   piano, 1982 France

1 When I try to answer this question, I get immediately stuck on the fact that there's no one "dream band." It's all contextual. How could I possibly choose without knowing what music I wanted to make? So many musicians I love! Fortunately we're limited in our choices of whom to work with in the real world. I can write something and think to myself, so and so would be perfect for this. Let's see if he or she is available. Thank goodness this is the way it works or I'd never be able to decide on anyone!

2 The things that stand out for me are the times I've realized a dream that at some point seemed impossible. Things like playing at Smalls with my trio, for the first time, in 2006; or at the Village Vanguard with Lee Konitz; or playing duo with a long-time inspiration of mine, Paul Motian. I've been lucky to play solo concerts in some magical places: Wigmore Hall in London, Sumida Triphony Hall in Tokyo, the MACC on Maui . . . I'll never forget the feeling of playing my own music in such special environments; I felt deeply honored. But perhaps the most memorable times, for me, are the premieres of big projects — when something you've been working on for a long time finally gets out into the world — like the first performance, at the Ravinia Festival two summers ago, of *Solar Spiral*, my new piece for string quartet and piano. Recently, I've been introducing my

algorithmic music project, Acoustic Informatics, to the world, and every one of those performances has been profoundly memorable to me, because it feels scary and exciting to present something so new and personal, to the world.

3 That we may learn to take care of this Earth we've been entrusted with. It's my hope that music, which has the power to bring us together and increase our empathy for each other and our environment, can help in some small but significant way.

Dan Weiss   drums, 1977 USA

1 John Coltrane and Nikhil Banerjee

2 When my daughter started to recognize and remember music. The first song she remembered and could ask for was "I Want a Girl" off the Count Basie and the Kansas City Seven, from 1962.

3 That it be mandatory for politicians to be exposed to great music from throughout the globe!!!

Daniel Humair   drums, 1938 Switzerland

1 Sonny Rollins, Cannonball Adderley, Louis Armstrong, Oscar Peterson or Keith Jarrett, Ray Brown or Jean-François Jenny-Clark. It's a weird choice but I think that Louis and Sonny, genius of swing and creativity, would make for a happy match.

2 My participation at the JATP (Jazz at the Philharmonic) in Nice, with Cannonball, Milt Jackson, Dizzy Gillespie, Lockjaw Davis, Al Grey, Niels-Henning Ørsted Pedersen and Oscar Peterson. To be accepted, and I believe, appreciated by all of them was a great accomplishment.

3 That we no longer use the word "jazz" at any time and any old time and wrongly. It's amazing to see performances, even in well-known

festivals, with musicians presenting sometimes rhythmic music, but derived from pop music unrelated to jazz, and of not very high quality, TOTALLY contrary to the basic rules (even if I do not like rules in general) swing, ternary implementation, improvisations, harmony, phrasing. Too many musicians, perhaps knowledgeable, but without knowledge of the "popular roots" of our music, are invited to attract often ill-informed spectators concerning jazz, and end up giving an outdated and inappropriate image of this misunderstood art form, which has survived for more than a century, without any real support from the non-specialized media. Unfortunately, there are also too many jazz musicians, often good ones, who seek commercial success by making themselves more popular through music with too many concessions, gratuitous effects that get the audience used to trivial and audience-friendly music. Unfortunately, I seem to hear this type of work more and more often. My wish is therefore to see influential people working to make known to a public, which isn't well informed, this great universal music that, when practiced by real professionals with knowledge and experience essential to stylistic accuracy (whatever the choice of the genre, because jazz is timeless and limitless in its creative variations), is a great source of pleasure and culture. Thus, jazz will continue to develop and introduce us to new creative musicians who will have found the necessary means for academic and practical knowledge. The history of jazz and the musicians of the past and present will be better understood by a wide and more discriminating audience.

Danilo Perez   piano, 1966 Panama

1 Trumpet: Dizzy Gillespie, Miles Davis, Freddie Hubbard, Claudio Roditi; alto sax: Charlie Parker, Kenny Garrett; soprano sax: Wayne Shorter and Steve Lacy; tenor sax: John Coltrane, Sonny Rollins; trombone: J.J. Johnson, Bob Brookmeyer; acoustic bass: Ron Carter, Jimmy Garrison, John Patitucci, Ben Street; electric bass: Jaco Pastorius, Meshell Ndegeocello, Alain Pérez; keyboards: Joe Zawinul; guitar: Jimi Hendrix, Lionel Loueke; drums: Elvin Jones, Tony Williams, Terri Lyne Carrington, Brian Blade, Horacio Hernandez, Adam Cruz; percussion: Roman Diaz, Zakir Hussein,

Airto Moreira, Giovanni Hidalgo; singers: Sarah Vaughan, Olga Guillot, Elis Regina, Milton Nascimento, Sibongile Khumalo, and Dianne Reeves; bandoneon: Astor Piazzolla.

2 In December of 1989, I had my first concert in Panama with my bandmates from the USA and Spain. The concert got canceled because two days after the band arrived, the U.S. invaded Panama. The entire country was in a state of war. We were fearful of the military intervention, and the future was uncertain. But we all decided to face the unknown, as happens in jazz, and we went forward with the concert, in the middle of the US invasion. With our musical shield, we were confident no bullets could enter our spirit. The club was packed with people for and against the invasion, who got together and decided to celebrate life. We laughed, hugged, and cried. On that day we had a country (in a small club) without an invasion for two hours. I learned then that the power of music could be an antidote against war, misunderstanding, hate and suffering, and that music is one of the most effective tools to redirect humanity in the quest for peace.

3 My wish for the 21st century is to create music that unites the world (just like Panama unites America and the world) and that many more artists would utilize Global Jazz as a tool to modify their surroundings for the betterment of society. I hope artists become the Guardians of the creative process that will enable humans to find adventurous proposals of great pedagogical, artistic, and social significance, in order to solve the challenges of the 21st century.

Danny Gottlieb   drums, 1953 USA

1 That's a very interesting question. There are so many great musicians and it's hard to just make one band. Well . . . when I think about it, maybe a large all-star big band, like Dizzy's world band and the Gil Evans Orchestra. I love playing with my Metheny bassist best friend, Mark Egan, and I loved playing with Pat Metheny and Lyle. So oddly enough I would probably keep that rhythm section. Bob Brookmeyer touched me so deeply when I had a chance to work with him, I'd add Bob. I'd add Gil Evans on a second keyboard, another master who touched me so deeply. Let's add John McLaughlin on guitar as

well. I would add my wife Beth on percussion, she's one of the greats as well. I'd also add Airto on percussion and his wife Flora Purim, who both touched me so deeply. I'd add Clifford Brown, Lew Soloff, Louis Armstrong, Jon Faddis, Randy Brecker, Frank Greene, Wayne Bergeron on trumpets, Lou Rawls, Sarah Vaughan, Joe Williams, Ella, Steve Lawrence and Sinatra on vocals. I'd add Tom Malone and Dave Steinmeyer on trombones, Miles Evans on trumpet, John Clark on French Horn, Dave Bargeron on Tuba, George Gruntz and Gil Goldstein on keyboards, Chris Hunter, David Sanborn, Mike Brecker . . . well . . . I guess that's enough for starters!

2 There have been so many. I would pick four off the top of my head. Metheny at Onkle Pö's in Hamburg, in 1978; John McLaughlin Mahavishnu first gig, at the Hammersmith Odeon, London 1984; Sting and Gil Evans, at the Umbria Jazz Fest, Italy, in 1987; Gary Sinise and Lt. Dan Band at the U.S. Capitol, Washington, D.C., on Memorial Day, May 27, 2018.

3 That all people help each other. That, somehow, education and the arts become a priority again.

Dave Liebman   saxophone 1946 USA

1 My "dream band" would be the John Coltrane Quintet, which Trane had as his working band for some months, in the early 1960s, when Eric Dolphy was in the group. With respect, I would've been more than happy substituting for Eric. Trane's group swung like hell; it incorporated the most sophisticated harmonies of the century along with more than a few memorable melodies. But beyond the musical elements, the group also hit the spiritual mother lode of what great art is about besides virtuosity: energy, beauty, depth of feeling and most of all complete honesty and sincerity.

2 There are two equally important concerts for me. With my first group as a leader ("Lookout Farm") that I put together after several years apprenticing with Elvin Jones and Miles Davis, we had just finished a tour of Japan and landed in Calcutta, India for American government sponsored concerts in eight cities. Getting out of the airport driving to the hotel, I noticed trucks stopping and going, a pungent odor and candles in tents on the streets, I was informed by the government rep that the trucks picked up dead bodies on a nightly basis. The whole band was quite shell shocked when we met the next day and began our activities. When we finally hit the stage that night, the vibrations from the people, as well as our emotions, were overwhelming.

The other event was a concert in 1987 (which Richie Beirach has written about for this survey) celebrating Coltrane's passing with Wayne Shorter, Jack DeJohnette, Eddie Gomez and Richie. When we began the duet portion of the program ("After the Rain" and "Naima") with the audience cheering, the spotlight on Richie and myself, a giant picture of Trane in back of us, playing with my best friend and a band of idols/friends remembering Coltrane, I thought to myself this is the Mount Everest of my life ... It doesn't get better.

3 The words might be a bit corny but peace and love, coupled with respect for cultural differences, alongside a feeling of empathy for the downtrodden, is what I would hope for.

David Binney saxophone 1961 USA

1 I like the bands I've had. Craig Taborn, Matt Brewer, Dan Weiss, Eivind Opsvik, Nate Wood, Justin Brown, Louis Cole, Ambrose Akinmusire, Brian Blade, Matt Mitchell, Tim Lefebvre, Zach Danziger. I can't imagine it getting better than that. And now with the younger guys: Luca Mendoza, Logan Kane, Anthony Fung, Ethan Moffitt, Ben Ring and new friends like guitarist Nick Reinhart et al. There are many people I would like/would have liked to play with ... Milton Nacsimento, Ivan Lins, Djavan, John Coltrane, Keith Jarrett, Squarepusher, Witold Lutoslawski, Charles Ives, Herbie Hancock, Alan Holdsworth, Merle Haggard, on and on and on ...

2. Again, too many to mention, but the top ones have mostly been my gigs at the 55 Bar and now at the Blue Whale. I've done many, many other things that I've loved, but none of them ever really reached the level of some of the 55 Blue Whale Bar gigs. I've had some really fun and great gigs with Simone Graziano's Frontal band in Italy, too. And a lot of fun gigs with Louis Cole. I've really enjoyed the solo and duo concerts I've been lately doing in Los Angeles. Had some fun ones with Mark Guiliana's Beat Music. There are just so many that have been amazing! It would be a very, very long list. All of these lists would be!

3. Do you mean in regards to me? To compose and record many more albums. To record my classical music. Release some of my electronic music. Both in the works, as I write this. I want to Produce a lot more records for others. I have had a lot of success producing, but I'd like to move into other areas of musical production because it feels natural for me to produce electronic records, rock, rap, singer songwriter; anything . . . it comes very natural to me. I'd love to record something for ECM. I'm not sure why that hasn't happened yet! I know more about the music on that label than probably anyone. I could make a great record for them . . . I hope that can happen.

I'd like to do more solo concerts. I'm working on making that happen too.

David Friesen bass, 1942 USA

1 Four different groups:
   - Thelonious Monk, Joe Henderson, Roy Haynes, Cecil McBee
   - Bill Evans Trio w/Scott LaFaro, Paul Motian
   - John Coltrane Quartet w/McCoy Tyner, Jimmy Garrison, Elvin Jones
   - Miles Davis group with Herbie Hancock, Wayne Shorter, Scott LaFaro, Tony Williams

   You can also put my dream band as follows: Wayne Shorter, Joe Henderson, Paul Motian and myself!

2 Playing eight of my original compositions with, and arranged for a 40-piece woodwind, brass and percussion symphonic band from Kiev. This concert, in June 2017, took place in Smela, Ukraine, the city where my mother was born... 1,000 persons attended, including the Mayor and other dignitaries! After the concert was over and after receiving a multitude of flowers from the public, he presented me with an honorary citizenship of Smela and other fine gifts.

3 For all of us who live in this world, that we may learn to live at peace with our neighbors close to us and far from us, without control or manipulation, showing forth kindness with mercy and forgiveness.

David Gilmore   guitar, 1964 USA

1 A rather eclectic band it would be (which I like!), but my dream band would consist of Sam Rivers, Freddie Hubbard, Bill Evans (the pianist), Jaco Pastorius, and Elvin Jones.

2 That would have to be during my time touring with Wayne Shorter, particularly the quintet consisting also of Jim Beard, Alphonso Johnson and Rodney Holmes. One performance particularly stands out for me, during the Summer of 1996, at The North Sea Jazz Festival. We played after Joe Zawinul's band, and I remember that the exchange of energy in the hall between not just the musicians on stage, but also the audience, was sizzling!!! It was a particular high that I have felt only a few times in my career. There is a video

of that concert, floating around somewhere, that I have never been able to track down, but I hope one day it appears!!! It was a great band, and unfortunately was short-lived, but I will always treasure those memories.

3 Musically? I wish for the medium of music to continue to act as a healing force in the world, bringing people of various cultures, languages and beliefs together, through the universal language of Sound. We often take music for granted and don't even contemplate what it really is, which is a language of frequency and vibration that operates on a cellular and unconscious level, bypassing the thinking mind. There is a potentially transcendent nature to this form of communication, which, if not usurped by the ego for its own gratification, can truly elevate the consciousness of humankind. True musicians, if they express from the Heart, and are not bound solely by commercial or personal gain in their musical pursuits, are true messengers of Light and Love.

David Hazeltime   piano, 1958 USA

1 My dream band has already existed as a band (more or less) featuring Billy Higgins, Sam Jones, Cedar Walton, George Coleman, (a band known in the 70s as "Eastern Rebellion") plus Freddie Hubbard, Slide Hampton, and Buddy Montgomery on vibes.

2 Actually, the trio recording I just made, this past May, with Ron Carter and Al Foster, had to be the most memorable for many reasons!

3 My wish for the 21st century is that love and fellowship, kindness and consideration, empathy and justice (all important elements in the creation of Jazz specifically, and all art in general) finally take their proper place at the top of human consciousness, throughout the world.

David Linx   vocal, 1965 Belgium

1 OK, for this I'll be a little gargantuesque. As orchestrators, I would like Maria Schneider, Philip Glass, Gil Evans, Morton Feldman, and Egberto Gismonti to sit around the table and work together on the concept of a project for this band, based on one of Arundhati Roy's

books: *The Cost of Living*. I'd love to have Lennie Tristano, Gonzalo Rubalcaba and Diederik Wissels on piano/keyboards together with Joe Zawinul; Brian Blade or Tony Williams on drums, Christian McBride on acoustic bass, and Jaco Pastorius on electric bass; Airto on percussion; The Georgia Mass Choir, Jimmy Hendrix and Charlie Christian on guitar, and a horn section with John Coltrane, Miles Davis, Louis Armstrong, John Zorn, Slide Hampton, Bob Stewart, Joshua Redman, Avishai Cohen (the trumpet player); James Baldwin to recite the poetry. All these artists, in different line-ups, throughout the project and/or evening. A couple of duets with Ray Charles and Betty Carter. And a producer to organize this whole crazy thing like Craig Street or Kip Hanrahan. I know they can handle it.

2 I have many different memorable moments. When you are young and starting out, it's a complete mind-blowing experience to find yourself one day performing or recording with the legends from your childhood, who initially triggered everything to start walking that path. Afterwards, it all helps you shape your own sound and skills to tell your story, and when that is recognized, because that's in the first place not why we do this, it is another memorable amazing feeling, I have to admit. It gives you a voice. My project with James Baldwin, reciting his poetry, for which Pierre Van Dormael and I gathered 20-some top-class performers such as Steve Coleman, Toots Thielemans, Slide Hampton... is one of those moments. Singing with the Count Basie Orchestra, in my mid-20s, with Frank Foster arranging my songs while having an occasional band, Natural Logic, with Steve Coleman, Bob Stewart and Pierre Van Dormael, that same year, is also a great memory. But one of the

most memorable events, in my artistic career, is my long-standing, over 30 years now, artistic partnership with pianist and composer, Diederik Wissels, "that" is my home, my niche, where I can tell my story every night. No glittering event could ever match this one.

3 My wish, one of 'em at least, is automatically linked to the current state of our planet, which in many ways is a direct metaphor of the state of our psyche in general, and also where we stand as a moral authority, a moral compass in high need of long-overdue repair, I fear. My wish would be that we take hold again of our minds, our spirits and our souls, teaching our young ones the language of the heart. Technology is only of good use if we, as human beings, are in control of the so-called progress it represents, with the center of our daily life-functioning being dictated by social media, to name just one example, so that as artists we can be satisfied again with being the witnesses of our era just by being excellent at what we do, by just being storytellers. Poets have done it so that we know about ancient Rome and Athens, artists yes, not politicians. That in itself is a political statement. I always think that the best tribute one can pay to tradition is to somehow perpetuate it. In these current times, where most of the artistic endeavors are focused solely on the pleasing (at all cost) factor, we tend to dabble in a stylistic still-water lake of the past where nothing can flow out to the sea to challenge ourselves with and confront new currents. The rhythm of society is in constant change, even turmoil, and has accelerated intensely in the past 70-odd years. And for me rhythm gives speech to the thoughts and the reflections we have. This is the perfect recipe for us to dance a new dance, sing a new song with ingredients of old. Musicians and artists everywhere should never underestimate the role they play. To entertain is one thing but we should keep the laboratories alive and open to any experiment with inspiration to stay alert at all times. It's not as much about having hope than as being "a" hope.

David Williams   bass, 1946 Trinidad and Tobago

1 My dream band would be John Coltrane, J.J. Johnson, Freddie Hubbard, Bud Powell, Paul Chambers and Max Roach.

2 My most memorable musical event is performing with Roberta Flack, with the Quincy Jones Orchestra. Featuring among other great names were Freddie Hubbard, Jerome Richardson; and Toots Thielemans, Ray Brown, George Bohanon, Chuck Rainey, the list goes on and on.

3 My wish for the twenty-first century is that the new generation will continue in the tradition and keep the integrity of the music, and to play from the heart and not so much from the head.

Dayna Stephens   saxophone, 1978 USA

1 Jack DeJohnette, Charlie Haden, Charles Davis on baritone sax, Herbie Hancock, Allan Holdsworth, Arve Henriksen, Betty Carter. If I made this list next week, it would likely look a tad different.

2 Playing with Herbie Hancock in Paris, in November 2002, as part of a UNESCO event while I was a student at the then Thelonious Monk Institute of Jazz, now the Herbie Hancock Institute of Jazz.

3 I wish that humans all over this planet remember that we all breathe the same air. I also hope we can grow a thick layer of compassion and empathy for one another, fueled by the realization that we can't choose our past traumas, or inspirations, that have brought us to this present, now. Musically, I hope to continue to enjoy the soulful journey that so many inspiring, unique artists take us on, every day.

Delfeayo Marsalis   trombone, 1965 USA

1 Soprano saxophone: Sidney Bechet, Branford Marsalis; alto saxophones: Johnny Hodges, Charlie Parker, Ornette Coleman; tenor saxophones: Coleman Hawkins, Lester Young, John Coltrane; trumpets: Louis Armstrong, Harold "Shorty" Baker, Dizzy Gillespie, Maynard Ferguson and Don Cherry; trombones: Kid Ory, Jack Teagarden, Vic Dickenson, Dicky Wells, J.J. Johnson, Urbie Green, George Lewis (me if necessary!); piano: Count Basie, Thelonious Monk, Herbie Hancock, Kenny Kirkland; bass: Jimmy Blanton, Charles Mingus, Ron Carter, Charlie Haden; drums: Baby Dodds, Papa Jo Jones, Art Blakey, Elvin Jones, Jeff "Tain" Watts; vibes: Lionel Hampton, Milt Jackson; harmonica: Toots Thielemans; vocals: Louis Armstrong, Billie Holiday, Ella Fitzgerald.

2 The last Japanese tour of Elvin Jones in January 2004. We arrived just outside of Tokyo for a concert in a small amphitheater that was perched on the side of a hill. Elvin had been having difficulties with his legs and couldn't walk up the stairs. A chair was tied on a dolly and Elvin carted up to the venue. It was raining. Once inside, Elvin said he couldn't play. There was a 10-year-old boy who offered to play. Many of the ladies were crying as the crowd chanted, "El-been, El-been, El-been", but Mr. Jones summoned up the strength that only a man of his fortitude and resolve could, mounted the throne, and the show began. His playing didn't have the strong, thunderous roars we were accustomed to, yet it was the most powerful performance I've ever participated in.

3 That the image of jazz musicians returns to being cool; and that all jazz musicians unabashedly embrace the African-American ingenuity of groove and spirit once again!

Dennis Chambers drums, 1959 USA

1 All depends on what style of music because, as you know, I love many styles of music, but here are two different styles I'm always interested in.
- Jazz music: Herbie Hancock, Jim Beard or Nick Smith on piano, Buster Williams or Ron Carter on bass, Bob Franceschini or Bill Evans on sax, John Scofield or John McLauglin on guitar.
- Funk music: Herbie Hancock, Jim Beard or Nick Smith on piano and keyboards, Rodney Skeet Curtis, Marcus Miller, Gary Grainger, or Anthony Jackson on bass, Dean Brown, or Kevin Oliver on guitar.

2 Is receiving my honorary doctorate degree from Berklee Music; and also playing with George Clinton Parliament Funkadelic, John McLaughlin, Steely Dan, John Scofield, George Duke and Stanley Clarke. I know, you said "one most rememberable moment," but it's hard to nail down one.

3 Peace and harmony on this planet.

Denny Zeitlin   piano, 1938 USA

1 I've been very fortunate, throughout my professional life, to be able to play with wonderful musicians, and have had a number of "dream" trios. If magically I could have been sitting at the piano in Miles Davis's second great quintet, with Wayne Shorter, Tony Williams, and Ron Carter, that would have been a "dream" band, indeed.

2 A pivotal event in my musical life was the opportunity to hang out with composer George Russell, in New York, in 1963. I was there, on a fellowship in psychiatry at Columbia Medical School, and spent many days with George, listening to music, and playing for him. His encouragement and belief in my music, coming from someone I admired and respected so deeply, was very precious.

3 My fervent wish for the 21st century is that, as a species, we find a way to make inroads on the tribalism that threatens to destroy us. On a personal level I hope to stay healthy; to continue to grow as a musician; as a psychiatrist to help my patients have more fulfilling lives; to stay curious and pursue my many interests; and to spend more and more time with friends and family.

Diane Schuur   vocal, 1953 USA

1 My dream band would be Buddy Rich on drums, Dave Holland on bass, Earl Bostic on saxophone, George Benson on guitar, Louis Armstrong on trumpet and George Shearing on piano.

2 One performance that shall forever be close to my heart was paying tribute to Stevie Wonder when he received a Kennedy Center Honor, in 2000. As he sat in the VIP mezzanine, I sang "I Just Called to Say I Love You" to him and the entire audience for this very special evening.

3 I wish for peace on earth, and that I and my fellow musicians may be partly responsible for helping make that happen.

Dick Hyman   piano, 1927 USA

1 I will give a list of my favorite musicians with pleasure, but it would not exactly be a performing orchestra, because not all of their styles would match.

However, here is a list — piano: Art Tatum; drums: Osie Johnson; bass: Milt Hinton; guitar: Howard Alden; trumpets: Bix Beiderbecke, Louis Armstrong; Clarinet: Benny Goodman; alto saxes: Charlie Parker, Johnny Hodges; tenor saxes: Coleman Hawkins, Ben Webster; baritone sax: Harry Carney; trombones: Urbie Green, Bill Watrous.

2 One of the most memorable events of my career was playing with the Benny Goodman Sextet, in 1948. Another was performing in recent years, in fact last week, as a duet with Ken Peplowski.

3 My wish for the 21st century would be peace and love for all.

Diederik Wissels   piano, 1960 Netherlands

1   Mathias Eick, Wayne Shorter, Pat Metheny, Eric Harland, Joe Sanders.
2   The creation of *Follow the Songlines,* writing for symphony orchestra with soloist David Linx, Maria João.
3   Tolerance, understanding, ecology, philosophy, joy, intelligence, beauty, respect, curiosity, humor, knowledge . . .

Diego Urcola   trumpet, 1965 Argentina

1   Joe Henderson: sax; Kenny Kirkland: piano; Ron Carter: bass; Jeff "Tain" Watts: drums.
2   Playing with Joe Henderson at the Blue Note for a week.
3   Hopefully to avoid World War III.

Dominique Pifarély   violin, 1957 France

1   The musicians I have been playing with in reality, because they all are responsible for who I am today.
2   My next performance, hopefully . . .
3   Justice, honesty, dignity: the end of exploitation.

Don Braden   saxophone, 1963 USA

1   Herbie Hancock: piano; Ron Carter: bass; Elvin Jones: drum; Freddie Hubbard: trumpet; J.J. Johnson: trombone; Cannonball Adderley: alto sax; (plus lucky me!).
2   I have had many, of course. But on this occasion I was on a Burkhard Hopper "Rising Stars" tour with my quartet: Darrell Grant on piano, Dwayne Burno on bass and Cecil Brooks III on drums, along with myself on tenor sax. A three weeks European tour with my own band — the good ol' days (90s) for sure! Anyway, in our first set at Birdland, in Hamburg, everything felt exactly right and ecstatic: the sound, technique, equipment, interaction with the cats, audience response . . . all of it. I was totally out of my own way, and the music and magic flowed unfettered. The listeners really got it, too. I have had many great gigs over the years, but none has yet matched the total human connection I experienced that first set that night. I'd hoped it would happen on the second set as well, but it merely went really

well, as usual! I dream of that happening again, and work towards it, every day. I want to let the music connect all our spirits!

3 My wish is that we humans take the next steps towards becoming mature. We have been growing and making progress in some significant ways, but we have a long way to go to reach our potential as mature Earth-dwellers.

For most of our civilization, our so-called leaders have been driven mainly by their addictions to power, money and sex. They have gotten a lot done in terms of innovation, and amazing things have been created and accomplished, but it's been a mess along the way: all kinds of wars and spectacular mistreatment of humans by one another, much of it fueled by those basic addictions. We all have been and still are burdened by the capitalistic hierarchical systems of business and government that these so-called leaders have built, mainly for their own gain, and thus they hold and hoard the bulk of the power and wealth, and constantly thirst for more. This makes absolutely no sense for the planet and most of its inhabitants, but it works for these leaders (so they think), and they're the ones in charge. Yet most of them are merely addicted, and acting like any uncontrolled addict: doing anything necessary to feed the addiction. Those of us who understand these systems can play along somewhat and do fine, but most of the planet is getting screwed over by this situation. And it's getting worse.

To me, all this is immature. We have the capacity to understand and manage our addictions, and our actual needs and wants. If we work together, we can build systems that would inspire and encourage (or force) us all, especially the leaders, to manage our addictions instead of merely feeding them, uncontrolled. Then the resources and power could be configured so that many more people could flourish (and by the way, the leaders could still have plenty). THAT would indicate real maturity, in my view. But the so-called leadership of the world has to look in the mirror, exert this capacity, understand and get control of themselves and their addictions, and be willing to take the steps.

This would be very challenging and take a lot of work, but my wish is that we start the process, then we will get there. And I think art in general and jazz in particular will be a big help; jazz is really about so many of the good qualities that connect all of us, including teamwork, empathy, spirituality, listening, supportiveness, leadership, creativity and democracy!

Donald Brown   piano, 1954 USA

1 Nat Cole, Cannonball Adderley, Freddie Hubbard, Milt Jackson, and Buster Williams.
2 Performing with Art Blakey and The Jazz Messengers in 1981-82.
3 I hope to be performing with my own band more often.

Donald Edwards   drums, 1966 USA

1 Donald Edwards: drums; Red Garland: piano; Ron Carter: bass; Freddie Hubbard: trumpet; Branford Marsalis: tenor sax; Cannonball Adderley: alto sax.

2 Seeing Art Blakey at the New Orleans Jazz Festival. Besides that, having the chance to play with Freddie Hubbard.

3 I wish for an end to racism. I wish for everyone to show love, peace and embrace our differences in culture.

Donald Harrison saxophone, 1960 USA

1 This is a hard question because I love so many musicians. If I had to choose a few of my favorite musicians for a dream jazz band of the musicians that inspire me every day, I would start with Sidney Bechet, Charlie Parker and John Coltrane on sax. I think the trumpeters should be Louis Armstrong, Dizzy Gillespie and Miles Davis. I would love J.J. Johnson on trombone. The drummers would be Baby Dodds, Joe Jones, Art Blakey, Roy Haynes, Elvin Jones, Billy Cobham and Tony Williams. On bass I would choose Slam Stewart, Ray Brown, Paul Chambers and Ron Carter. On piano how about Jelly Roll Morton, Duke Ellington, Count Basie, Bud Powell, Eddie Palmieri, McCoy Tyner and Herbie Hancock? The next band would be the funky bunch but we don›t have time for that one. This question is akin to asking a person to choose between seeing only a few people of those they love. I have played with over three hundred masters of jazz in addition to multitudes of masters of Classical music, funk, Afro-Cuban, New Orleans traditional jazz, New Orleans funk, soul, jam bands, Afro-New-Orleans-cultural music based on the offshoot sounds that came from Congo Square, Brazilian and many other styles of music. My real dream band would include all of them.

2 I have had many memorable events that inform the way I play. They color my musical emotions, intellectual understanding, and the physicality of my approach. I can even go back to the memory of my experiences in my present being to use as though they are happening at any moment I choose. A few of those experiences would include playing with Roy Haynes, Art Blakey, McCoy Tyner, Eddie Palmieri, Fred Wesley, The Headhunters, The Funky Meters, Leo Nocentelli; composing Classical orchestral works and playing with The Chicago Symphony Orchestra, The Moscow Symphony Orchestra, The Thailand Philharmonic Orchestra, etc . . . , Tony

Williams, Ron Carter, taking Johnny Hodges place in The Duke's Men, singing the lead chants as the Big Chief of The Congo Square Nation Afro–New Orleans Cultural Group, mentoring and having many rap battles with the king of NY hip-hop The Notorious BIG, having people on my bandstand like Christian McBride, Esperanza Spalding, Christian Scott, Mark Whitfield, Cyrus Chestnut, Jonathan Batiste, Dr. John, Bill Summers, Mike Clark, George Coleman, Lenny White, Allen Toussaint and many others.

I also treasure being directed as an actor in a movie by the great Academy Award–winning director Johnathon Demme, and working as an actor and script consultant for two characters based on me with Emmy Award–winning and MacArthur Fellow writer/director David Simon on his HBO drama *Treme*.

3 That we, as human beings, work collectively for the good of all, and for me to be the best I can be.

Doug Weiss   bass, 1965 USA

1 Joe Henderson, Thelonius Monk, Art Blakey, and myself.

2 The most memorable event in my career was during the recording of Chris Potter's record *Sundiata*, in 1994. The date was going pretty good as I recall, and about mid-way through I found myself playing a chorus on "Body and Soul." I happened to glance over at the drum booth. Al Foster was peeking at me under his cymbal, and his smiling eyes gave me the encouragement I needed right at that very moment. The years of our playing together started with that date. We have supported each other through many changes over the period of almost 25 years, and counting. He's been a mentor to me, and also someone I am proud to call my friend.

3 For the 21st century, for humanity, I wish all humans to live in peaceful accord with themselves. Peace will come when it is engaged internally. Musically I hope the music I and my friends and associates make can be transformative and helpful in this process. As artists we have a special calling of service, to help break old patterns of thought to allow new ones to manifest in the world. Through our music and our actions, may this become so.

Dr. Lonnie Smith   organ, 1942 USA

1. My "dream band" would be playing with an orchestra! Doc mentioned Gil Evans, Ravel and Oliver Nelson.
2. The most memorable events were my early years, playing along side popular Motown groups such as Gladys Knight, Curtis Mayfield, etc. I've also had the honor, throughout the years, of playing with many Jazz giants such as Jimmy Smith, or Monk. Of course, being honored, in 2017, by the National Endowment for the Arts was a most memorable musical event.
3. My wish for the 21st century is to bring Jazz back and mainly to the US, its birth place. Jazz is more respected in Europe and Asia. But here, most of the old Jazz clubs are gone, which is sad. A musician has nowhere to go, and just hang and jam. Jazz festivals have turned into pop festivals. Jazz is becoming lost to hype and commercialism.

Dré Pallemaerts   drums, 1964 Belgium

1. Wayne Shorter, Keith Jarrett, Charlie Haden.
2. Playing and touring with Mr. Yusef Lateef.
3. That, in its evolution, music does not lose its integrity and spirituality.

Eddie Daniels   clarinet, 1941 USA

1. Bill Evans, Scott LaFaro, Al Foster.
2. Getting an Honorable Doctorate from Oberlin College last year.
3. All acoustic music . . .

Edward Simon   piano, 1969 Venezuela

1. My dream band is my quartet Afinidad, with Scott Colley on bass, Brian Blade on drums and Dave Binney on alto sax.
2. Having the opportunity to join and play with the SFJAZZ Collective has been a memorable landmark. The year I joined, the band was Eric Harland, Matt Penman, Mark Turner, Miguel Zenón, Robin Eubanks, Avishai Cohen and Stefon Harris. Having your music played by some of the best musicians on the scene is truly a joy.
3. This question could be answered on many levels. My wish is for a more joyful, peaceful world. A more equitable society where the arts are a top priority, valued and supported, much like other professions. In general, I would say my wish is for awakening for all living beings.

Eli Degibri   saxophone, 1978 Israel

1. Herbie Hancock, Ron Carter, Tony Willams, Wayne Shorter, Miles Davis!
2. Around the year 2000, while already being a part of Herbie Hancock's band, he was asked to play a big concert in his hometown (Chicago) and to introduce a young musician of his choice to his audience. The concert was at an outdoor park. Herbie chose me and featured my

compositions to thousands of people including his parents! This was for sure one of the most memorable events in my career.

3 For people to get along just like musicians do for thousands of years — playing together in harmony! Wouldn't that be wonderful?

Eliane Elias piano, 1960 Brazil

1 I am actually playing with one of my dream bands almost every night: Marc Johnson on bass, Rafael Barata, and Rubens de La Corte on guitar. My special guest would include Frank Sinatra in his mid-1950s prime. If we could go back further, I would say, piano duets with Maurice Ravel or Bill Evans would be special.

2 There were two in recent memory. Two sold-out nights at Rose Theater in New York's Jazz at Lincoln Center titled *From Bill to Brazil*, where I programmed the first half of the show dedicated to the music of pianist Bill Evans, performing in trio with Marc Johnson and Joe LaBarbera (the last two members of Bill's trio). And the second half of the evening when I showcased my Brazilian quartet performing selected works from an extensive repertoire of original works and Brazilian classics. There was another night: a sold-out show in Paris, at Le Châtelet, where I performed with my same "dream quartet" and included Toots Thielemans as a special guest.

3 I have many wishes for the 21st century, but one word might sum them up: peace. Peace would encompass people living safely, without fear, having love, food, education, housing, medical attention, opportunities, and freedom to create what most matters to them in their lives.

I also hope that music will continue occupying people's hearts and homes, and bring to them comfort and inspiration.

Eliot Zigmund   drums, 1945 USA

1 Born in 1945, having grown up in the 50s and 60s in New York City, I was especially drawn to the bop and post-bop music that was happening at that time. It is still the music that most excites me after all is said and done. There was a sense of discovery, urgency, and living evolution of the music that was very unique to the time. I feel very lucky to have been witness to, and later part of that music.

Below would be one of my dream bands, heroes from my youth, but I should say there are so many others I would love to play with as well, from earlier and later eras. This is but one of those dream bands. Saxophone: Hank Mobley; trumpet: Lee Morgan; bass: Sam Jones; piano: Wynton Kelly.

2 One of my most memorable musical events was the first time I played the Village Vanguard with Bill Evans. Magical club, magical band. A dream come true.

3 For the 21st century. I can't imagine the challenges that will be facing the world and mankind as we move through this century. We are at a point in time when we need the most enlightened political, scientific, moral and ethical leadership to navigate and survive the challenges we will be facing with environmental degradation, mass migration, nuclear proliferation, population, food production, etc. Needless to say, especially in America, our leadership is lacking many of these qualities. We need to move beyond capitalism and authoritarianism and find new solutions to the world's problems. I'm hoping that with more enlightened younger generations and advances in technology, mankind and the world can survive these great challenges. There will be a great transformation and change in this century, the question is whether it will be into the dark or the light.

Elisabeth Kontomanou   vocal, 1961 France

1 The Duke, Mingus, Art Blakey, Louis Armstrong, Charlie Bird and Coltrane would have been my dream team.

2 Memorable experience: the recording of the album *Secret Of The Wind* with Geri Allen.

3 Peace to the world is my wish.

Ellis Marsalis   piano, 1934 USA

1 My dream band would be Branford, Wynton, Delfeayo and Jason on drums with Reginald Veal on bass (no nepotism intended).

2 The most memorable musical event occurred in New Orleans, at a club called Vernon's, when James Black (drummer/composer), his

wife Brenda, my wife Dolores and I went to hear the John Coltrane Quartet with McCoy, Elvin and Jimmy in 1963.

3 With an increase in Jazz studies programs at the university level, I hope the music curricula will reorganize the standard approach to the study of Western art music to recognize and include the oral tradition of Jazz improvisation.

Enrico Pieranunzi   piano, 1949 Italy
1 Charlie Parker, J.J. Johnson, Django Reinhardt, Scott LaFaro, Brian Blade — and Pieranunzi on piano, and arranging, of course.

2 July 2010: when for the first time I played at the Village Vanguard, New York, as a leader of a trio including Marc Johnson and Paul Motian, and recorded with them my first *Live at the Village Vanguard*.

3 That jazz keep living as long as possible . . . and that I keep being able to play it well, as long as possible.

Enrico Rava   trumpet, 1939 Italy

1 It happened already: Miles, Wayne, Herbie, Ron Carter and Tony Williams. Obviously it would be fun to put together Armstrong with Parker, Art Tatum, Jimmy Blanton and Elvin Jones, but I'm pretty sure it would not work.

2 Difficult question. Probably in 2014, at the Torino Jazz Festival where I played with a symphonic Orchestra my suite *Rava on The Road,* in the main square of the town, in front of about 30,000 people, and the whole thing sounded so good! . . .

3 Regarding the future: I hope they find a planet where we can go running away from pollution, wars and overpopulation.

Eric Grávátt drums, 1947 USA

1 My dream band would have been comprised of Thelonious Monk, Ron Evaniuk, James Allen Ford, Grachan Moncur III, Robert Rockwell, Fats Navarro and Eric Kamau Grávátt.

2 My most memorable experience was that of having spent three tours of duty with McCoy Tyner.

3 The three words of the 21st century are: wanted, dead, (or) alive.

Eric Reed piano, 1970 USA

1 Freddie Hubbard, Charlie Parker, Joe Henderson, Paul Chambers, Tony Williams.

2 Any time I played my composition *Wish,* written for my father.

3 My wish for the 21st century is that everyone would begin to think critically.

Ernie Watts saxophone, 1945 USA

1 Elvin Jones: drums; Charlie Haden: bass; Keith Jarrett: piano; Freddie Hubbard: trumpet.

2 In 1966, I was a student on a *DownBeat* magazine scholarship at the Berklee College of Music in Boston, when the Buddy Rich big band came into town on tour. Their alto saxophone player quit then, and Buddy needed an immediate fill-in player to finish the tour, but didn't think he could find who he needed in Boston on the spot. Buddy's manager called Phil Wilson at Berklee, asking for a bright student player as a temporary member to get the band back to New York. Phil recommended me, and I left school for Buddy's band. It was an amazing, remarkable experience to suddenly be part of an incredible ensemble like that, the tightest big band I ever played with before

or since, led by the person still considered to be the best drummer of all time. They just kept me; I was with them two years, toured the world with them, and recorded three albums. It was a transformative time for me; I learned a lot, from the individual band members and, of course, from Buddy too. I became a professional musician on that tour.

3 My wish is for world peace and understanding among all people.

Essiet Essiet   bass, 1956 USA

1 So to say "favorite" is relative to what your objective was at that time. I thought about my #1 group and I have more than one dream band. One of my dream bands would be Art Blakey: drums; McCoy Tyner: piano; Charlie Parker: alto sax; John Coltrane: tenor sax; Clifford Brown: trumpet; J.J. Johnson: trombone; Wes Montgomery: guitar; and Bobby Hutcherson: vibes. Another would be Tony Williams:

drums; Phineas Newborn: piano; Cannonball Adderley: alto sax; Joe Henderson: tenor sax; Freddie Hubbard: trumpet; George Benson: guitar, and Milt Jackson on vibes. And yet another one could be Elvin Jones: drums; Herbie Hancock: piano; Dexter Gordon: tenor sax; Dizzy Gillespie: trumpet, and Pat Martino: guitar. There are a lot of other players who would also be great in a dream band to me. Charlie Christian: guitar; Wynton Kelly: piano; Wayne Shorter: tenor sax; Red Garland: piano; Woody Shaw: trumpet; Mulgrew Miller: piano; Kenny Garrett: alto sax; Kenny Kirkland: piano. Probably more, but that might take all day.

2 I would have to say that playing in Art Blakey and the Jazz Messengers band was the highlight of my career, and I'm not sure if it will ever get any better.

3 My wish for the 21st century would be to get my group, International Bushman's Organization, working as much as possible, and to get a chance to play with the top players and groups of today's scene. I would also wish that jazz becomes more popular to the U.S. audience.

Eumir Deodato   piano, 1942 Brazil

1 Regarding the question about my "dream band," it would be unfair to name only a few musicians, since all the musicians that I have worked with, during my life as an arranger, producer, performer, etc., were very good and dedicated to the music they were playing!!!! I am a blessed person, and I thank the creator for letting me have the chance to exist (first of all) and to be able to have worked with so many GREAT artists, players and in so many GREAT PROJECTS!!!! I would need a thick book just to name a few of them . . .

2 I think it was when I was 12 years old and played the accordion, in pajamas, Rimsky-Korsakov's "The Flight of the Bumble-Bee" in a big theater stage, with little children dancing around me, all dressed as bumblebees . . .

3 My wish for the 21st century is that the music business around the world, return to a sustainable business level so the musical art becomes a doable career for young people to follow as a means of working!!!

Evan Parker   saxophone, 1944 UK

1 Every band I play in is a dream band. Many of my wishes have been realized, maybe some more will.
2 Playing with Cecil Taylor.
3 The end to senseless wars.

Fay Classen   vocal, 1969 Netherlands

1 My dream band — piano: Thelonious Monk; keyboards: Joe Zawinul; bass: Jaco Pastorius; drums: Elvin Jones; trombone and arrangements: Bob Brookmeyer; harmonica: Toots Thielemans; tenor sax: Michael Brecker, Dexter Gordon; vocals: Betty Carter and myself :-)
2 I am so happy and grateful to have had so many opportunities to work with some of my big heroes, like Barry Harris, Toots Thielemans, Michael Abene, Kenny Wheeler and many others. I always love interpreting music written especially for me, and also writing my own music. One of the most memorable experiences was when Bob Brookmeyer asked me to sing his incredible versions of songs only from the American Songbook, on his last album *Standards,* with his New Art Orchestra.

3 I'm convinced that everybody loves jazz, some just don't know it yet. So, my wish for this exciting century and the centuries to come is that jazz, with all its varieties, from intellectual to popular, always reaches the people. I wish that jazz gets more and more recognition for its own quality and profoundness thanks to the creativity of all the great jazz artists around the world; all those musicians who preserve and develop this unique art form.

Fay Victor   vocal, 1965 USA

1 Thelonious Monk on piano (Jaki Byard could sub!), Wilbur Ware on bass and Elvin Jones on drums, with Roy Eldridge on trumpet and Sidney Bechet on soprano saxophone.

2 Performing a poem of the incredible poet-activist Jayne Cortez, in duo with pianist Randy Weston, as part of his 91st birthday celebration.

   Ms. Cortez had performed this poem once with Mr. Weston, and is featured on his Blue Nubia recording. It is also the last public performance of Jayne Cortez before she transitioned.

3 My wish is for human beings to truly embrace our "humaneness," truly embrace our similarities instead of differences, and come together. If we don't, we may not survive. We need each other, this is a fact.

Ferenc Nemeth drums, 1976 Hungary

1. It's a difficult one, because of all the amazing musicians :) but let me try. It would have to be Miles Davis, John Coltrane, Wayne Shorter, Herbie Hancock, John Patitucci and Lionel Loueke.
2. I have a couple of them; in order of preference they would be: Carnegie Hall, Hollywood Bowl, Jazz à Vienne.
3. My wish is: Humanity among people, world peace, acceptance of all cultures and religions by everyone.

Flora Purim vocal, 1942 Brazil

1. My dream band would be Hermeto Pascoal, Ron Carter, Airto Moreira, and Joe Farrell.
2. My favorite events in my musical life was to sing with the Gil Evans Band at the inauguration of the Kennedy Center for the performing Arts. And the two years I spent traveling with the Dizzy Gillespie United Nations band.
3. My wish for the 21st century is that music keep the world united in Peace.

Foley bass, 1962 USA

1 Oh! Wow . . . this is such a Great Question! Well, this band would be HUGE!! Ummm, Shit . . . wow . . . Lemme Think:
Drums: Lenny White, James "Diamond" Williams; keys: Herbie Hancock/Bernie Worrell/Sly Stone; guitar: Jef Lee Johnson/Leroy "Sugarfoot" Bonner, Freddy Stone; horns: Miles Davis, Sonny Stitt, Fred Wesley (section of LIFE); vocals: Rance Allen, Aretha, Mavis Staples, Sly Stone; strings: London Philharmonic Orchestra; percussions: Steve Thornton; DJ: BHB.

2 Paris, July 1991, when Miles agreed to play with all of his alumni musicians. I felt like I'd been a part of something that could NEVER be taken away from me, I BELONGED THERE . . . Miles MADE IT SO . . .

3 EVERYONE . . . WOULD LOG OFF . . . (their phones, their computers, etc.) and simply get their LIVES BACK! Maybe it helps in decision-making? From hating each other to remembering WHY they're on Earth to begin with? It's NOT gonna happen . . . but I can Dream.

Franco D'Andrea   piano, 1941 Italy

1. With me: Tony Scott, Roswell Rudd, Paul Motian, Don Cherry as a special guest. And Thelonious Monk inspiring all of us.
2. Listening to my first jazz record: Louis Armstrong playing "Basin Street Blues" with Barney Bigard, Trummy Young, Bud Freeman, Billy Kyle, Arvell Show, and Kenny John. That sound gave a soul to my musical life.
3. Swing, colors and explorations.

François Couturier   piano, 1950 France

1. The music I'm currently playing may not sound like jazz. But, deep inside, I feel like a jazz musician. The question is thus very difficult! Talking about my idols (Coltrane, Miles Davis . . .) would be a little too easy. When I think about it, I would opt for a quintet: Jimmy Giuffre, Wayne Shorter (I'm an absolute fan of his current band), Charlie Haden and Paul Motian. I would offer them a quiet and very open music.
2. In September 2008, I recorded a solo piano album at the auditorium of the Swiss Italian Radio, in Lugano, for the ECM label. The first day went well, I had prepared especially written pieces. At the end of the recording, Manfred Eicher offered me the option to improvise freely. It then, turned into a kind of miracle for me. I felt as though in a musical bubble, with no stress, and played for two hours. The *One Day So White* CD consists of most of these pieces. More generally, I must say that my collaboration with ECM (11 CDs to date), a dream come true for a musician, at least for me, will remain paramount for me.
3. Continue playing with my close friends with whom I have shared the stage for 15 years. Duet with cellist Anja Lechner, the Tarkovsky quartet that I founded 15 years ago. Always invent new music, new projects with, for example, Jean-Paul Celea, Michele Rabbia and others, to widen this circle of friends.

Frank Gambale   guitar, 1958 Australia

1. For a jazz group it would be John Coltrane, Lennie Tristano, Jaco Pastorius and Elvin Jones.

   For a more fusion/rock group: Mitch Mitchell, Stanley Clarke, Jan Hammer, with Maurice White singing!!!

2. There are many... The first time hearing my music on public radio; auditioning for Chick Corea; the making of all my albums; playing on the stage at Jazz à Vienne (in a Roman Amphitheater!); playing Sydney Opera House with Return to Forever, to a sold-out house with my family in the 9th row... that was pretty cool for a kid from Canberra!... There are more, but I think that's more than one.

3. Guitar becomes cool again.
   - Music is only played on musical instruments by real people;
   - Popular music has more than one key;
   - Arts and music become as important as Maths, Geography and Science in school education;
   - More appreciation for Jazz and Classical musicians;
   - Humans find ways to solve the world's biggest problems such as poverty, environment, disease, etc. Again there's more but that's a good start!!!

Fred Hersch piano, 1955 USA

1. Sonny Rollins, Charles Lloyd, Miles Davis, John Hébert, Billy Hart.
2. The night I opened, as a leader with my own trio, at the Village Vanguard, in 1997.
3. An end to racism and homophobia.

Fred Wesley   trombone, 1943 USA

1 I'm living my dream since my current band, The NEW JBs, is my dream band: Bruce Cox on drums, Dwayne Dolphin on bass, Peter Madsen on piano (all three since 1990), Reginald Ward on guitar and Gary Winters on trumpet (both since 1999), and Phillip Whack on sax, since 2010.

2 The music festival that accompanied the 1974 "Rumble in the Jungle" between Muhammad Ali and George Foreman, in Zaire. You can see scenes from the event in the documentary movies *Soul Power* and *When We Were Kings*.

3 More melody.

Freddy Cole   piano and vocal, 1931 USA

1 Louis Armstrong, Duke Ellington and Stan Kenton would be my dream band!

2 It hasn't happened yet!

3 My dream for the 21st century is for Jazz to keep "swingin!"

Gary Smulyan   saxophone, 1956 USA

1 My dream band — this is really challenging by the way as my band would have dozens of musicians in it!! — would be: Charlie Parker/Pepper Adams, Kenny Dorham/Thad Jones, Bud Powell, Paul Chambers, Philly Joe Jones.

2 A major highlight was the day spent in the studio on December 18, 1991, with the great Tommy Flanagan, to record my CD, *Homage*, playing the compositions of Pepper Adams. This was an extreme honor because, at this point in his career, Tommy wasn't often recording as a sideman but agreed to be a part of this project ... It remains one of the most exciting, profound, and inspiring musical experiences I've ever had.

3 My wish for the 21st Century is to begin to create a more peaceful, tolerant, enlightened, and empathic world so we can make the planet a better place for all future generations ...

Geoffrey Keezer piano, 1970 USA

1 This is based on musicians that I didn't actually get a chance to play with, but would have loved to. It may not be a realistic combination!

Elvin Jones: drums; Jaco Pastorius: bass; Allan Holdsworth: guitar; Charlie Parker: alto sax. (A very odd band indeed!)

2 I was playing with vibraphonist Joe Locke in a duo at the Bach Dancing & Dynamite Society in Half Moon Bay, California. The venue is in a beach house, right on the Pacific Ocean. During our set, it began raining. As the rain grew in intensity, the sound of the raindrops on the roof of the house became like a "third instrument" and contributed a beautiful, percussive effect to the music we were playing. The rain mixed with our music, and combined with the stunning visual element of the rolling and crashing waves on the shore that we could see through the giant window in the venue, made this moment one of the most special in my life.

3 That we can truly evolve as a species to fully appreciate each other's diversity and uniqueness as human beings, and allow everyone to co-exist peacefully, without regard for skin color, gender, sexual orientation, economic status or any other mode by which we artificially separate ourselves from others.

George Cables piano, 1944 USA

1 I've had the good fortune to have played with many great iconic musicians. And I'm still playing with great musicians. So I'd have to say my dream band would be the guys I'm working with now, that is Victor Lewis and Essiet Essiet. Add: Freddie Hubbard, Dexter Gordon, and Bobby Hutcherson on vibes would complete the band.

2 Sometime in 1970 I was playing with Sonny Rollins in the garden of a museum in Los Angeles. It was a beautiful setting and a beautiful day. Sometime early in the performance, I happened to look at the audience and not only saw everyone smiling, but I could have sworn I saw something like a rainbow emanating from the audience. It was visible evidence of music giving joy and bringing people together.

3 It is that people can be open to each other and ready to understand and embrace their differences.

Gil Goldstein   piano and keyboards, 1950 USA

1 My dream band would be more like a dream duo. I love the opportunity to play in a duet with great players, as it gives me the opportunity to become an on-the-spot arranger. To pick duet partners on piano or accordion, I would put at the top of the list: Jaco, Pat Metheny, Bill Evans, Keith Richards, and Chris Daddy Dave.

2 Quincy Jones asking me to reconstruct the classic Gil Evans arrangements, in Montreux, featuring Miles Davis. All the concerts with Michael Brecker's quindectet, which I arranged and played electric piano. Being the main orchestral arranger and conductor for Sting and Trudie's Rainforest Concerts since 2006 at Carnegie Hall, doing at least 20 arrangements in about a three-week period and then conducting it, and watching it all come together.

3 To have the receptive universe that I saw in the twentieth century, always looking out for interesting projects for me, and putting me in touch with people that recognized my strengths and allowed me to exercise my abilities in projects. I feel like I'm at the top of my game now at my ripe old age, and therefore more experienced and wise about what I do, so there seems that there should be more opportunities coming down the pipeline. As Gil Evans said to me once, "Every day I wake up and say a prayer: God, I hope I'm lucky today!" I adopted that wish.

Gilad Hekselman   guitar, 1983 Israel

1 I wasn't sure if you meant to have a band for me, or just in general. If it's just in general, there are a few bands that are already dream bands, like the Miles quintet, Wayne shorter band to speak no evil, John Coltrane quartet, etc. If it's for me to play with, it's so hard to choose, but I think it would be with Elvin Jones, Wayne Shorter, Billie Holiday and Charlie Haden.

2 So many to choose from, but recently I did international Jazz Day and got to hear Herbie for the first time, just a few feet away from me. His sound and presence were inspiring and life-energy filling.

3 I hope for more compassion and open-mindedness to be re-found in the world. For people to connect to one another, more eye contact, more real-life experiences and . . . world peace. Can I ask for world peace too? I want world peace.

Giulio Carmassi   multi-intrumentalist, 1981 Italy

1 John Guerin: drums; Eddie Gomez (70s and 80s): bass; Michel Petrucciani: piano; Lyle Mays: synths; John Scofield: electric guitar; Pat Metheny: acoustic guitar; Joe Farrell: tenor sax; Jan Garbarek: soprano sax; Lew Soloff: trumpet; Gary Valente: trombone; Norma Winstone: vocals. In a band like that I'd be a multi-instrumentalist,

singer and arranger. Probably: synths, Hammond organ, vocals, sax, flugelhorn, percussion, vibraphone, arrangements.

2 I remember two very vivid out-of-body musical experiences. One is when I was on stage, in Japan, with Steve Gadd. I was the multi-instrumentalist in that band (with Will Lee and Chuck Loeb), and in that particular tune I was just playing the shaker. I remember the feeling of locking with Steve on a Bill Withers' groove and feeling one of the highest musical highs of my life, just listening. Another similar memory was when I was in studio with the Pat Metheny Unity Group. I was in the booth with Pat's Steinway, and I was hearing the band playing live with me through my headphones, and I remember for a minute getting to this other place and thinking, "oh this is the new Metheny group record, it's cool! Wait I'm playing piano on it! I am making choices as to where this bar will go or not go!"

3 Globally, one cannot but hope for a reversal of climate and environmental destruction. Or at least for plateau. And on a slowing down of the insane economic inequality making this world so angry and making people feeling left out. Personally, I do hope making art will remain a viable job for the young generations, as streaming, new technologies and the lack of any governmental or union protection (at least in Italy and the U.S.) has made it look less and less like a realistic life commitment.

Greg Osby   saxophone, 1960 USA

1. Geri Allen: piano; Oteil Burbridge: bass; Jack DeJohnette: drums; Hermeto Pascoal: soprano saxophone, percussion and keyboards; Gretchen Parlato: voice; Greg Osby: alto and saxophones.

2. One of the most memorable musical events of my career was to sit, with Wayne Shorter, all night, in a hotel in Japan, and to have him interview ME about my perspectives on music and life. At the time I was 28 years old, and he told me that I was a good thinker, and that I was on the right path. He also was one of my many idols, and HE told me that I was like the "son that they never had." That statement will resonate with me forever.

3. I am hopeful that artists that produce popular music, study the fundamentals of music again, so their songs will once again have form, development and substance — instead of simply loops and beats. Jazz musicians used to regularly improvise on popular music, which gave them familiar material that audiences could identify with. This, in turn, helped to popularize jazz because audiences respond favorably to instrumental music that is based on well-known themes.

Gregoire Maret   harmonica, 1975 Switzerland

1. Duke Ellington on piano, Charlie Christian on guitar, Charlie Haden on bass, Billy Higgins on drums.

2. The first time I played with Herbie Hancock. It was on a jazz cruise.

3. Hoping things will get better past the Trump era . . . and music will still be going strong and getting more exciting . . .

Guinga   guitar, 1950 Brazil

1. Piano players "changing places": Vladimir Horowitz, Duke Ellington, Bill Evans, Oscar Peterson, Art Tatum; as "horns": Charlie Parker, John Coltrane, Miles Davis, Clifford Brown and the Brazilians Nailor Proveta, Paulo Sérgio Santos, Jessé Sadoc and others. Bass: Charlie Mingus; guitar: Brazilians — Baden Powell, Hélio Delmiro,  Lula Galvão, Marcus Tardelli, Raphael Rabello; male vocals: Brazilians — Cartola, Paulinho da Viola, Milton Nascimento, Djavan, Caetano Veloso; female vocals: Brazilians — Mônica Salmaso, Leila Pinheiro, Fátima Guedes; international vocals: Ella Fitzgerald, Billie Holiday, Esperanza Spalding. This is a very difficult question! I would like to mention so many other artists that are, and were, very important for my career and for my musical appreciation, as listener.

2. I have had a lot of memorable musical events in my more than 50 years as an active musician! . . . I had many encounters with amazing artists that gave me the honor to play my songs. I would like to mention two: my meeting with the Choro master Pixinguinha, and the concert that I gave, a few years ago, with the Los Angeles Philharmonic at the Disney Concert Hall.

3. I would like to bring back to life many composers that touch my heart: Heitor Villa-Lobos, Gershwin, Tom Jobim, Leonard Bernstein, Duke Ellington, Pixinguinha, Ernesto Nazareth and many other great Classical composers.

Gwilym Simcock piano, 1981 UK

1 Michael Brecker, Toots Thielemans, John Scofield, Jaco Pastorius, Brian Blade.

　A mixture of heartfelt melody and music making, incredible command of the instruments and great groove!! — I'm not sure, sadly, that I'm good enough to be part of this, although I would be very, very happy to sit there and listen!!

2 Playing a piano concerto I wrote at the BBC Proms, at the Royal Albert Hall, London (and live on BBC television) in 2008.

3 That enough politicians around the world have the courage to take the necessary drastic steps to save the planet, so there actually is a future for our children and their children. Or else everything we do seems a bit meaningless — in the light of the impending catastrophes that await the world if nothing is done . . .

Hal Galper   piano, 1938 USA

1. The quintet I had with Mike and Randy Brecker, Bob Moses on drums and Wayne Dockery (whom we just lost) on bass.
2. Playing duo on "Con Alma" with Dizzy for seven nights in a row.
3. Resurrecting the Oral Tradition for future students.

Hal Singer   saxophone, 1919 USA

1. For a quartet, there would have Big Sid Catlett, Slam Stewart, Art Tatum and me. For a septet, Max Roach, Paul Chamber, Oscar Peterson, Lester Young, Miles Davis, Charlie Christian and me.
2. I can't answer that question. I have been with too many bands, on too many occasions, in too many countries and have so many great memories.
3. I'll leave the answer to that question to today's musicians.

Hamilton de Holanda   bandolim, 1976 Brazil

1 Pixinguinha: sax; Tom Jobim: piano; Nico Assumpção: bass; Luciano Perrone: drums; Nana Vasconcelos: percussion; HH: bandolim.

2 It was to see Hermeto Pascoal for the first time.

3 All kids around the world in school, for a good education, with a nice home, health and food.

Harold Danko   piano, 1947 USA

1 Louis Armstrong, Earl Hines, Lester Young, Charlie Parker, Bud Powell, Thelonious Monk, John Coltrane, Wayne Shorter, McCoy Tyner, Elvin Jones, Scott LaFaro — would be interesting, particularly with the piano chair alternating.

2 Playing for the first time at Carnegie Hall, with Chet Baker, in 1976 — I think. Also, my first trip to Europe, with Chet in 1975.

3 That the USA will return to civilization, but not much hope. I do hope there is more real person-to-person communication without all of the falseness imposed by electronic media. Maybe there will be some recognition for artists, particularly improvising jazz artists (not necessarily the current stars) who are off the spotlight radar.

Hein Van De Geyn   bass, 1956 Netherlands

1 This is a very difficult question, since there are a few musicians that I absolutely would love to play with — yet I can see the incompatibility between them as well — meaning that the mention of their names would not lead to a dream band after all ;-). If I were able to create a band with Kenny Wheeler, John Abercrombie, Enrico Pieranunzi and Jon Christensen, I believe that a band like this could have sounded amazing, if we had had the chance to play between 1980 and 1990.

2 The Tokyo concert with Chet Baker, Harold Danko and John Engels, in 1987, might be the most memorable concert I ever played. When I hear the recording I can still (after more than 30 years) remember the decisions I took, the thoughts I had during the performance.

3 If you mean musical wish: I would say that I hope that, although I basically stopped my career as a performing musician, I will have the time and inspiration to write some interesting music in which composed elements and improvised elements are woven into a coherent unity.

Helen Merrill   vocal, 1930 USA

Your questions are very difficult for me to answer, because every place I stopped in the world and worked, it was always with the finest musicians. I am a New Yorker and had so many wonderful musicians to choose from, here.

I would say recording with Ennio Morricone and Torrie Zito. Unbelievable sensitivity. Both magnificent arrangers.

Meeting Torrie Zito and working at a recording that I produce, called *Casa Forte;* his arrangement of *Natural Sounds* was magical.

A dream band . . . piano: Teddy Wilson or Bill Evans. How about two pianos equal one? Bass: George Mraz, Lester Young. I used to listen to him for his wonderful phrasing. (I suggest that all musicians listen to these amazing musicians!)

I realize this is not the answer you needed, but it is as close as I can answer with your guidelines.

Henri Texier   bass, 1945 France

1 I have had the chance to play with many great French masters, Europeans, Americans . . . and what really counts is to play with musicians who give you the joy of expressing yourself fully; that's why I would cite the members of my current "Sand" quintet: Sebastien Texier, Vincent Le Quang, Manu Codjia and Gautier Garrigue.

2 In the 90s, during a tour in Mali, with A. Romano, L. Slavis, G. Le Querrec and C. Caratini, we went, as we were accustomed to, to play impromptu in Korokoro a village in the Mandingo region. We set up our instruments on the village square made of earth and straw, very simple, shabby boxes. Spontaneously the villagers came to listen to us and by chance, just in front of me the oldest ladies, some of whom were shirtless and others smoking clay pipes, stood there. Suddenly I felt as though I were in a black and white film. . . . We started playing as we always did wherever we were, and, when we played one of my compositions, "Idemo," during my improvisation. The old ladies began to clap their hands in rhythm that seemed to me to go back

to time immemorial. I felt an extremely intense emotion, I was on the verge of tears to feel this deep sensation of being as close as we could to the sources of our music, and to share this music with these ladies who did not, who will probably never know who we were.

3 That suicidal bastards be annihilated and that, at last, people of good will make it understood that these same bastards can go ahead and commit suicide without killing us into the bargain, and without messing up every form of life on this planet.

Hubert Laws   flute, 1939 USA

1 Herbie Hancock: keyboard; Chick Corea: keyboard; Ron Carter: bass; Ralph Penland: drums; David Budway: piano.
2 Hollywood Bowl with Jean-Pierre Rampal in 1978.
3 Peace, Security, and Music Improvisation.

Ingrid Jensen   trumpet, 1966 Canada

1 Wayne Shorter, Geri Allen, Herbie Hancock, (yes, two pianists), Joni Mitchell, Jaco Pastorius, Jeff Watts.
2 I have had so many incredible moments making music that it is almost impossible to choose. A musical memory, that will always remain as a "big one" in my life, was sitting in with my idol Clark Terry at the Village Vanguard, in 1990. I was incredibly nervous because he didn't know me at the time and I wasn't sure I could calm my nerves enough to play in front of him, the Vanguard audience, and Clark's musical pals from the Ellington band that were there. It was an exciting night and we became great friends from that point on. He would always ask me to sit in if I was in the room and, every time, it was a swinging and wonderful affair.
3 I wish for more compassion, communication and calmness in every aspect of our civilization. Musical and beyond. We seem to be in a panicked state thanks to the direction of our current political direction, and people are forgetting about love and all of the amazing outcomes that take place when we stop thinking singularly, and start sharing all of our gifts and means with one another. More arts in education, music in the schools for everyone, and endless free concerts and gatherings where people can feel safe and freely express

their individual characters. When I think of all of the influential people in my life, this is why they taught me to do and be. To be me and to celebrate who I am, and what I have to say.

Iro Haarla   piano and harp, 1956 Finland

1 My present quintet — with Trygve Seim: sax; Hayden Powell: trumpet; Ulf Krokfors: double bass; Markku Ounaskari: drums — is an ideal line-up for my music; kind of a dream band. However, if I should make some other choice, I wish to perform my ballads with Jan Garbarek and strings (with a string quartet or with a chamber orchestra).

2 The most memorable musical event was: I had a concert with Norrlands Operans symphony orchestra and Iro Haarla Quintet at Umeå jazz Festival in Sweden, in 2012. I had composed a four-part commission work, *Ante Lucem,* (released for ECM four years later). Beside the enthusiasm of playing, I had a very strong feeling of sorrow while performing, for private reasons: during the period of eight months of composing the work, I also took care of my sick and old mother, at my home. She passed away two weeks before the performance. My mother was an opera singer, and a piece, by the name of *Songbird Chapel,* is dedicated to her. In the concert, while playing the tune, I could hear the voice of my dear mother, who would never sing

anymore — only in the chapel of songbirds — as an allegorical meaning. I can still hear the sound of a big symphony orchestra at the moment, in my ears. That, I will never forget.

3 I wish to record still one recording for ECM records, produced by Manfred Eicher. It would consist only of my ballads, with different line-ups. It would be a recording as a statement of my profound desire to protect nature. I wish to be able of doing something for the protection of nature — share peace and love, trying to make something good through the beauty of music. It is possible!

Ivan Lins vocal and keyboards, 1945 Brazil

1 Me: rhodes+voice; Pat Metheny: guitars; Bill Evans: piano; Dave Holland: bass; Vinnie Colaiuta: drums; Miles Davis: trumpet; John Coltrane: tenor sax; Wayne Shorter: alto and soprano sax; Bob Brookmeyer: trombone; Hubert Laws: flutes; Toots Thielemans: harmonica; Paulinho Da Costa: percussion; Milt Jackson: vibes. Wow!!!!!!!!

2 The International Jazz Day, last year (2017), in Havana, Cuba.

3 Besides peace on the planet, that musicians and composers of very good music (where jazz is highly included) of the whole planet, would receive, from the internet, the royalties they deserve, instead of the disgraceful fees they are getting, indicating a dark future. Composers and musicians produce the raw material through which digital platforms, multinational companies make huge amounts of money. At least 50 percent of the gross money from the digital commercialization should go to composers and musicians! This is what I would like to see, if possible, happen in the 21st century.

Jacques Morelenbaum   cello, 1954 Brazil

1. Miles Davis: trumpet; John Coltrane: sax; Hermeto Pascoal: everything; Bill Evans: piano; João Gilberto: guitar; Charlie Haden: bass; Tony Williams: drums; Gil Evans: arranging; Antonio Carlos Jobim: composer, and Jacques Morelenbaum: cello.
2. My first concert ever in Antonio Carlos Jobim's band, on March 28, 1985, in Carnegie Hall, NYC.
3. That mankind finally achieve peace and win its battle against hunger and extreme inequality.

Jacques Schwarz-Bart   saxophone, 1962 Guadeloupe

1. For me, the ultimate rhythm section is the John Coltrane quartet's: McCoy, Jimmy and Elvin... They are the only musicians that matched Coltrane's intensity and ability to constantly channel spiritually, from the absolute serenity of a ballad, to the controlled chaos of a modal tune, or the joyful bliss of a blues. If I try to imagine what it must feel like, I would compare it to sailing an unsinkable ship in the middle of a hurricane...

2 I will give a twofold answer to this question: first interpreting the word event as synonymous with accomplishment. Then I will take it as meaning: *anecdote*.

I was blessed to participate in new movements in music: Neo soul with D'Angelo, Urban jazz as a co-founder of the RH factor . . . odd meters post bop with Ari Hoenig and James Hurt.

But my greatest satisfaction was to initiate two musical genres that have since inspired many young talents: Gwoka jazz with the CD *Sone Ka-La,* and Voodoo jazz with *Jazz Racine Haiti*. Making these two projects made me feel that I brought my own little building block to the giant edifice of modern music, that I said something that no one else could say at the time. Since then, I have seen a blossoming of projects by great young Caribbean Jazzmen who are not afraid to embrace their roots . . .

My most cherished anecdote was the night when I met Roy Hargrove. I had just moved to NY and I was going to jam sessions every night. As I was walking out of a club, in the Village, my friend, Bruce Flowers, told me that Roy Hargrove and Chucho Valdés were playing at Bradlee's. A rush of adrenaline just took over my senses. Bruce and I walked a couple of blocks to Bradlee's. As we got to the door, the magic of the music put me in a trance. I felt the overwhelming urge to join this amazing musical feast on stage. As I was starting to assemble my horn, Bruce looked increasingly worried. He told me that if I played unsolicited, I would be quickly blacklisted on the NY scene. I brushed off his advice. As I jumped on stage, Chucho thought I was a friend of Roy's, and Roy thought I was a Cuban and part of Chucho's click. They both looked at me and signaled me to take a solo. I played with such abandon that two weeks later, I was on the road with Roy's band.

3 The music industry is experiencing a cruel transition: recorded music has now lost all monetary value since it can be streamed and often downloaded for free. CDs are becoming a thing of the past, as well

as record labels. I just hope that future generations of musicians will be able to enjoy the fruits of their labor and creation, just like we did up to 10-15 years ago.

An invigorated live scene could be one solution. If venues start multiplying, more talents can reach their full potential and bring about new waves of musical innovation. Having the government fund such a revival would be a breath of fresh air compared with the current era of cutting cultural programs.

It is time for the arts, and music in particular, to be treated as essential to human life and civilization, because no one can be happy without a song in their heart . . .

Jaleel Shaw   saxophone, 1978 USA

1 That's difficult. McCoy Tyner, Christian McBride, Roy Haynes.
2 I've had many. Hard to really describe just one. Performing with Roy Haynes with guests Ron Carter and Chick Corea at The Blue Note was definitely one of them.
3 Peace.

James Carter   saxophone, 1969 USA

1 The choices are so infinite with such a vast time frame! But let's see: Rhythm Section: Charles Mingus, Don Pullen, Ted Dunbar and Philip Wilson. Horns: Lester Bowie, Jabbo Smith, Sydney Bechet, Don Byas, Charlie Parker, Dicky Wells, Rahsaan Roland Kirk, Eddie "Lockjaw" Davis, early Lester Young, Louis Armstrong, Harry Carney, and Kenny "Pancho" Hagood as vocalist for openers!
2 I would have to say that one memorable event for me was to share studio time and space with the "elders" on my CD!! In particular, Harry "Sweets" Edison and Buddy Tate, from Count Basie fame, I had met 10 years prior to that session, in Detroit at a "Save Paradise Valley" concert, and told them, at 17 years of age, that I wished to record and/or jam with them! Total rite of passage for me!

3 My wish for the 21st century and beyond is for humankind to cherish ALL things that are beneficial to the fine arts, and never take them for granted, and to personally continue to strive, to be relevant, for many years to come!

James "Jimmy" Heath   saxophone, 1926 USA

1 During my career, I have been lucky enough to have played with most of my heroes, except for Duke and Basie. Over the last couple decades, I have had a big band, and that is my love now, at 91. Playing with these younger people, who are reachers, preachers and teachers, is heavenly. Saxophonist and doublers: Antonio Hart, Mark Gross, Bobby LaVell, Sam Dillon, and Gary Smulyan. Trumpets: Frank Greene, Mike Mossman, Diego Urcola, Freddie Hendrix (or Greg Gisbert). Trombones: John Mosca, Steve Davis, Jason Jackson and Douglas Purviance. Piano: Jeb Patton. Bass: David Wong. Drums: Lewis Nash or Evan Sherman. Vocalist: Roberta Gambarini.

2 One of the most memorable events in my life is taking my first flight. It was to Paris, in May of 1948, at the age of 21. The headliner of the festival was the Grande Coleman Hawkins who had John Lewis on piano and Kenny Clarke on drums with him. The Slam Stewart Trio with Erroll Garner on piano and John Collins on guitar. There was a singer, Chippie Hill. I was playing with Howard McGhee and his Sextet De BeBop. On bass was my brother Percy. The tenor sax man was Jessie Powell, the drummer, Specs Wright, the pianist, Vernon Biddle, and me on alto. I was in a dream world. Never forgotten.

3 The continuum of the Afro-American Classical Music called Jazz.

Jamie Baum   flute, 19— USA

1   This is a difficult question because there are so many musicians, both that have passed and are no longer with us, and that are alive today, that I would have loved to play with or would love to play with going forward. It is really impossible to narrow it down to one dream band! There are also many fantastic, younger musicians creating interesting and exciting music, that I would love to play with, and could be listed as my "dream band." However, I am very fortunate to have the musicians in my current band, The Jamie Baum Septet+, (featuring Amir ElSaffar, John Escreet, Jeff Hirshfield, Brad Shepik, Chris Komer, Sam Sadigursky, Zack Lober), who, besides being great musicians individually, have now played together and with me for nine years, and are very connected. They have become my "dream band" because they create such magic every time we play together. They interpret and bring so much creativity, spirit, passion and energy to my music! Nonetheless, if I could have played with Miles Davis and his quintet with Herbie Hancock, Wayne Shorter, Ron Carter and Tony Williams (or Jack DeJohnette), that would be one of my top "dream" bands. (Though some of his later bands would have been a "dream band," too).

2   Aside from many memorable concerts with my band "The Jamie Baum Septet+" and a very memorable duo tour with

pianist Richie Beirach in 2014, I was chosen in 2002 to be a U.S. Jazz Ambassador by the Kennedy Center/U.S. State Department, to tour in South Asia for six weeks, in a trio with Jerome Harris and Kenny Wessel. The U.S. State Department organized a concert for us in collaboration with one of the top Indian percussionists, Karaikudi Mani and his eight-piece band. We rehearsed his music with him and his band, and then performed a concert that was nationally televised. The level of musicianship of Guru Mani and his group was extraordinary, and performing with them in Chennai was very exciting, and something I will never forget.

3 In general: peace, tolerance, equality and compassion. For myself, as a musician: to continue to be able to play and collaborate with great musicians, compose, record, tour, grow and evolve.

Jane Bunnett   saxophone, 1956 Canada

1 Elvin Jones, Charles Mingus, Charlie Parker, Don Pullen, Woody Shaw, Jimmy Knepper, Chano Pozo . . . Jane Bunnett.

2 Most memorable musical moments:

- Playing with Don Pullen at the Havana Jazz Festival '91 . . . and later dancing to Los Van Van and Son 14.
- Playing and hanging with the legendary Slim Gaillard in Toronto Canada, from 87 to 91.
- Performing with Brazilian great Egberto Gismonti in Toronto Koerner Hall in 2014.
- Playing MJF in Montreal, Canada, in1992 with Don Pullen.
- Performing with Merceditas Valdés and our group Spirits of Havana in celebration of our CD first recording in Cuba, at Womad Toronto in 1991.
- Performing with Charlie Haden, Don Pullen, and Dewey Redman in Toronto, in 1994.
- Recording with pianist Paul Bley: *Double Time* in 1996.

3 As Dizzy Gillespie said: "A jazz club in every city in China," and peace and love to the world!!!!!

Jane Ira Bloom   saxophone, 1955 USA

1 Billie Holiday, Bill Evans, Miles Davis, Charlie Haden, Ed Blackwell.

2 Performing my NASA commissioned work, at the Kennedy space center, with astronauts John Young and Robert Crippin in attendance.

3 That live improvised music performed on this planet or others, in zero gravity and beyond, continue to move people in meaningful ways.

Jane Monheit   vocal, 1977 USA

1 This is such a hard question for so many reasons! A difficult one to narrow down. I don't know if I'd put these musicians together in a band, but each one would be worth the price of a time machine to play with! For piano, definitely Bill Evans. I've been just this side of obsessed with his music since I was a teenager. Bass would have to be Ray Brown, the most swinging of all time! Drums, now that's the hardest one, since I'm married to a brilliant drummer. Let's skip that chair and add a horn player, definitely Ben Webster.

2 The most memorable events of my career have always been about who I was playing with. I've been incredibly fortunate to have opportunities to play with so many of the greats ... and to get my butt properly kicked by them on the bandstand. Tommy Flanagan, Ray Brown, Ron Carter, Ivan Lins, Herbie Hancock, Wayne Shorter ... sometimes I think about it and it doesn't even seem real.

3 My wishes for the world right now have little to do with music, that's for sure! Things are hard all around. If anything, I hope our music can be part of the solution, whether it's because it brings people together and encourages understanding, or because it remains a source of joy and solace when those things are desperately needed.

Jason Lindner piano, 1973 USA

1. Aretha Franklin: vocals; Notorious B.I.G.: rap; Clarence "C" Sharpe: alto sax; Angus Young and Arsenio Rodriguez: guitars; the New York Philharmonic Orchestra of 1940 conducted by Igor Stravinsky and featuring the Bulgarian State Radio and Television Female Vocal Choir; Cachao: bass; Clyde Stubblefield and Tony Allen: drums; Doudou N'diaye Rose and his sabar drum; Aphex Twin: electronics and robotic MIDI-programming; Karlheinz Stockhausen: experimental electronics. I play synthesizers, Hohner clarinet D6 and Imperial Bösendorfer piano.

2. Arriving on the stage of Carnegie Hall to perform with Angélique Kidjo in the first performance of the Talking Heads "Remain in Light" music, looking out to a sold-out house — me, being from New York and remembering having performed on that stage as a teenager — had me extremely emotional.

3. Avoiding and/or curing cancer and Alzheimer's disease would be a good start.

Jay Clayton vocal, 1941 USA

1. Hard to say . . . I am about to turn 77 so you can imagine that I have played with some of my dream musicians. So I don't actually have a dream band, I just want to continue the projects I have going already.

2. I have to say, if I had to pick one, it would be when Muhal Richard Abrams asked me to perform with him, for his 80th birthday, at Roulette . . . a real honor!

3. I just want to continue performing and touring more, with the projects I am already doing:

   - Jay Clayton Quintet: I would be choosing from Julian Priester/Jane Ira Bloom/Ed Neumeister to name a few;
   - Jay Clayton/Jerry Granelli *Sound Songs* duo voice/drums;

- Vocal summit: Jay Clayton, Ursula Dudziak, Norma Winstone, Michele Hendricks — we are planning a reunion tour;
- Jay Clayton, Sheila Jordan *Bebop to Freebop;*
- Jay Clayton, Ken Filiano Double Duo;
- Jay Clayton "singing and saying the poets" solo voice with electronics.

Jean-Luc Ponty violin, 1942 France

1 I have had musical experiences with several dream bands throughout my life, so, I am afraid another "imaginary" dream band could turn into a nightmare . . . You never know . . . LOL! I will say that collaborating with pianist Bill Evans would have been another dream. When I discovered jazz, in my youth, I was very moved by his emotional playing, and such noble use of harmony, and I still am today.

2 Oh! I have quite a list of memorable moments, so I will pick one from my beginnings. Around 1966, I was 23 years old playing at

the Caméléon, a famous but small jazz club in Paris, when I saw Cannonball Adderley and Joe Zawinul walk in and sit in the front row, right in front of me. I became a bit nervous, but the look on their faces was so positive, smiling and bobbing their heads while I played, that my nervousness turned into excitement: I felt so honored by their presence. I learned later on that they had just landed in Paris for a show on the next day, and had asked the jazz promoter who picked them up at the airport: "Who is playing in town?" When Cannonball heard my name, he asked to go to the club before going to the hotel, bringing along Joe, who was the pianist in his band at the time. I had not yet played in America, so I was very surprised that they would even know my name.

3 I love democracy and applauded when artists from poor American neighborhoods were able to reach out to large audiences, with the way they use their talent to create simple forms of music, rap, hip hop, etc. But it is another thing when a mass of mediocre music is being exploited worldwide. Scientific research has confirmed that the highest forms of musical expression from geniuses in the Classical world, and jazz, have a very positive impact on the development of very young children's brains. We also know that highest standards of music have had an influence on societies in the past. So I wish that those standards be kept alive by the numerous, very talented, young musicians that are coming up in jazz and Classical, and not die out in our current and future world.

Jean-Michel Pilc   piano, 1960 France

1 I consider myself very lucky, having felt more than once that I was, indeed, playing with a dream band. I have been honored to share the stage with quite a few musicians whom I consider as masters, even geniuses. I couldn't wish for more, so I'll refrain from fantasizing and mythologizing (something jazz is very prone to), and I'll just be grateful for the actual dream that I have experienced with these exceptional artists.

2 Every concert for me is a unique moment, which feels like the first, the last and the only. Choosing one of them would be reductive, and

impossible anyway. To me it's a continuous process, not distinct moments which you can single out or hierarchize. This being said, in recent months, my duo piano performances with Martial Solal at Sunside jazz club, in Paris, have been particularly emotional. For me, since I was young, he has been the epitome of piano playing, of musical integrity, and of endless creativity. So it felt like coming full circle, so to speak.

3 I hope my children will live happily, in a world where freedom, respect, knowledge and reason will prevail over oppression, intolerance, ignorance and superstition.

Jeff Ballard   drums, 1963 USA

1 Let's limit the list to one big band, otherwise it would be way too long of a list.

Trumpets: Louis Armstrong, Miles Davis, Fats Navarro, Johnny Coles, Ambrose Akinmusire; trombones: J.J. Johnson, Curtis Fuller, Frank Rosolino, Richard B. Boone; alto saxophones: Charlie Parker, Logan

Richardson; tenor saxophones: John Coltrane, Mark Turner; baritone saxophone: Chris Cheek; pianos: Duke Ellington, Brad Mehldau; bass: Jimmy Blanton, Larry Grenadier; guitar: Bill Frisell; vocals: Ray Charles, Billie Holiday.
2 Playing with Ray Charles.
3 That we don't destroy ourselves.

Jeff "Tain" Watts   drums, 1960 USA

1 Although I have been fortunate to participate in what I consider dream bands, with the Marsalis brothers, Kenny Garrett and others, one dream band for me would be with Wayne Shorter, Charles Mingus, Kenny Kirkland, Jimi Hendrix and Aretha Franklin.
2 I treasure the time I spent with McCoy Tyner.
3 My wish for this century is for general human understanding between all peoples. This will enable us to strive to help each other, and to move forward and evolve.

Jeremy Pelt   trumpet, 1976 USA

1 I'd say my dream band would consist of Herbie Hancock: piano; Paul Chambers: bass, and Philly Joe Jones: drums! (Just a quartet!!)
2 I've had more than a few memorable events in the past 20 years, but a standout is playing a quartet gig with Mulgrew Miller, Bob Cranshaw, and Roy Haynes!
3 My wish for the 21st century, ironically enough, is that people take the time to listen and care (for melodies, in some cases) the way we did in the 20th century! I'm all for technical advancements, but I feel like the soul of music has been lost because people want a "quick fix." Who listens to full albums anymore??

Jessica Williams   piano, 1948 USA

1 On electric bass, Stanley Clark. On acoustic bass, Paul Chambers. On drums, Tony Williams. We have played together and loved each other's playing, but never recorded together.
   See, I never really took to jazz as a format, always trying to get my musicians to incorporate the steady time and fierce groove of Black soul musicians of the 60s and 70s. They made social music,

something that only Miles had the courage to model his music after. He loved Al Green and Curtis Mayfield. I grew up on the East Coast, where the time was sacred and soul music was popular!

2 The end of it. Brain damage from a spinal operation that occurred when I died in surgery. I woke up and I had a very vague idea of what jazz was, but could never play it again. On the other hand, I had played Rach 3 at Peabody Conservatory, and I did that just fine. What to do? At 70, it seemed the time to stop playing jazz. I never felt accepted in jazz, being different. I'm a matrilineal Jewess, white, tall, and very female. Oh! . . . and a post-operative transsexual? OMG! The sky is falling and the aliens have landed. My message to those whose lives revolve around their own prejudices: Get over it.

3 World Peace in our time. Barring that, a general awakening of our species to change, Newness, Humanism, Science, Space Exploration, leaving our cradle and becoming adults in a vast network of other worlds and other ways. Less childhood reliance on ancient religions and dirty politics, and an end to war, which can only happen with the inclusion of women in all fields, with less pressure on males to be macho, warlike aggressors. And stop killing black folks because of their color. Please wake up and ask what is right and what is plain wrong!

Jim Beard   piano, 1960 USA

1 I find this question impossible to answer. I have been a member of many dream bands and they have all been unique, and fulfilling musically. I am currently working in a dream band. It seems you could ask this question to anyone: a sports figure, an actor, a chef (who would make up your dream sports team, cast or kitchen staff). What's the point? Why not ask me a question about me and my music? Having said that, it WOULD be fun to play some straight ahead with P.C. and Jimmy Cobb. A bit with James Jamerson and Richard Allen wouldn't hurt.

2 This question also seems redundant. How and/or why should I have to choose between all of the amazing moments I've had and pick just one? But, there's being with Wayne and Joe reuniting in San

Sebastian after Weather Report broke up (and the party afterward). Also, there's my first professional record date with Dave Liebman. Certainly, something I will never forget is recording Toots Thielemans on *East of the Sun*. I flew to Brussels to record him on the rhythm section tracks that were recorded live in the U.S. When it came time for him to play "Diana," he asked if I would come into the live room and sit next to him while he recorded. He played just one take and when he finished, there were tears coming down his face. I will never forget that.

3 It has nothing to do with music but humanity in general. I hope we, as humans, find a way to become less reliant on devices and more reliant on each other. And I hope that we can ultimately understand that we are one race; the human race. And that we ALL occupy this speck of rock whizzing through infinite space.

Jim Black drums, 1967 USA

1 My music is made with my friends that speak a personal, shared, and common musical language, therefore I have been living a dream situation for the last 30 years, starting with our still working first

post-college band Human Feel (Andrew D'Angelo, Chris Speed, Kurt Rosenwinkel, and myself.) Sure it would have been fun to play with John Coltrane, but what kind of honest communication/musical understanding could we really have? I've been lucky to play with almost all of my "in my lifetime" heroes, except for one, Mr. Bill Frisell . . . we have never played a note together . . . so I'd book a gig with him and my friends if I could, just to experience the music we could make together.

2 Improvising with Steve Coleman for a week long tour, on the West Coast, was a concentrated musically affirming experience at a mid-life moment . . . But nothing beats all these years of recording and touring, with your own bands made up of your close friends, playing for our fans across the globe.

3 A world where all citizens are protected by enforceable, global, human rights laws: the right to proper living wage, the right to health care, and the right to proper food, clothing and shelter. That would indeed be a miracle to behold.

Jim McNeely   piano, 1949 USA

1 Saxes: Charlie Parker, Eric Dolphy, John Coltrane, Sonny Rollins, Pepper Adams. Trumpets: Snooky Young, Dizzy Gillespie, Thad Jones, Dave Douglas. Trombones: J.J. Johnson, Bob Brookmeyer, Slide Hampton, Dave Taylor (bass trombone). Rhythm Section: Me, Rufus Reid on bass, and Mel Lewis on drums.

   The ensemble work might be a little sloppy, but the solos would be *magnificent!* Plus several of those musicians were tremendous composers/arrangers — I wouldn't have to write much for this band!

2 The premier of my arrangement of "Sing, Sing, Sing" with David Liebman and the Carnegie Hall Jazz Band, in 1993. The band was incredible. Some people loved it; some people walked out.

3 I wish that by the end of the twenty-first century (2099) the human race is still alive, and that people have finally learned how to emerge from their individual tribes and get along with each other. It sure ain't happening now!

Jim Rotondi   trumpet, 1962 USA

1. Well, my dream band has, maybe, already existed, and I guess you might be hoping for a list that crosses timelines and eras, but for me, a band with Freddie Hubbard, George Coleman, Jackie McLean, Curtis Fuller, Herbie Hancock, Ron Carter and Philly Joe Jones would be sublime.
2. Well, there have been quite a few, but recording with George Coleman and Harold Marbern in George's octet, at Rudy Van Gelder's studio, was certainly one of them. Making a recording with Cedar Walton was another.
3. That Donald Trump only has one term! Oh, and maybe that all of us musicians are consistently treated with the respect we deserve.

Joanne Brackeen   piano, 1938 USA

1. Probably because I have a long history, I should mention Dream Bands I've led or been in:
   - Michael Brecker, Cecil McBee, and Billy Hart.
   - Joe Henderson, Eddie Gomez, and Jack DeJohnette.
   - Stan Getz, Clint Houston and Billy Hart.
   - Perhaps a future Dream Band would be: Ravi Coltrane, Ugonna Okegwo and Rudy Royston.

   (All-women bands seem to be popular now, if that were the choice it could be Grace Kelly, Linda Oh and Terri Lyne Carrington). There now are so many possibilities! Many of your above mentioned musicians would also make up an awesome dream band!!!
2. I think receiving the 2018 National Endowment for the Arts Jazz Masters Award, and having James Francies, Christian McBride and Terri Lyne Carrington play two of my compositions was a tremendous Musical Event.

3 To share my music with many people on earth is my priority! Performances, compositions, recordings!!! To continue to create and learn new musical concepts and ideas, and share through new performances, compositions, recordings, etc. with the largest amount of people possible, is certainly my wish for the 21st century. Perhaps music is the highest art form we currently have on this planet!!!

Joe Chambers   drums, 1942 USA

1 I cannot answer the "dream band" question.

2 Most memorable event was recording my first large orchestra CD, where I did all of the orchestration.

3 My wish for the 21st century is that jazz is alive and flourishing.

Joe LaBarbera   drums, 1948 USA

1 I truly feel as if I have already experienced my dream band with Bill Evans and Marc Johnson, but since you have expanded the time frame, my other dream band would include Lester Young and Nat Cole. I have reconsidered my response to question 1, and would prefer to play with Ben Webster and Nat Cole.

2 The most memorable moment of my career to date is performing at Carnegie Hall with Bill and Marc in 1980, as part of the Newport Jazz Festival in Manhattan, where we shared the Stage with Sarah Vaughn and her trio including Jimmy Cobb, on drums. What makes this date so memorable is that Bill arrived backstage 15 minutes before the start of the concert (very unusual for him) with stitches on his forehead, his left arm in a sling and a cast on that arm from the elbow to the finger tips! You can imagine the reaction from all of us, including manager Helen Keane, as we saw Bill enter the stage door. The audience reaction was a collective gasp, but once Bill seated himself at the piano and removed his arm from the sling placing it on the keyboard it was as if there was absolutely nothing wrong. His performance was flawless in spite of a serious fracture and head injuries which were the result of a car accident on the West Side Highway in Manhattan.

3 My hopes for the 21st century is that humanity rights itself worldwide. A good start would be to end hunger everywhere, and then proceed up that ladder improving healthcare and education to ensure that everyone can live in peace.

Joe Locke   vibraphone, 1959 USA

1 Kenny Kirkland: piano; Pino Palladino: bass; Adam Rogers: guitar; Lisa Fischer: voice; Terreon Gully: drums.

2 Playing a duet concert in Italy with pianist Cecil Taylor. It was like walking on a high wire without a net below!

3 My wish for the 21st century is that we are able to turn away from the encroaching neo-conservative right-wing wave that is spreading in

the world today, and embrace a philosophy of inclusion and kindness, as opposed to isolation and selfishness. It is a dream I truly hope is not out of reach.

Joe Lovano   saxophone, 1952 USA

1 My dream band would be Don Cherry, Thelonious Monk, Dave Holland, Charlie Haden, Paul Motian, Elvin Jones.

2 At 23, in 1976, being part of the Woody Herman 40th anniversary concert, and recording at Carnegie Hall, playing along side some of my saxophone heroes and influences, Flip Phillips, Stan Getz, Zoot Sims, Al Cohn, Jimmy Giuffre and Frank Tiberi . . .

3 A world where everyone embraces each other's contributions to humanity, and creates more of a universal song and dance . . .

Joel Frahm   saxophone, 1970 USA

1 Brad Mehldau, Charlie Haden and Billy Higgins, with me and Freddie Hubbard in the front line.

2 Playing the Monterey Jazz Festival as a leader, for the first time, with Peter Erskine, Billy Child and Scott Colley.

3 My wish is for human beings to soften their hearts, one by one, and start treating each other as brothers and sisters with gentleness and patience.

Joey Baron drums, 1955 USA

1 My dream band is always the band that i am making music with, at that moment.

2 Unloading my first drum set (used) with my father and mother, setting up in our living room, and playing along with the record player, and looking up to see the look of happiness on my parents' faces. If that's not nice, i don't know what is.

3 One of my many wishes for the 21st century is that music will still be made by musicians who care and are not afraid to be generous.

Joey Calderazzo piano, 1965 USA

1 Me, John Coltrane, Miles Davis, Tony Williams; as far as bass players: Dave Holland, Jimmy Garrison.

2 I have been very lucky to play with some of the best. Playing with Elvin Jones was such an honor. Another show I played was in Vienna. It was a duo show with Branford. It was as perfect as we ever played. Very special night that I will always remember.

3 My wishes would have nothing to do with music and more to do with overall humanity.

John Clayton   bass, 1952 USA

1 My dream band would be huge! It would include:

Trumpets: Louis Armstrong, Freddie Hubbard, Lee Morgan, Snooky Young, Harry "Sweets" Edison; trombones: J.J. Johnson, Curtis Fuller, Murray McEachern, Frank Rosalino; saxes: Cannonball Adderley, Gene Ammons, Al Cohn, John Coltrane, Pepper Adams; piano: Oscar Peterson; guitar: Wes Montgomery; vibes: Milt Jackson; organ: Jimmy Smith; bass: Ray Brown and John Clayton; drums: Art Blakey; vocals: Sarah Vaughan.

This is only ONE dream band. I can make at least ten other dream bands, easily.

2 My memorable events continue. But it's playing with my heroes that is most memorable to me. These were people I've admired for sometime before I was gifted with the opportunity to play with them. Playing with Milt Jackson, who was co-leading the first live band I had ever heard, in a jazz club (Shelly's Manne-Hole in L.A.), playing with Monty Alexander — my dream from the first time I heard him when I was 17; playing with my mentor, Ray Brown; touring with Count Basie, Carmen McRae, Nancy Wilson, etc. I pinched myself each time, not believing it was really happening.

3 My wish for the 21st century is that musicians are inspired to follow their hearts, regarding their music, take responsibility and be creative about building opportunities for themselves to share their art.

John Patitucci   bass, 1959 USA

1 John Coltrane, Miles Davis, McCoy Tyner, Wes Montgomery and Elvin Jones.
2 One of my most memorable events, so far, would have to be any of the gigs with the Wayne Shorter Quartet.
3 The things I pray for the most are an end to gun violence, racism, and any oppression of the voiceless peoples in the world.

Johnathan Blake   drums, 1976 USA

1 McCoy Tyner: piano; Ron Carter: bass; Joe Henderson: tenor sax; John Coltrane: soprano sax; Woody Shaw: trumpet.

2   Meeting Elvin Jones when I was 14 years old at the Blue Note Jazz Club, in New York, and having him place me on top of his hardware case to watch him while he played his second set. Also having the honor of playing with the great Clark Terry.

3   To rid the world of racism and guns.

Jon Balke   piano, 1955 Norway

1   I work with my dream musicians: Audun Kleive, Per Jørgensen, Bjarte Eike, Helge Norbakken, Pedram Khavarzamini, Derya Turkan, Mona Boutchebak. For me its important that I have good personal communication with my fellow musicians. And that is often difficult with the big stars :-)

2   I have had many strong experiences on stage, so maybe the most memorable ones are in special settings: performing on a snow stage on a mountain top with Jaap Blonk and my group Batagraf; performing *Siwan* in Cairo; the strange and beautiful concerts with Jøkleba.

3   Peace and prosperity on earth, and acknowledgment of the importance of culture in illuminating the minds of people, globally.

Jon Faddis   trumpet, 1953 USA

1   Wes Montgomery: guitar; Milt Jackson: vibes; Jimmy Smith: organ; Duke and Count: splitting the piano chair; Ray Brown: bass; Mel Lewis: drums parts; Philly Joe Jones: solos.

Trumpets: Louis Armstrong, Sweets Edison, Dizzy Gillespie, Clifford Brown, Miles Davis, Fats Navarro, Clark Terry, Snooky Young, Me?

Trombones: Tricky Sam Nanton, J.J. Johnson, Slide Hampton, Frank Rosolino, David Taylor, Douglas Purviance, and Bob Stewart: tuba.

Saxes: Charlie Parker, Johnny Hodges, Benny Carter, Lester Young, Sonny Rollins, John Coltrane, James Moody, Jimmy Heath, Pepper Adams, Gary Smulyan.

Vocalists: Ella Fitzgerald, Sarah Vaughan, Billie Holiday, Dinah Washington, Aretha Franklin, Fats Waller, Johnny Hartman, B.B. King, Frank Sinatra.

Composers and Arrangers: Duke, Thad Jones, Billy Strayhorn, Lalo Schifrin, Gil Evans.

2 The first time that I played with Dizzy . . . I was so nervous that I almost fainted! After that night, I knew that I was going to be a musician.

3 Peace and a healthy earth.

Jon Gordon saxophone, 1966 USA

1 So many to choose!
- Small group a) Mulgrew Miller, Dave Holland, Al Foster, Tom Harrell, Joe Lovano, John Scofield. b) Duo with Art Tatum; c) Trio with Lennie Tristano and Kenny Clarke; D: Jaco, Omar Hakim, Zawinul, Allan Holdsworth.
- Big Band a) sax section-Cannonball: Phil Woods, Joe Henderson, Sonny Rollins, Bob Gordon. b) rhythm section: Hank Jones, Dennis Irwin, Eddie Locke; trumpets-pops: Roy Eldridge, Dizzy, Clifford Brown. c) trombones: Al Grey, Benny Powell, Eddie Bert, Bobby Pring. I could easily do 10 more of these bands!

2 Many memorable musical events I'm thankful for, too many to mention. But one of the most important early ones was getting to sit in with Eddie Chamblee's band, at the Saturday brunch gig, for many years at Sweet Basil, as a teenager into my 20s. I learned so much from Eddie, Ernie Hayes, Jimmy Lewis, Belton Evans and Khalil Madhi! Also met and worked with many other great musicians through that, including Doc Cheatham, on Sundays.

3 I wish for peace, sanity and a livable, sustainable environment for the 21st century. For the music, I wish for deeper appreciation of jazz, it's history and significance, and the musicians.

Jonathan Kreisberg guitar, 1972 USA

1 This is a tough question, because the musicians that I play with, today, are incredible as well, and we all speak the same language, musically. So I truly already have a great dream band! But if I could have that wish, I think I would put together a group that would be a wild combination of personalities and eras. How about Lennie

Tristano, John Coltrane, Jack DeJohnette and Charles Mingus? Wow, that would be fun!

2 I've been fortunate to have had many wonderful experiences and opportunities over the course of my career, but I think one of the greatest was a true "learning experience" I had while still fairly young. At around 18 years of age, I was nearing the end of a period where I had studied, and emulated, many great players with great detail. On one particular day, I was performing a Pat Metheny composition, titled "Have You Heard," with a group in Miami. I prepared to launch into the solo section of the tune with my Pat Metheny ideas in full display . . . There was only one problem. As I looked into the front row of people in the audience, I was greeted by a familiar smile and aura-like hair style that all we know and love. Indeed, it was Sir Metheny himself! In that moment I was taught a lesson that stood with me for a lifetime. At some point (and for me, this was the time!) every player needs to break free from their influences and find their own path and voice . . . and then pursue it with great passion.

3 My hope is that Jazz continues to be a beacon of light to young fans. In my perception, the rush of technology and information is changing the relationship of music fans, consumers and artists. As they are confronted with a sea of mediocre information. It is my hope that Jazz will be seen as an alternative path. A great Jazz musician lives and breathes creative excellence and focus in a time when many other qualities seemed to be given more importance and attention. It is my hope that this will raise the art form to another level both musically and socially.

Jorge Rossy   drums and piano, 1964 Spain

1 Dream band with Nat King Cole on piano, Harpo Marx on the harp, Olivier Messiaen on the organ, Kenny Dorham on trumpet, Lester Young on tenor sax, Wilbur Ware on bass and Kenny Clarke on drums. Not everybody would play in every tune; I would experiment and the music would be sometimes swinging and sometimes very dreamy and open; I might play some vibes or drums in some of the combinations, but mostly just listen.

2 Too many memorable moments to choose only one! It feels wrong to choose one! It feels untrue to the nature of life experience with the constant flow of magical events . . .

3 For this century I just wish for the survival of human civilization. In other words: the end of capitalism, militarism and fake collective identities. The arrival of global humanism. What John Lennon described in the song "Imagine."

Joseph Magnarelli   trumpet, 1960 USA

1 I have played with so many great big bands, I have already lived that dream, so I will keep the band sextet: Paul Chambers, Duke Ellington, Roy Haynes, Charlie Parker, Ray Barretto (Roy Haynes loved Ray, he would come to hear the band in NY and sit right up front), me. :)

2 Playing JVC/Fuji Jazz Festival, with Ray Barretto's New World sextet, Carnegie Hall, June 2005. Many others too, but, this stands out, as we opened the show with "Persistence," my composition. We recorded it under the title *Mags*. That was a real thrill.

3 People will start talking to each other more, in person, showing love and compassion for one another. Also, that we make it in One Piece to the 22nd century.

Joyce Moreno   vocal and guitar, 1948 Brazil

1 For a start, Bill Evans on piano. That was my lifetime dream and it almost happened in 1977, when I did a project produced and arranged by Claus Ogerman. Unfortunately the album never came out, but Claus wanted Bill playing the piano on my song "Feminina." It would have been marvelous! As a Brazilian musician, I always believe the rhythm section should be from Brazil. So, alongside my own guitar, I would still choose Tutty Moreno as the drummer for this band, Naná Vasconcelos on percussion, and a good Brazilian bass player (could be Rodolfo Stroeter, who currently plays with me, or some good Brazilian bass player from the 1960s). I would be very pleased if I could jam with Django Reinhardt on a two-guitar basis. In my dream band, however, my second guitar choice would be Barney Kessel. All arranged and conducted by Johnny Mandel.

2 I've been lucky enough to have plenty of those. But I have to say that the 2015 concert at Berklee School of Music, with an orchestra of graduate students that arranged and played my compositions, was a beautiful moment for me. Performing at a Jobim tribute at Carnegie Hall (NYC, 1995) or having played twice at the Théâtre de la Ville (Paris, 1990/1991), or playing with my group at Barbican Hall (London, 2006/2008) were also great moments. I've had so many of those wonderful occasions in my life, and I truly believe that certain concert halls have a magic of their own: nothing can go wrong there.

3 Apart from world peace? More music in this world. "Peace and music" has been my motto for many years, and I still believe in both things as being intertwined.

Julian Joseph   piano, 1966 UK

1 Armstrong, Miles, Cootie Williams, Booker Little, Charlie Parker, Ornette, Coltrane, Shorter, Pepper Adams, Benny Goodman, J.J. Johnson, Frank Rosolino, Wycliffe Gordon, Dennis Rollins, Wes Montgomery, Butch Warren and Tony Williams. I'd try writing for a big band with these flavoursome musicians.

There are many more players to exchange and try like Dizzy, Fats, Clifford, Kenny Dorham, Lee Morgan, Freddie, Woody Shaw, Wynton Marsalis, Byron Wallen, Russell Bennett, Jackson Mathod, Sidney Bechet, Cannonball, Dolphy, Benny Golson, George Coleman, Johnny Griffin, Joe Henderson, Branford Marsalis, Gerry Mulligan, Tony Kofi, Jean Toussaint, Steve Williamson, Ned Goold, Soweto Kinch, Patrick Clahar, Nadim Teimoori, Vincent Gardiner, Chris Crenshaw, Elliot Mason, Frank Lacy, George Benson, Pat Martino, John McLaughlin, John Scofield, Pat Metheny, Bill Frisell, Mark Whitfield, Ray Brown, Ron Carter, Dave Holland, Jaco Pastorius, Reginald Veal, Charnett Moffett, Rodney Whitaker, Eric Revis, Christian McBride, Alphonso Johnson, Anthony Jackson, Paul Jackson, Marcus Miller, Mark Hodgson, Carlos Henriquez, Neal Cain, Art Blakey, Max Roach, Roy Haynes, Elvin Jones, Freddie Waits, Joe Chambers, Harvey Mason, Leon Ndugu Chancellor, Jeff Watts, Billy Kilson, Mark Mondesir, Eric Harland, Arthur Latin, Justin Faulkner and many, many more!

2 Playing the Royal Festival Hall on November 16, 2002, premiering my piece the *Great Sage* combining my Big Band with the strings of the BBC concert orchestra. The first half featured a sextet with legends Johnny Griffin and George Coleman added to my regular quartet of the time with Adam Salkeld, Jeremy Brown and Mark Mondesir. It marked a compositional progression from my Big Band concert at the BBC Proms in 1995, which is also a hugely memorable musical event for me. I've quite a few if I'm honest, and can't not include

premiers of my operas *Shadowball* — about the U.S. baseball Negro Leagues — and my first one, *Bridgetower,* about the gifted violin prodigy at the time of King George III.

3 I wish for greater tolerance in a world struggling to let go of old ways and old prejudices. I wish for an expansion of the jazz universe, with musicians and composers drawing even more on the remarkable wealth of talent that exists. My wish is that we all have a little more patience with one another, and raise our consciousness to give space, appreciation and even more support to beautiful and great things on this planet, so we aspire to the very highest possibilities of our imagination, creativity and humanity.

Justin Faulkner   drums, 1991 USA

1 I would have loved to play with Lee Morgan in one of his configurations. I loved growing up listening to Lee Morgan with my father. His music has had a huge place in my life. I would've loved to play with Shirley Horn and Coleman Hawkins as well.

2 I think the most memorable moment of my musical career was the two days that I spent with Mr. Ornette Coleman at his home, in NYC. We recorded a project with the great bassist Jamaaladeen Tacuma.

3 One wish would be for humanity to embrace honesty, empathy, compassion, patience and forgiveness. In this season of my life I'm working on each of these ideals. Fortunately, music, as well as my faith, has collectively contributed to the process of learning how to implement these ideals.

Karin Krog   vocal, 1937 Norway

1 Hampton Hawes: piano; Red Mitchell: bass; Billy Drummond: drums.

2 Recording and working with the Don Ellis Band in 1967.

3 That we still have music with melodies and harmonies!

Kenny Werner piano, 1951 USA

1 Paul Motian, Charlie Haden, and Dewey Redman.
2 Can't think of any. But many good ones.
3 That we realize we are all one entity, one connection.

Kevin Eubanks guitar, 1957 USA

1 Miles Davis: trumpet; John Lee Hooker: vocals; Larry Young: organ; Elvin Jones: drums; Meshell Ndegeocello: bass.
2 When I played in front of Mom and Dad in New York City. It was one of those great nights of music.
3 That the power of love will transcend and dissolve the love of power.

Kevin Hays   piano, 1968 USA

1 Miles Davis, Roy Haynes, Ron Carter.
2 I was working with Sonny Rollins, around 1994, and we were playing at an amphitheater in Istanbul. The power went out, but Sonny just kept playing in a kind of eastern "call to prayer" sort of way, and when the power came back on, the crowd roared with joy.
3 Peace among men and nations.

Kit Downes   piano, 1986 UK

1 I wouldn't want to hear myself in it, but my dream band would be John Coltrane's classic quartet — give me a time machine and seeing that band play live would be high up on my list.
2 Seeing John Taylor play a duet with Charlie Haden — it was the last time I saw Charlie Haden play, and one of the last times I saw John play as well, and time stood still, completely. I'm grateful that my wife and I got to hear that together.
3 A healthier relationship with our environment.

Kurt Elling   vocal, 1967 USA

1 Freddie Hubbard, Dexter Gordon, Herbie Hancock, Ray Brown, Roy Haynes.
2 Getting to record a duet with my 10-year-old daughter on a holiday record.
3 That the human race will come to its senses regarding the many potentially catastrophic challenges we face, and confront them in creative unity, and with compassion for all beings.

Kurt Rosenwinkel   guitar, 1970 USA

1 Charlie Parker, Bobby Hutchinson, Bud Powell, Joe Henderson, Paul Chambers, Elvin Jones.
2 Playing at Madison Square Garden with my band and special guests Allan Holdsworth and Eric Clapton. When the stage rotated around and we were in front of 20,000 people it was literally a dream come true, and slightly terrifying. Making one note on my guitar and hearing it roll through the arena was like nothing else. Not a good place for bebop though . . .

3 I wish that human beings evolve before they destroy themselves. I wish that peace and the pursuit of love, truth and beauty are the champions of men's minds. Or, if not, then a shift to a matriarchal governing body wherein man's aggressive nature can be tempered and kept in check. And then, of course, endless, ever-evolving music.

Lakecia Benjamin   saxophone, 19— USA

1 This is a hard question so I'll make a super-sized band. Drums: Roy Haynes; bass: Marcus Miller; piano: Les McCann, McCoy Tyner; alto sax: Lakecia Benjamin; tenor sax: John Coltrane; trumpets: Freddie Hubbard, Clark Terry; trombone: Fred Wesley.

2 One of my most memorable experiences was when I was playing, at the Inaugural Ball, with Regina Belle. The music director asked me if I wanted to go play another ball with Stevie Wonder. I said, "yea, right..." but agreed to do it. We ran about half a mile in the freezing cold without coats, in black tie evening wear. We finally get to the show and play an hour and a half warm-up set. I am convinced that Stevie Wonder is not coming so I am ready to leave. Finally, he comes and sings a song: I'm delighted. He apparently likes the band and ends up playing another hour and a half set of his own music, with us! On the song "All I Do" there is a famous alto solo. He screams in the mic: "somebody solo," and I start off with that line: yes goes

yeeeaaaaaaaaaaa!!! The whole band was cheering me on. After, he wanted to meet us and speak with us. Best night ever.

3 I wish that artists be allowed more freedom to create genuine, authentic music, without having to deal with the music business, politics, and side game. That the music and art truly come first.

Larry Coryell (with Tracey Coryell)   guitar, 1943-2017 USA

Tracy was Larry's wife and manager. She kindly sent the answers her late husband would have most likely provided.

1 Larry loved many musicians and played with many that he admired. But I can say that, in the last year or so, he was extremely passionate about opera and fusing jazz and Classical. He even wrote three operas of his own, and had two of them world premiered . . . a Larry most didn't know, but this was his new pioneering phase.

   Here is the fantastic dream band I know Larry would have loved to perform with, on stage: Maria Callas, George Gershwin, Charles Mingus, Yo-Yo Ma.

2 The World Premiere of Larry's first opera, *War and Peace*, based on Leo Tolstoy's most famous novel.

3 That the world become a more peaceful place; that he made a difference in people's lives and contributed to their happiness and inspiration, through his musical accomplishments and endeavors.

Larry Grenadier   bass, 1966 USA

1 Start with the trio: Duke Ellington on piano, Elvin Jones on drums. Add some horns . . . Joe Henderson on tenor, Charlie Parker on alto, Fats Navarro on trumpet. Maybe bring in Jimi Hendrix for a solo, and Oscar Pettiford on cello.

2 There are so many memorable, musical moments. I guess I'm always hoping the next gig will be the most memorable.

3 I wish that the world reconsiders what its most pressing problems are, and use our commonalities to solve them.

Larry Koonse   guitar, 1961 USA

1 Bill Evans: piano; Charlie Haden: bass; Paul Motian: drums — talk about empathy and taking the music into fresh directions!

2 Playing a duo gig with Charlie Haden at the age of 21. I quickly found out that there was a dimension to music that was bigger than myself, and that the source for that deep connection resides in a place that has nothing to do with intellect, knowledge, or experience.

3 My wish is that more younger people will embrace live performance over easily accessible video performances. Nothing like hearing and feeling powerfully creative musicians in three-dimensions!

Laurie Antonioli   vocal, 1958 USA

1 I've already worked with some of my dream players, and I love my band here in California. With that said, a band with Keith Jarrett or Marc Copland, Brian Blade or Paul Motian, Renaud Garcia-Fons, Michael Brecker, Kenny Wheeler and Nguyên Lê would be fun. Lots of possibilities with those musicians!

2 In 2006, in Leipzig, Germany with Richie Beirach. We performed at the Gewandhaus, and the choir director, Morton Schmidt, had arranged Richie's songs with my lyrics, for the choir. I stood in front of the heavenly voices, hearing my lyrics and singing with Richie, who was playing on a concert grand piano, in a beautiful hall. It was otherworldly. That was the year the World Cup was held in Leipzig

and the team from Mexico was staying in our hotel. We had Secret Service–type guys walking us out to our car, and we drove into a sea of people, on all sides of the car. Even though the crowd was there for the World Cup, it felt like we were rock stars on the way to the concert hall. It was surreal and memorable.

3 I hope that the dark times in our current political environment create a need, and sense of urgency, for truth and beauty. I hope that my grandchildren, and all children, will have days with nothing but sun and clean air, warm sand and fresh oceans — days with no computer screens — days where they can dream and grow.

LeeAnn Ledgerwood   piano, 1959 USA

1 My dream band to play with:
Steve Grossman: tenor sax; Jimmy Garrison: bass; and Billy Hart on drums.

2 One of my happiest and most memorable times in my career was the recording of the trio record *Transition* with Matt Penman on bass, and Jaz Sawyer on drums. I felt very strong within myself, and connected to these young and truly great players.

3 My hope for the 21st century is very clear. All of the major countries, in terms of pollution and greenhouse gasses, need to stop using, and investing in oil and its byproducts. We must stop destroying our planet. Nothing will survive this continued scourge of the earth, whether it be art or humanity. It absolutely must change.

Lenine   guitar, 1959 Brazil

1 It would be a big band: Tom Jobim: piano; Marcus Miller: bass; Django Reinhardt: guitar; Ravi Shankar: sitar; John Bonham: drums; Naná Vasconcelos: percussion; Dominguinhos: accordion; Toots Thielemans: harmonica; Pixinguinha: saxophone; Dizzy Gillespie: trumpet; Raul de Souza: trombone; Nina Simone, Tina Turner and Beyoncé on the vocals; Björk: doing whatever she wants . . . and a string quartet playing an arrangement of Heitor Villa-Lobos.

2 A concert we played at Le Zénith in Paris, with the Orchestre National d'Île-de-France, under conductor David Levi, with a choir of 1,300 young local students.

3 A planet without borders and in peace, committed to preservation and sustainability. And music, always.

Lionel Loueke guitar, 1973 Benin

1 Tony Williams, Dave Holland, Herbie Hancock, John Coltrane, Wayne Shorter.

2 My performances at the White House for The First Lady and President Barack Obama.

3 No boundaries in Jazz and in any style of music.

Logan Richardson saxophone, 1980 USA

1 I live my dreams. I have already documented my dream band. This documentation already exists in the form of my debut album on Blue Note Records. The title of this documentation, and record is *Shift.* This album includes Pat Metheny on guitar; Nasheet Waits on drums; Jason Moran on piano; Harish Raghavan on bass; and myself on alto saxophone.

2 Learning how to play the saxophone.

3 I live my wishes. Kansas City Cultural Arts (KCCA) is located in Kansas City, Missouri, my home town. To build the 21st century platform that artists of all disciplines, and the communities alike are able to mutually foster and develop from the inside. I am in the process of building this venue. KCCA is a vehicle for the incubation of the social, intellectual exchange that has always sprouted opportunities

professionally, artistically, and personally for the world's community of artists, and enthusiasts alike.

Lorraine Feather   vocal, 1948 USA

1 I am not a musician, but I am a lyricist. My dream band would be one of the "small big bands" used by Duke Ellington up till 1940 or so, but since we are time-traveling, I'd like to have Billy Strayhorn on the scene for all of it, and to write songs with both of them. I know, that sounds rather nervy, but it's my dream!

2 I don't know if you'd called it an "event," since it took place over the course of a couple of years, but the creation of my *Ages* album, which I began in 2008, was a turning point for me. I had produced half a dozen albums for myself as a singer, mostly writing lyrics to pre-existing music by legends such as Fats Waller and Duke Ellington . . . but also some songs written with composers I knew. The material for *Ages* was created entirely with living composers, including Eddie Arkin, Russell Ferrante, and Shelly Berg. It was the most personal project I had done. I loved working with these guys, and the album brought me my first Grammy nomination. I was sitting, watching reruns on TV, in my house on Orcas Island, when I saw the nominations on my laptop; I burst into tears, thinking of my late mother and father. I had been in the music business for over 30 years, and to do something I felt so good about, and have it acknowledged in that way, was memorable.

3 For music, or in general? My wish for jazz music is that musicians, singers, and songwriters, of all ages, find their own creative breakthroughs and make music that is truly original. Of course there are always people who are doing that! But I mean a groundswell of originality, a whole new golden age of jazz. For civilization, I would like us to save this planet, stop befouling it — and become truly compassionate toward other human beings and to animals.

Lou Donaldson   saxophone, 1926 USA

1 It would be a big band! Clifford Brown, Freddie Hubbard, Blue Mitchell, Gene Ammons, Dexter Gordon, Eddie "LockJaw" Davis, Charlie Parker, Johnny Hodges, Sonny Stitt, Harry Carney, J.J. Johnson, Curtis Fuller, Benny Green, Herman Foster, Idris Muhammad.

2 *A Night At Birdland* in 1954 (concert with the Jazz Messengers, Art Blakey's Quintet).

3 More straight-ahead jazz music!!

Louis Hayes   drums, 1937 USA

1 I can't identify a "dream band." That's like asking who you love the most, your mother or your father, or which of your kids you love the most. There are too many great artists, that I love and respect, to mention.

2 For me, there is no single event. I would say, it has been the unforgettable experiences of musically making myself, the artists I have played with, and the audiences, happy.

3 Stay healthy.

Louis Moutin   drums, 1961 France

I get your questions but, in keeping with the book of the baroness, I wanted to simply offer you three wishes.

1 To be able to continue to play music my whole life long.

2 To love and be loved by people who are dear to me, until the end of my life.

3 To see the world of human beings give prime importance to intelligence.

Luciana Souza   vocal, 1966 Brazil

1 Oh, this is very hard to choose ... Tom Jobim, Herbie Hancock, Wayne Shorter, Milton Nascimento, Lionel Loueke, Scott Colley, and Vinnie Colaiuta.

2 Oh, there have been so many. In 2017, I performed a new contemporary piece called *The Blue Hour*, with an orchestra from

Boston, called A Far Cry. The piece was composed by Rachel Grimes, Angelica Negron, Shara Nova, Sarah Kirkland Snyder, and Caroline Shaw based on a poem by Carolyn Forché.

3 It is a bit ambitious, but I do wish for a great enlightenment; for everyone inhabiting the planet to develop more acceptance and kindness towards each other — only then can equality and real progress be achieved by all.

Luis Conte
percussion, 1954 Cuba

1 Chucho Valdés: piano; Israel "Cachao" Lopez: bass; Steve Gadd: drums; Grant Green: guitar; Clark Terry: trumpet; Paquito D'Rivera: woodwinds, trombone; Shorty: trombone; Andy Narell: steel drum and auxiliary percussion; Dianne Reeves: vocals, and Me on percussion.

2 I've been blessed with many, but going back to my home land of Cuba, after 40 years, and playing with "la Conga de San Agustin" a local carnival ensemble of my home town, Santiago de Cuba, that is unforgettable . . .

3 Peace on Earth and more Music!

Luis Perdomo piano, 1971 Venezuela

1 John Coltrane, Hermeto Pascoal, Jorge "El Niño" Alfonso, Albert Stinson, Elvin Jones, Jimi Hendrix.

2 Playing piano, right next to Alice Coltrane on organ, was definitely a highlight; the time I got to compose for Tom Harrell; having Jack DeJohnette on my *Universal Mind* CD; playing with Ray Barretto in both his jazz and salsa bands . . . being a member of Ravi Coltrane and Miguel Zenón quartets . . .

3 Hoping that this primitive and savage humanity won't blow up the planet . . .

Lynne Arriale piano, 1957 USA

1 There are so many iconic jazz musicians that I would have loved to play with, that it is very difficult to narrow it down to form one band! Having said that, some of the musicians and groups that have most inspired me are the bands of Miles Davis, John Coltrane and so many others . . . too many to list. To play in any group that they led would be an experience of a lifetime.

2 I found great inspiration touring in Japan with the 100 Golden Fingers tour. To listen to and play with Hank Jones, Tommy Flanagan, Cedar Walton, Kenny Barron, Junior Mance, Roger Kellaway, Monty Alexander, Ray Bryant and Harold Marbern was a transformative experience; I am so grateful to have participated. I was fascinated to hear each pianist play every night, and to see how they approached the same nightly repertoire in a different way, during each performance. Also, hearing different pianists play the same pianos was really striking; for example, hearing Tommy Flanagan's touch and then listening to Hank Jones or Kenny Barron on the same piano was a great learning experience, as each musician had their own unique sound. I also learned so much from recording and touring with Randy Brecker, whose brilliance elevates every musical group he plays in.

3 My wish for the twenty-first century is to have a renaissance in consciousness; people taking a stand for truth, kindness and compassion.

Mads Vinding
bass, 1948 Denmark

1 Egberto Gismonti, Bill Evans, Stan Getz, Gary Burton.

2 There are too many to mention. Maybe the recording of the movie *Round Midnight* with Dexter Gordon. Or duo concerts with female singers.

3 Peace! — and that musicians play from their heart, keep evolving and get better paid.

Makoto Ozone   piano, 1961 Japan

1 Oscar Peterson, Erroll Garner, Buddy Rich, Thad Jones, Phineas Newborn, Quincy Jones, Henry Mancini, Sergei Prokofiev, Leonard Bernstein, Gary Burton, Chick Corea, Antonio Carlos Jobim, Astor Piazzolla, Keith Emerson, Rick Wakeman, and more… I have included non-jazz musicians because I truly adore their music and have been heavily influenced by them.

2 1983 Debut Concert at Carnegie Hall,

2005 Piano Duet with Herbie Hancock, at Montreux Jazz Festival;

2009 Performing at La Roque d'Antheron Festival with my Big Band, No Name Horses;

2013 Playing at "Quincy Jones 80th celebration Concert" in Tokyo, with my Big Band, No Name Horses;

2016 Piano duet concert tour, with Chick Corea, in Japan;

2017 The last concert in Tokyo, with Gary Burton on his Final Concert Tour;

2017 Performing at the New York Philharmonic Subscription

Concert series, as part of Bernstein Centennial Celebration.

3 To break down the wall between genres, as all the great musicians have succeeded in doing. And to always keep on creating new music. As a musician, it is so easy to stay in your comfort zone. But, regardless of genre, we need to keep on trying to create something we have not done before. It might be familiar on the surface to certain people, but it doesn't matter. We have to remind people that sharing Love with people is all we need, through this beautiful language called *Music*. And JAZZ, especially, is to me the most powerful and direct language that connects people's heart and Spirit.

Manu Katché   drums, 1958 France

1 Being a 20-year-old again, and being able to start again from the beginning, and living again all these past years!!!
2 Freedom and respect for everybody on this planet.
3 Having three more wishes, if it's possible . . .

Marc Copland   piano, 1948 USA

1 Drew Gress and Joey Baron. Piano trio is really intimate and loose; there's not a lot that feels better than playing a ballad with a trio. Drew and Joey are special players — with them the music can go anywhere.
2 The two partnerships I had, over several decades, with John Abercrombie and Gary Peacock, were really life-changing. In both these cases, I connected with a musical alter ego on a different instrument. The depth and character of understanding was special.
3 That more young players continue to work hard at their craft to try and advance this music; and that these players remain true to themselves, and make the most honest music they can.

Marcin Wasilewski piano, 1975 Poland

1 John Coltrane, Jack DeJohnette, Scott LaFaro and me ;-)
2 Meeting with Joe Lovano in 2006: my trio played with him during a two-and-a-half hour concert at the Bielska Zadymka Jazzowa (Poland).
3 To be still able to play and record my music, and cooperate with the best jazz musicians in the world . . .

Marcus Miller bass, 1959 USA

1 Hi-hat: Papa Jo Jones; ride cymbal and hi-snare: Philly Joe Jones; bass drum and low-snare: Dennis Chambers Jones; acoustic piano: Herbie Hancock; electric piano: Chick Corea; upright piano: Art Tatum; organ: Jimmy Smith; synthesizers: George Duke; guitar: George Benson; tenor sax: John Coltrane; alto sax: Cannonball Adderley; soprano sax: Wayne Shorter; trumpet: Louis Armstrong, Miles Davis, Freddie Hubbard; Producer/Arranger: Marcus Miller!
2 Playing for Miles Davis, Aretha Franklin and Luther Vandross on the same day (I almost missed the Miles gig, that would NOT have been cool!)

3 My wish is that jazz continues to grow; incorporating new ideas and allowing each generation to add to this beautiful language. My other hope is that human beings don't obliterate themselves with nuclear weapons.

Marilyn Crispell   piano, 1947 USA

1 I do not have a dream band. I've loved playing with my many colleagues these past years, but I do wish I could have played duo with Cecil Taylor. Also, that I could play sometime with Pharoah Sanders, and that I had accepted Ornette Coleman's invitation to come play with him, at his NYC studio.

2 Playing in Anthony Davis's opera, *X,* with the New York City Opera.

3 That people will learn to get along, solve their differences, and create peace on earth. And that they will respect, nurture and help to heal our planet.

Marilyn Mazur   drums, 1955 Denmark

1 I have formed several of my own dream bands through the years, and also had the experience of playing with some of my absolute favorites. Actually I am always making up dream bands, beginning with some kind of musical concept, and choosing musicians because of their sound and personality, human quality, sensitivity and vibes, and their telepathic ability to blend and agree on where the music leads us! It's not important for me to make my dream band with famous stars, as the music springs from what we can do together. But if I were to create a fictional new band now, selecting from the "spirits from the past" and also living greats (with some names that people know about), I might consider Miles Davis, Bill Frisell, Esperanza Spalding and Jan Garbarek. I'd like to add two more — yet

nameless — members, as I am always, i.e., searching for keyboard wizards and interesting singers, from other parts of the world.

2   Wow, there are several strong memories that pop up. Here are three!
- Living in Denmark since I was 6 years old, I returned to New York for the first time when I was 30 years old; two days later I was playing on the Pier in New York with Miles Davis!!! That was in 1985.
- Gathering my 14-piece unit for three concerts when I received the Jazzpar Prize, in 2000.
- Creating and meeting and playing with SHAMANIA, my wonderful present group of 10 female musicians, plus a dancer, since 2015.

3   That all people be resourceful, creative and generous, humble, respectful and good to each other. Musically, my wish is that there continue to be strong, individual, live musicians expressing their visions, and that the world enjoy and appreciate them, so it also becomes possible to have good (although hardworking) lives.

Mark Whitfield   guitar, 1966 USA

1   My "dream band" is Elvin Jones: drums; Paul Chambers: bass; McCoy Tyner: piano; John Coltrane: tenor and soprano saxophones; Freddie Hubbard: trumpet, and . . . if they allow it, I will play guitar!!! LOL!!

2   I toured with Carmen McRae for a few months, nearly 30 years ago, and while I was with her, we opened her show,

every night, by performing voice and guitar duets! I've had many amazing musical experiences but none greater than this!!

3 I finally feel like I have developed my inner voice, and my ability to express it through my guitar in a way I can be proud of, and I'm looking forward to continuing to travel the world, sharing my music and my love for music, with people everywhere!!

Markus Stockhausen   trumpet, 1957 Germany

1 Since I only live in the NOW, I tremendously enjoy playing with my fellow musicians like Tara Bouman on clarinets, Florian Weber on piano, Christian Thomé on drums, Jörg Brinkmann on cello, Angelo Comisso, also on piano, Ferenc Snétberger on guitar, Arild Andersen on bass . . .

2 Hard to say, because with so many projects, I have had really great concerts. My appearance as solo trumpeter "Michael" in my father's opera *Donnerstag aus Licht* at La Scala di Milano, in the spring of 1981, surely was one of the outstanding events of my life. But also many smaller concerts have been totally inspiring and have reached some people's hearts, which is the most important thing.

3 Respect each other no matter what religion, nationality, race, etc. — humans respecting humans. We all have so much more in common

than what makes us different. We all want to have enjoyable lives, shelter, enough healthy food, education for our children, etc. It is quite possible to live in peace with everybody, if only we wish so, and act accordingly.

3.2 Stop all wars, stop all weapon making, which in the end will always kill somebody. Immediate abolishment of all atomic bombs.

3.3 Each human being should feel responsible for the whole world, regarding nature, food, resources, water, energy, waste, etc. We all inhabit one and the same planet, and we have to share it justly and wisely.

3.4 We should only use harmless technology that does not do any damage to our health (regarding 5G).

3.5 Every child should already be taught how many people we are on earth, and that more than seven billion people do not make life easier on this planet, that fewer would be favorable. We all should be conscious of this fact, especially when thinking of having large families.

Regarding music, I have no special wishes: there is so much activity going on in all fields, it is wonderful. I, personally, promote the Intuitive Music a lot, which gives the musician the utmost freedom, yet it demands the highest skills and musicianship, as well as social qualities.

Martin Taylor   guitar, 1956 UK

1 Bill Evans: piano; Ray Brown: bass; Max Roach: drums.

2 Working with Stéphane Grappelli for 11 years (1979–1990) was an incredible time for me, and I have so many happy memories of Stéphane. Probably the most memorable single musical event was performing my *Spirit of Django Orchestral Suite* at the Royal Albert Hall, for the BBC Proms, with the Britten Sinfonia. It was such an incredible experience to hear my music played by that great orchestra, in such an iconic venue!

3 My personal wish is to continue creating music for as long as I can, and pass on the knowledge and experience that I've accumulated over the years to young players. My wish for music, generally, is that young musicians never lose sight of the magic of creating music, and how deeply it can touch the hearts of people.

Martin Wind   bass, 1968 Germany

1 Here is my "dream band"– trumpet: Miles Davis; tenor sax: Wayne Shorter; guitar: Pat Metheny; piano: Bill Evans; drums: Philly Joe Jones.

2 Well, there are honestly several, if not many highlights — such as a couple of trio concerts with Pat Metheny, or playing with Hank Jones, Benny Golson, the Metropole Orchestra directed by Vince Mendoza and special guests Randy and Michael Brecker... But if I'd have to pick one, I would go with a concert that happened in 2013,

in Jesi, Italy; it was with my own quartet featuring Scott Robinson (tenor sax), Bill Cunliffe (piano) and Joe LaBarbera on drums plus the Orchestra Filarmonica Marchigiana under the direction of Massimo Morganti. The program was called *Turn out the Stars — Music Written or Inspired by Bill Evans*. It featured my first arrangements written for orchestra: the title track "Turn Out the Stars" (Bill Evans), "My Foolish Heart" (Victor Young), "Memory of Scotty" (Don Friedman, dedicated to Scott LaFaro) and "Blue in Green" (Bill Evans). Scott Robinson and Bill Cunliffe each contributed a chart as well. The concert took place in a gorgeous old theater in this little Italian village, just outside of Ancona, and the atmosphere was magical! To be hearing my arrangements in this incredible environment, played by these wonderful musicians, and to experience the joy that the audience was having makes it unforgettable! I'm so happy that we were able to document this repertoire on the self-released CD.

3 Again I'm not really sure about your question; do you mean what I'm wishing for myself artistically or for the world that we are living in? Well, for myself I'm wishing to stay healthy so that I can continue to do what I've been doing for the past 20 years: trying to grow as a musician, bassist, arranger, composer, educator AND a human being. For our world, I'm hoping for the return of tolerance, peace and kindness — the last few years have been extremely discouraging and frightening, with nationalism and greed on the rise again.

Marty Morrell

drums and vibraphone,
1944 USA

1 Bill Evans and Scott LaFarro.
2 Concert in Buenos Aires in 1973. Bill played extraordinarily well. Wonderful audience.
3 More awareness of the arts in the US.

Mathias Rüegg   piano and arrangements, 1952 Switzerland

1 A duo with Billie Holiday and pianist Bill Evans; and writing the arrangements for an added string quartet.
2 An American gospel choir singing "Round Midnight," outdoors in an old ruin, at the Perugia jazz festival in 1989.
3 I hope a realistic one: that every single human being, in the whole world, has at least $16 a day (today's value).

Matt Mitchell   piano, 1975 USA

1 Re dream bands:
I consider NOW to be my ideal time for creating music with bands, as I have the resources of music history from which to draw, and an array of truly remarkable musicians with whom I am fortunate to play. The breath of possibilities that this combination allows for is staggering. But, in staying within the specific parameters of the question/exercise: I've often fantasized about the directions Eric Dolphy would have taken, had he not passed on so young. Sometimes, I imagine Sam Rivers as a pairing with him. So, maybe them for a front line, with Richard Davis and Tony Williams as a rhythm section. That's one of many possible examples from the "jazz" continuum.
2 My primary goal is to be able to document my work as a composer and pianist, so any chance I get to record and release my music is especially significant.
3 Peace. Higher collective consciousness for humanity, or at least the chance for all to freely access that.

Matt Penman   bass, 1974 New Zealand

1 I would love to have a quartet with Duke Ellington on piano, Questlove on drums, and Dewey Redman on alto sax. I've always

been attracted to musicians who were not necessarily virtuosos on their instruments, but amazing nonetheless. And I love the way great composers improvise — it really sounds like a beautiful act of construction. I just know that everyone would come up with something great, so maybe we would just freely improvise. Although who's going to turn down some new Ellington material . . . ?

2   It would have to be the time I played with Wayne Shorter's quartet in 2016 — that was a dream come true. A pure, musical conversation, with one of the masters of the music, in which I was so fortunate to take part.

3   I hope that robots don't end up playing better solos than humans! Seriously, I hope that with the way technology is progressing, we come to value that which is human above all else. This may sound obvious, but it could also be naive; it depends on which way we go. We are reaching a time when what it is to be human will be questioned repeatedly. Hopefully our examinations will lead to greater empathy; before you enlist technology to problem solve, you first have to choose which problems! To me, playing jazz music

is one of the most human endeavors I have come across, so I would like to see it become more universal, and more inclusive. It would be good for our world.

Matt Wilson   drums, 1964 USA

1 I would call it: Universal Spirits, with Duke Ellington: piano; Geri Allen: piano; Coleman Hawkins: tenor sax; Ornette Coleman: alto sax; Lee Morgan: trumpet; Ray Nance: violin; Jimmy Giuffre: clarinet; Sam Jones: bass; Oscar Pettiford: bass/cello; Gabor Szabo: guitar; Bobby Hutcherson: vibraphone; Carmen McRae: voice; Doris Day: voice; And I would love to have Jonathan "Papa Jo" Jones, as a drumming partner.

2 So many, but a trio concert at the 2004 Montreal Jazz Festival with Dewey Redman and Charlie Haden, stands out. These two grand spirits were both important mentors to me and we were family. I played with Dewey from 1992 until he died in 2006. One of my triplet sons, Max, has Dewey as his middle name. I played with Charlie from 2004 until he died in 2014. We both were proud parents of triplets plus one: eight kids but just four ages. Dig that? During that concert, I recall stopping playing, pinching my leg and exclaiming out loud, "This is not a dream, I am really here!"

3 More love, kindness, acceptance in our world. We need music and the arts to welcome "human moments" that everyone can share and use as a connection to each other.

Melissa Aldana   saxophone, 1988 Chili

1 I would love to have had the chance to play with the Miles Davis Quartet with Herbie Hancock, Ron Carter and Tony Williams.

2 When I got to meet my hero, Sonny Rollins, at the Apollo Theater, a few years ago.
   Sonny is the reason why I play tenor and not alto. I remember when I was around 12 and I heard him for the first time . . . I knew then that my voice as a musician was on the tenor saxophone and, since then, I have never looked back.

3 Peace in the world, I know that sounds like a cliché but that is the first thing that comes to my mind during these troublesome times.

Michael Formanek   bass, 1958 USA

1 My dream band would include: Lester Young on tenor saxophone and clarinet, Jaki Byard on piano, and Ed Blackwell on drums.

2 There are many, but the one I truly remember is a set that I played at the Village Vanguard, in the mid-1980s, with Elvin Jones, Tommy Flanagan and Lee Konitz. It was literally thrown together while we were all at a celebration for the 50th anniversary of the Village Vanguard, and I happened to be playing there later that night, so I had my bass there. I don't necessarily remember the music as being particularly great or anything, but just playing with Elvin and Tommy together had such a sweet feeling that I'll never forget it.

3 I assume you mean for jazz in the twenty-first century, because otherwise my wish for the twenty-first century is that our planet survives until the twenty-second century! For music, I hope that the twenty-first century is a time when the labels that are given to different styles of music completely disappear and musicians are free to play, compose, listen to, be influenced by, and respect any music or art that they choose to, without feeling that they need to defend their choices in any way. Many musicians have already reached this point, but they have to be very confident. Maybe this can only happen once we arrive at a time where race, gender, religion, and other differences people may have become completely irrelevant to any human interaction. I'm not overly optimistic that it will ever happen, but it's a nice goal nevertheless.

Michael Gibbs   trombone & arrangements, 1937 Zimbabwe

1 Trying to come up with a lineup for a dream band is difficult because, for me, it's the nature of the project, performing situation that defines the selection of players.

But, as I think back, it was when I arrived in the USA, in 1959, to start my studies at Berklee that I heard Horace Silver on his piano. He is the one who so thrilled me and inspired me the most initially, and whom I most remember with such fondness.

Being a trombone player, J.J. Johnson was always my favorite trombonist and inspiration, whom I met in 1960 at the Lenox Summer

School. I even had a few lessons with him. I did really love Benny Green also, and did both hear him and meet him.

Without a doubt Miles Davis has been the most inspiring trumpet virtuoso, but I also love Claus Stötter, Kenny Wheeler, Percy Pursglove, Cuong Vu, Julian Sanchez.

As for tenor sax, the field is vast, but Paul Gonsalves never fails to touch me deeply. For alto sax, Charlie Mariano has always also touched me, deeply, from the first note of anything he plays.

Right now, the drummer, who has been grabbing my ear in startling and always delightful ways, is Jonas Burgwinkel. But Adam Nussbaum has been my stalwart jazz drummer of choice for many years!

Bass? So many who thrill me — but I'm most drawn to opportunities to work with, and listen to Steve Swallow.

As for guitar — I've been so fortunate to perform and write for so many — but Bill Frisell, John Scofield and John McLaughlin whom I've known the longest. Yes, My BIG MUSIC album comes close to the dream band for me — and that has five guitars playing on it!

2 I was stunned when, after only two years at Berklee, Herb Pomeroy asked me to join his small/big band on trombone . . . That was in 1961-63. We played every Tuesday and Thursday nights at The Stables jazz club. The band included Sam Rivers, Ray Santisi, and Alan Dawson. We also played other outside events — festivals etc, and one concert. Coleman Hawkins joined us as a guest.

3 I'll be 82 at my next birthday — and find that thinking further than the end of the current week is about as far as I care to think. However, several really wonderful projects have arrived which will take me to January 2021 — bewildering, daunting — but, I find just thinking that far ahead too heady an exercise, and don't think much further than that.

Michal Urbaniak   violin, 1943 Poland

1 Herbie Hancock, Marcus Miller, Lenny White, George Benson, Kenny Garrett, Miles Davis, Stanley Turrentine, Mtume, Michal Urbaniak.
2 Recording on *Tutu* with Miles Davis.
3 More popularity for real jazz music.

Michel Benita   bass, 1954 France

1. So many fantastic musicians to choose from! Nearly impossible. All I can say is that I'm lucky enough to already play in a band I dreamed of: Ethics, with Eivind Aarset, Mieko Miyazaki, Matthieu Michel and Philippe Garcia.
2. My first recording session with Manfred Eicher, for ECM Records.
3. Two things: find the opportunity and time to write a piece for string quartet, and leave a clean and safe planet to my kids.

Michel Camilo   piano, 1954 Santo Domingo

1. From the great jazz legends that are no longer with us, I would have loved to have had Art Blakey on drums, Ray Brown on bass, and Chano Pozo on congas for my rhythm section! And for the horns, Clifford Brown on trumpet, Dizzy Gillespie on trumpet, J.J. Johnson on trombone, Charlie Parker on alto sax, Cannonball Adderley on alto sax, John Coltrane on tenor and soprano saxes, and Gerry Mulligan on baritone sax. What a wonderful sound that combination would have been!

Three Questions

2 There are so many that it is hard for me to pick just one, but among the highlights, I have to include the concert at the BBC Proms at the Royal Albert Hall in London, performing my *Piano Concerto No. 1*, as well as Gershwin's *Rhapsody in Blue* with the BBC Symphony conducted by maestro Leonard Slatkin! Performing with Tito Puente at the Montreal Jazz Festival. Jamming with Dizzy Gillespie, Jaco Pastorius, Herbie Hancock, Paquito D'Rivera, George Benson, Mongo Santamaria, Roby Lakatos, Chucho Valdés, Gonzalo Rubalcaba, Hiromi, Arturo Sandoval and many more. Also, a few solo piano concerts that were truly special at the Queen Elizabeth Hall (London), The Royal Concertgebouw (Amsterdam), Auditorio Alfredo Kraus (Las Palmas); the *Caribe* live album, and the memorable live streamed concert with my Big Band at the Marciac Jazz Festival (France). The Duo concerts with Tomatito at Carnegie Hall, Montreux Jazz Festival, Teatro Real (Madrid) and Palau de la Musica (Barcelona). Performing *From Within* with my Trio for the award-winning jazz documentary film *Calle 54*. And last year, my "Artist in Residence" symphonic, big band and duo performances at the Vienna Konzerthaus. Great fun!

3 We are living in amazing and exciting times with many discoveries and inventions happening really fast, so it would be fitting, for us in music, to evolve and advance as well; starting by "opening up" to new avenues of expression, more collaborations with no category or label of what type of music you are or are not playing ... Wishing for more "open minds" and much more freedom of creativity with infinite possibilities!

Miguel Zenón   saxophone, 1976 Puerto Rico

1 The Miles Davis Quintet (Miles, Trane, Red Garland, PC [Paul Chambers] and Philly Joe).

2 I've had many, but every time I get to perform in Puerto Rico it feels special. Not only because I get to play in front of my family and friends, but also because of the fact that I get to contribute to the cultural activity in my country. On those instances, it feels like I've actually accomplished something through my hard work.

3 My wish is that our world survive the twenty-first century and make

it to the twenty-second. We need to take better care of our planet before it's too late.

Mike LeDonne   piano and organ, 1956 USA

1 If I were playing piano, it would be Paul Chambers on bass, Billy Higgins on drums, Kenny Dorham and Freddie Hubbard on trumpet, Curtis Fuller on trombone, Charlie Parker on alto sax, John Coltrane on tenor, Pepper Adams on baritone sax, Milt Jackson on vibes, and Wes Montgomery on guitar.

2 When Milt Jackson passed away, George Wein gave me the honor of producing a memorial concert at Symphony Space, here in NYC, as part of the JVC Festival. I wrote some three-horn arrangements of Milt's tune for the first half. The band was composed of Jimmy Heath: tenor sax, Slide Hampton: trombone, Jon Faddis: trumpet and vibist, Steve Nelson in the front line with Bob Cranshaw, Mickey Roker and myself in the rhythm section. During the intermission John Lewis played solo piano. The second half really took the cake,

though. The band included me, Bob Cranshaw, Mickey Roker with Stanley Turrentine on tenor and Etta Jones singing. The last tune was a blues, and when Bob and Mickey heard Stanley start playing the blues, they lit on fire. The feeling of swing was so deep that Etta Jones, who usually never scatted, came over to me while I was playing, and asked if she could get a piece of it, and she went to the mic and started scatting her butt off. It was one of the few times I actually thought the roof was going to come off the building. The audience went nuts. For weeks after that, when I was up in that neighborhood, I had complete strangers coming up to me, on the street, saying that they had been there, and would never forget it. Neither will I.

3 I have a disabled daughter named Mary, who is the biggest blessing in my life. I've learned and grown so much from being around her. I created the Disability Pride Parade in NYC in hopes of raising awareness around the issues that plague the community she is part of. My hope is that the world will finally wake up to the fact that people like Mary are not damaged human beings to be pitied, feared and ignored, but are simply another beautiful and diverse aspect of humanity.

Mike Richmond   bass, 1948 USA

1 If I were to play bass in a dream band, and in this case an imaginary large ensemble, I would include:

Piano: Herbie Hancock, Chick Corea, Bill Evans, Wynton Kelly, McCoy Tyner, Thelonious Monk, Kenny Barron; drums: Elvin Jones, Jack DeJohnette; sax: John Coltrane, Cannonball Adderley, Joe Henderson, Charlie Parker, Phil Woods; trumpet: Miles Davis, Freddie Hubbard, Woody Shaw, Kenny Wheeler, Nat Adderley, Art Farmer; trombone: Slide Hampton, J.J. Johnson, Jimmy Knepper, Bob Brookmeyer; guitar: John Abercrombie, Wes Montgomery, Pat Metheny, John Scofield; bass: Mike Richmond. By the way, if there was room on stage, I would include a least a dozen other bassists . . .

2 It is difficult to name one event. There are *many* memorable musical events. Performing with the following musicians has enriched my

life beyond words: Miles Davis, Stan Getz, Dizzy Gillespie, Horace Silver, Joe Henderson, Elvin Jones, Jack DeJohnette, Roy Haynes, Billy Hart, Ravi Shankar, Gil Evans, Hubert Laws, Henry Mancini, Chet Baker, Michel Legrand, John Abercrombie, Pat Metheny, Toots Thielemans, Lee Konitz, Roland Kirk, Phil Woods, Art Farmer, Milt Jackson, Thad Jones and Mel Lewis Big Band, Tommy Flanagan, Charles Mingus Big Band/Orchestra/Dynasty. Life changing musical "jazz" events were, for me, to go to performances by the Miles Davis Quintet, John Coltrane, Lee Morgan, Jimmy Smith, Dave Brubeck, Charles Mingus, Art Blakey, Duke Ellington, and Count Basie, when I was in college.

3 It is for "peace and sanity in the world."

Mike Stern guitar, 1953 USA

1 My dream band would be playing with Miles Davis, Jaco Pastorius, John Coltrane and Bill Evans (on piano).

2 They are all memorable, and I am so fortunate to have played with so many great musicians. To name a few highlights: Michael and Randy Brecker, together and separately, Miles Davis, Jaco Pastorius. There are so many more!

3 My wish for the 21st century is first, to see Donald Trump out of office. Then we have much more hope for this century. Musically, however it evolves, it evolves. I'm not so worried about that. We NEED music, especially now.

Mike Walker   guitar, 1962 UK

1. Dave Holland, Chris Potter, Brian Blade, Keith Jarrett — or James Gadson, Willie Weeks, Donny Hathaway and Eddie Harris.

2. Most memorable moment? Listening to Kenny Wheeler Cadenza when I was touring his Music for Large and Small Ensembles band. Playing the Library of Congress with George Russell and him asking me to "Blues" him. "Blues me, Mike," he whispered to me, in front of a packed house. So I did.

3. It is that we learn to find out the truth of things *before* we assume, and then judge others. Our judgment of others often gives us an air of superiority. We don't like to admit it, but I think it's true.

Monty Alexander   piano, 1944 Jamaica

1. There is no dream band and at the same time every band is a dream band.
2. Seeing Louis Armstrong when I was a child in Jamaica.
3. More love and less fear.

Nadje Noordhuis   trumpet, 1980 Australia

1. At the moment, my dream band is my quintet — with Maeve Gilchrist on harp, Jesse Lewis on guitar, Ike Sturm on bass, and James Shipp on synths/percussion. I'm having such a lovely time writing for each of these musicians. Aside from them, perhaps a fun band would be

Dave Holland on bass, John Taylor on piano, and Johnathan Blake or Obed Calvaire on drums.

2. The one that springs to mind was the first time I played with the Maria Schneider Orchestra — my dream band for the last fifteen years. Another one was playing in a student concert band when I was teaching at a summer camp in New York — we were playing "Danny Boy" and the conductor had just explained the meaning behind the song. Halfway through the song, I hear some sniffing and looked over at my 12-year-old student who was crying as he played. Of course, then I started crying, and then when the conductor saw what was going on, he teared up too. Oh! The power of music.

3. Naturally, world peace would be amazing. Living in a world free from racism, sexism, homophobia, and classism would be beyond incredible. And I wish that music continues healing us all, as we strive towards that common goal.

Nathalie Loriers piano, 1966 Belgium

1 Not easy to answer the question of what my ideal group would be, because there could be several answers. I would opt for Jarrett's European rhythm section, namely Palle Danielson and Jon Christensen, and while we are at it, with Garbarek on saxes . . . A trio with Jim Hall and Charlie Haden would have been fine with me.

2 I have had a lot of beautiful moments with my trios, and the meeting with Tineke Postma was immediately magical at the first concert that gave rise to our first CD . . . But, one of the most beautiful music I got to play is Maria Schneider's, with the Brussels Jazz Orchestra (Maria directed, of course). This event will also be repeated in October for the 25th anniversary of the orchestra . . .

3 I would like all the beautiful music found in jazz, and other types of music, to be made more widely available to the general public. It is deplorable to see that commercial music takes up almost all the space on our airwaves, and that it sometimes becomes the only reference to a listener's ears.

I think we trust that the listener is "able" to hear and appreciate more . . . But, imagine a world where we would talk, on the street, about the release of Chick Corea's latest album, rather than the score of the Belgium vs Panama soccer game! I also hope that jazz will remain a music of the heart and freedom. But, if this question was more general, I obviously have this utopian dream that, one day, men will stop their bullshit and reach a degree of wisdom that will make them live in peace, with respect for this planet. In this event, music will certainly have a different position . . .

Nathan East bass, 1955 USA

1 Wes Montgomery: guitar; Bill Evans: piano; Cannonball Adderley: saxophone; Charlie Parker: saxophone; Chet Baker: trumpet; Elvin Jones: drums; Pat Metheny: guitar.

2 There are many including Sammy Davis Jr.'s 60th Anniversary Celebration with Ella Fitzgerald, Frank Sinatra, Stevie Wonder, Michael Jackson, Quincy Jones, etc. But possibly the most memorable was performing on the steps of the Lincoln Memorial for the Inauguration Concert of President Barack Obama.

3 That integrity, respect, peace and love become the pillars of our culture, and that music survive.

Nguyên Lê guitar, 1959 France

1 So many! Let's keep it to living musicians: Herbie Hancock, Wayne Shorter, Jack DeJohnette, Avishai Cohen.

2 In 2011, I was invited to play my music in Hanoi, Vietnam, for the first time by myself with local musicians. When I started to play, I felt so much love from the packed audience that I understood that my quest for identity was achieved, and a new path for sharing and making my music flourish could start.

3 Jazz was born in America, but now is going global. I wish every culture of the world would use that universal language to create more diverse, rich and unique colors of music and thus would help to foster peace on earth.

Niels Lan Doky piano, 1963 Denmark

1 It is indeed a difficult question. I have a lot of dream bands, many of which I have already played with — but here is one with which I haven't and will not (as most of the musicians are dead) — Freddie Hubbard: trumpet; Michael Brecker: tenor sax; Buster Williams: bass, and Elvin Jones on drums. Guests: George Benson on guitar and Sarah Vaughn, vocal.

2 Playing my first gig with Thad Jones in 1979 when I was only 15 years old. A life-changing experience.

3 Love, harmony and cooperation. A paradigm shift in values. Health, joy and laughter. Wisdom, experience and intelligence. Courage, vision and ambition. Science, knowledge and imagination. Spontaneity, creativity and improvisation. Cultural diversity and sustainable development. Free health care and education available to all. The permanent end of all wars, poverty and famine. A resource-based economy replacing the current monetary  system. Sustainable affluence and abundance for all. Respect, love and support for all species relationship. Skills as a part of basic school curriculum. Passion, admiration, excellence and awe-inspiring encounters with alien civilizations. Spiritual enlightenment.

Nils Landgren trombone and vocal, 1956 Sweden

1 Miles Davis, Duke Ellington, Charles Mingus, Jack DeJohnette.

2 A concert at Jazz Baltica, in Germany, together with Esbjörn Svensson on piano, Lars Danielsson on bass, Wolfgang Haffner on drums, Pat Metheny on guitar and Michael Brecker on tenor sax. It's all on YouTube, and it's epic!

3 A world without war, free from racism, hatred, bigotry and borders. Peace, love and Jazz.

Nils Petter Molvaer   trumpet, 1960 Norway

1. I already play with my dream bands. But other than them, maybe Jon Christensen/Jack DeJohnette: drums; Holger Czukay: megaphone; Christian Fennez: guitar; Eno/Lanois: electronics; Leland Sklar: bass; Nana Vasconcelos: percussion.

2. Hard to say, but the concert together with Herbie Hancock's band, at Tokyo Stadium, was a fantastic experience. But there are so many . . . it's hard to name one.

3. That my children and grandchildren can grow up on a planet that is clean, and that politicians actually work as public servants. And that the idea of "illegal" human beings are just part of our shameful history.

Norma Winstone   vocal, 1941 UK

1. The problem for me with this question is that I have *been* a member of a "dream" band, "Azimuth." Any band with John Taylor on piano, and Kenny Wheeler on trumpet and flugelhorn cannot be improved upon. I guess this is not the answer you are looking for so I propose:

   Herbie Hancock on piano, Dave Holland on bass, Jack DeJohnette on drums, and Mike Walker on guitar.

2. My 75th Birthday concert at The Cadogan Hall, as part of the 2016 London Jazz Festival, featuring my

European trio of Glauco Venier (piano) and Klaus Gesing (saxophone and bass clarinet) and including my two sons Leo and Alex Taylor on drums and voice respectively. This was followed by a set of arrangements by the late Steve Gray, for orchestra and big band. Magical!

3 To keep singing well, and being involved in interesting musical projects. Also peace for those poor people suffering in the wars in this troubled world.

Omar Sosa   piano, 1965 Cuba

1 Don Cherry, Carlos "Patato" Valdes, Bola de Nieve (Ignacio Villa), Richard Egües: flute; Emiliano Salvador: piano; and Charles Mingus. I would like to listen to what would have come out of a creation with these musicians . . .

2 It is very difficult but, following my instinct, what comes to mind is September 12, 2003, at Zankel Hall at Carnegie Hall with my Octet. It was a magical experience and, at the same time, it went by so quickly, everything happened so fast that maybe that's why it's always so present.

3 Peace, consonant harmony between beings, consensus, respect and freedom . . .

Orlando Le Fleming   bass, 1976 UK

1 Miles Davis, Wayne Shorter, John Coltrane, Keith Jarrett, Elvin Jones, (Charlie Haden, if two basses allowed!)

2 Playing with the Branford Marsalis Quartet in Gdynia, Poland. I was 23 and still living in London at the time. Eric Revis couldn't make the gig and Jeff Watts recommended me as they were looking for a last-minute replacement. I was not ready and underprepared. Branford gave me a hard time, but overall saw my potential, so it was still encouraging even though I sucked on the gig! It was a big venue and the whole experience was filled with extreme emotions and was over too quickly. This single event really helped shape the rest of my career. Branford encouraged me to move to NY, and then I went on to play extensively with bands led by Jeff Watts and Joey Calderazzo, also occasionally, with Branford's quartet.

3 More critical thinking and less motivated reasoning. Less identity politics and polarization. Caution on A.I. and care with climate change. My musical wishes for the 21st century would be: increased revenue for record sales, broader and longer attention spans for young listeners, less soulless factory produced music, and everlasting appreciation of live music.

Paco Sery   drums, 1956 Ivory Coast

1 Mozart
2 All the time that I spent on my career: I loved it.
3 Compose my symphony this year.

Paolo Fresu   trumpet, 1961 Sardinia

1 I would have liked to be in the Miles Davis band for the recording of *Kind of Blue* with Miles (or without Miles . . .), but with the same relaxed atmosphere and the same beautiful sound. With Coltrane, Cannonball, Bill Evans and the others.
2 It was my tour in Sardinia, my native land, on the occasion of my 50th birthday. 50 free concerts on 50 consecutive days, with 50 different projects, in 50 memorable outdoor venues. Without stages and without chairs for the audience. All this powered by solar energy and 140,000 people, and the demonstration that jazz is not music for just the happy few.
3 Continue to make music with passion and without commercial constraints. Also have the opportunity to travel with my mind. Visit places, see the world and meet new musicians with whom to make music with passion. But, especially, keep discovering myself through music.

Paquito D'Rivera   clarinet, 1948 Cuba

1 Wynton Marsalis, Chick Corea, Victor Provost, Dave Samuels, Giovanni Hidalgo, Romero Lubambo, Mark Walker and John Patitucci.
2 Touring as a guest artist in 2003 with Yo-Yo Ma, playing the music of the Grammy-winning CD *Obrigado Brasil*.
3 To perform in a democratic Cuba, free of communist rulers in power.

Pat Martino guitar, 1944 USA

1 John Coltrane, Lee Morgan, Gonzalo Rubalcaba, Richard Davis, Elvin Jones.
2 Aside from the depth of this moment, the formation, and reformation of the "Joyous Lake" ensemble, as well as its international performances.
3 That they all begin to realize how their constant focus, and creativity within "Now" has a greater importance than their pondering upon the past, or the future.

Patricia Barber piano and vocal, 1955 USA

1 Emma Dayhuff on acoustic bass, Victor Lewis on drums, Paul Desmond on alto saxophone.
2 Playing on Marian McPartland's show, meeting her, getting to be good friends with her until the end of her life.
3 My wish for the 21st century is that people put streaming away and begin to cherish music in physical and mental form again. Streaming is making people ignorant about music. It is hurting music and

devastating composers, conductors, ensembles, musicians and all associated with music. The old "precious object of music" was something we valued — we had to save money for it, we had to go to a store to find it — sometimes, a Betty Carter record was very hard to find; it took patience, resourcefulness, detective work; while sifting through bins, we learned about the music in a broader context. With our prize chosen and paid for, at home we opened the LP or CD, read the liner notes, read about the musicians, saw the tracks, the names of the songs, and listened in a knowledgeable way to the recording. We learned to love the artists as well as the music. We formed a relationship with them, the musicians, the conductors, the band leaders, their influences, the history of the music, the thoughts of the artist. This knowledge compelled us to seek out other recordings, related to the musical artists we heard and read about on the LP/CD. It encouraged further exploration and education about music. We set up special places in our homes to house the music we loved. Like the books we love, our homes were filled with these artists. Our shelves were lined with intelligence, humor, history, the sublime. Our lives were enriched with the presence and knowledge of the humanities, music being one of the pillars of the humanities. That which makes us human.

I have no illusions that this will happen, but it is what I would want for music in the 21st century.

Paul Jackson   bass, 1947 USA

1 Guitar: Jeff Beck; drums: Michael Clarke; tenor saxophone: Donald Harrison; keyboards: Herbie Hancock; bass: Marcus Miller and Paul Jackson.
2 Playing "Actual Proof" at Wally Heider Studios, in San Francisco, in August 1974 with the Head Hunters.
3 To be alive!

Paulinho Da Costa   percussion, 1948 Brazil

1 Question "impossible" for me to answer!
2 One event that is not only memorable, but the most important of

my musical career is NOT actually a musical event. It is when I met my wife in 1970 and she started to manage my career.

3 My wish is to have a non-violent world and to eliminate hunger from the face of the earth.

On a lighter note, let music lift our spirits and bring us some happiness.

Pee Wee Ellis   saxophone, 1941 USA

1 I'd like, in my dream band, Oscar Peterson, Paul Chambers, Elvin Jones, Herb Ellis, Johnny Griffin, Sonny Rollins, Benny Golson, Christian McBride, Michael Brecker, George Benson, Freddie Hubbard, and me!!

2 One of the most memorable musical events in my career, so far, would be meeting Sonny Rollins on the street, in midtown NYC, and asking for a lesson, winding up spending most of the summer of 1957 studying with him . . .

3 My wish for the 21st century is that I can play with more people, and help influence young people to savor the good things we have, and share the wealth of the world: Music!!

Peter Erskine drums, 1954 USA

1 I'm not sure that my time/space travel continuum fantasy can come up with anything better than the actual bands of Duke Ellington, Count Basie, Dizzy Gillespie and Charlie Parker, Max Roach and Clifford Brown, Art Blakey, Miles Davis, John Coltrane, Cannonball Adderley, Bill Evans, Charles Lloyd, Thad (Jones) and Mel (Lewis), et al . . . I imagine that any dream band would include Lester Young. And Michael Brecker. Sorry, I'm not very good at this game.

2 Tonight's concert was pretty great (May 30, 2018 at the Duc des Lombards, Paris). I would also include the recording with Joni Mitchell and orchestra that was done in London around the year 2000. I've also really enjoyed getting to play the concerto for drum set and orchestra titled *Erskine* composed by Mark-Anthony Turnage, with symphony orchestras in Los Angeles, Germany, the UK, Finland and Japan.

3 That the world returns to an orientation of win-win solutions for all to benefit from. My wish is that we honor those who fought for liberty and freedom, honoring their sacrifice by being kind and decent to one another. In other words, my wish is for man to evolve. We were tantalizingly close during the Obama era. My wish is for the pendulum to swing back. My wish is also for governments to fix broken things, and find a way to support more music in schools and in our society.

Phil Markowitz piano, 1952 USA

1 Tony Williams: drums; Eddie Gomez: bass; Michael Brecker: tenor sax; Dave Liebman: soprano sax.

2 There are SO many, it is hard to choose. Fabulous audiences all around the world, in various situations, but the Phil Markowitz–Joe Locke group at Carnegie Recital Hall, NYC, in the early 80s was the first "real" gig I had as a leader (with Joe) that elicited such a tremendous response. It was very reassuring that going out and

playing music could be such a great experience and success. Of course, having Eddie Gomez and Keith Copland in the band, at that time, made it unbelievable. We were very young and yet we had a rhythm section that was so brilliant and experienced!

3 Peace Prosperity and Communication. Let's hope we can keep our message of the world's greatest example of civic comportment "MUSIC" alive and well!

Philippe Baden Powell   piano, 1978 France

1 Bass: Esperanza Spalding; harp: Dorothy Ashby; percussion: Paulinho Da Costa; drums: André Ceccarelli; soprano sax: Wayne Shorter; vocal: Milton Nascimento; guitar: Baden Powell.

2 That is a hard one. All musical moments are special, but I keep remembering three of them which make me want to keep dedicating my life to music:
- The first concert that I ever played with my brother and my father in the Un, Deux, Trois jazz club in Rio de Janeiro.
- Playing as a keyboardist with Airto Moreira and Flora Purim.
- Playing as a finalist at the Montreux Piano-solo Competition.

3 My wish for the twenty-first century is that we all become the change that we want to see in the world.

Philippe Le Baraillec   piano, 1965 France

1. I don't want to embarrass anyone with my dreams, so to avoid any risk, and since I want to play the game, I'll only choose musicians who have already died! Charlie Haden, Ben Riley, Frank Sinatra, João Gilberto.

2. Next one . . .

3. Peace in the world; teaching philosophy in grade school; lots of polar bears that hug seals that hug new Eskimos 2.0; fields of organic zPhone; a new Dow Jones of non-profit companies. In sum, a world outside this world . . . so a kind of knife with neither handle nor blade!

Ralph Alessi trumpet, 1963 USA

1 John Coltrane, Tony Williams, Ornette Coleman, Charlie Haden, Paul Bley, Stevie Wonder, DJ Olive.

2 Playing with Steve Coleman at the Hot Brass, in Paris, in 1995.

3 To heal the planet.

Ralph Towner guitar, 1940 USA

1 I'll just pick some musicians that I would find musically compatible to fit in a group together. This is limited to jazz musicians that I have already played with, or would like to hear together, a group in which I wouldn't sound too strange. Scott LaFaro or Gary Peacock on bass, for sure. Keith Jarrett on piano. Joey Baron or Jack DeJohnette on drums. Collin Walcott on percussion. Miles Davis on Trumpet. Paul McCandless on woodwinds. John Abercrombie on electric guitar.

I have left out all the musicians that shaped my playing starting with the swing bands with Goodman, Glenn Miller, then Nat King Cole on piano, Louis Armstrong for my Dixieland period, Duke Ellington, Victor Feldman…Now I'm entering into my era. This can't become a list of all the musicians that influenced me, because I find it strange to have them all playing together from such stylistically different eras.

2 I have so many memorable events in the 70-plus years of being immersed in music, that this is a bit difficult to choose just one. But I am fond of one particular event: Around 1976 my band, Oregon, was in the midst of doing a sound check for a concert in Berklee Jazz Auditorium, in which Bill Evans was to be the opener, playing solo piano. (I had been living in NYC since 1968, and had met Bill and even shared some concerts with his trio. His trio of Scott and Paul had completely turned me around upon hearing them on records in the 60s.) Bill came rushing onto the stage, having just made it to Boston, and headed straight for the piano where I was still doing the sound check. He was saying excitedly as he approached, "Ralph, Ralph, listen to this!!!" and sat next to me on the piano bench and began playing the most amazing Bartokian sounding passages, very harmonically angular and complex. I was stunned, but I eventually had to say to him: "I'm sorry Bill, but we have to finish our sound check." He graciously gave the piano back to me. The irony of having to tell this legend and musical guru of mine, that he had to stop and let us finish our sound check was beyond anything I could have imagined happening when I was trying to emulate his playing, so many years before.

3 I would be happy if the music, that my generation of the 70s and 80s, in New York City, composed and played, would be recognized for its originality and given its place of importance in the evolution of improvisation. And of course, would continue to flourish in the 21st century.

Ramsey Lewis   piano, 1935 USA

1 Art Tatum, Dizzy Gillespie, Ray Brown.
2 The first time playing Carnegie Hall.
3 Peace on earth.

Ran Blake   piano, 1935 USA

1 Chris Connor, Mahalia Jackson, Abbey Lincoln, Ray Charles, and Al Green: vocals; Louis Armstrong: trumpet; Jimmy Knepper: trombone; Johnny Hodges: alto; Coleman Hawkins: tenor sax; John Coltrane: soprano sax; Serge Chaloff: baritone sax; Stevie Wonder: harmonica; Robert Pete Williams: guitar; Charles Mingus: bass; Max Roach: drums; Bobby Hutcherson: vibes; Mary Lou Williams and Thelonious Monk: piano; Jason Horowitz: violin.
2 Hearing Mahalia Jackson and Mildred Falls at Newport. I was a lifeguard at the Newport Jazz Festival that year and she started at midnight. That was in 1958!

3 That there are real peace and tolerance in the world. That more time is spent on hearing recordings, and for young people to appreciate History.

I met Nica (*Pannonica De Koenigswarter*) when I was a waiter at the Jazz Gallery, in the fall of 1960. More details can be found on Robin Kelley's biography of Monk.

Randy Brecker   trumpet, 1945 USA

1 OK Lilian, here's what I think. In 1961- 66 this question might have had some relevance since it was a pre YouTube, Facebook world and the history of the music was a mere 65+ years. Now, where every musician has instant access to just about every other musician on the planet, and also every musician who *ever played* in the now almost 120-year legacy of the music, which, in the interim, has been totally globalized, so there are great musicians all over the world playing it now, from Siberia, to unknown cities in China, to

wonderful players throughout Africa, and Eastern Europe, there are just too many players out there to make a hypothetical "dream band" and the question becomes rather absurd, that's the way I see it, kind of like the question about "which 5 records would you take to a desert island" ... well, maybe I'd take 500. I am remembering my brother "refusing to go there" when asked that question. But having said all this, if you could make Miles Davis disappear for a night (we're dealing with hypotheticals here) and drop me in the middle of his band doing a night at Birdland with Trane, Cannonball, Wynton Kelly on the first set, Bill Evans on the second set, and Paul Chambers and Jimmy Cobb — that would make me very happy. Also the same with the Coltrane Classic Quartet with McCoy, Elvin and Jimmy Garrison, but Coltrane would need to be there too! Also with the Sonny Rollins band he used on *Our Man in Jazz*: Don Cherry, Bob Cranshaw and Billy Higgins . . . and while you are at it, stick me in the middle of some Louis Jordan "soundies" of the 30s and 40s, so I could learn how to swing my butt off and entertain at the same time. And just for a pinch of God, stick me in the middle of the choir at the New Bethal Baptist Church with Rev C.L. Franklin at the helm and daughter Aretha singing all the lead parts . . . and all that would be enough . . . just for now!

2 My most pivotal/memorable musical event was writing for, and forming the original Brecker Brothers Band in 1974-5. This *was* my Dream Band at the time. Mike Brecker, Dave Sanborn, Don Grolnick, Bob Mann and Steve Khan, Will Lee, Harvey Mason and Chris Parker and Ralph MacDonald. I had written nine tunes and arrangements expressly for this personnel, and was just getting ready to record a demo, and start shopping the music, when I got a call from a man named Steve Backer who informed me that he was a record producer who had a new production deal with a newly formed label, Arista, headed by the great Clive Davis, a genius in the business. Steve said he'd been hearing about the music I had written, as had Clive. Clive had told him if I called the band "The Brecker Bros" he would sign me, and I wouldn't have to start shopping a demo. At first I protested since I wanted it to be a solo "Randy Brecker" record, but I relented, it was too great an opportunity, and the "Brecker Brothers Band" was formed with that moniker. Then Clive insisted we also do a single. I protested again, saying, "First, I gave up it being a solo work, now he wanted to add a tune to the nine tunes I had envisioned?" Well, he drove a hard bargain (like not releasing it at all!), so I trudged back to where we rehearsed, told the guys what had happened, and in less than 3 or 4 hours we jammed up a tune called "Sneakin' Up Behind You" which he stuck on the record. Clive loved it. Well that tune shot

up to #2 on the urban *Billboard* charts and, as a result, that album ended up in the Top 50 Albums Chart and also in *Billboard* magazine. The record sold close to 300,000 copies . . . I'm still living off that now, doing many of those tunes to this day. "Some Skunk Funk," which was also on the record, has around 32,000 hits on YouTube and almost as many *versions* on YouTube: Serbian tap dancers, string trios and quartets, Japanese all-female orchestras, marching bands, and ice skaters on the *Donny and Marie* show. It became a "rite of passage" song for many aspiring musicians. So that was, by far, the most pivotal and memorable musical event in my life.

3 I wish for the 21st century to see the 22nd century!

Raul De Souza   trombone, 1934 Brazil

1 Forming the group of my dreams would be great with the following names: John Coltrane, Freddie Hubbard (who played and recorded with me), Jack DeJohnette (Jack recorded with me too), Red Garland, Paul Chambers and Raul de Souza.

2 When I arrived in the United States in 1974, I had the great privilege and the honor to record my first album with Milestones in 1975. The great Cannonball Adderley was playing next to me! The arrangements were written by trombonist J.J. Johnson. Can you imagine my happiness and satisfaction? Even in a dream, when I was in Rio de Janeiro from '56 to '57 (I was 22-23 years old), listening to them on the radio program of Mr. Paulo Santos (Radio Jornal do Brasil), I would not have imagined having this privilege!

3 That human beings respect one another, listen to good music, so that they can feed and comfort their souls. That they live thus in PEACE. The Universe needs this as soon as possible.

Ray Anderson   trombone, 1952 USA

1 Louis Armstrong, Duke Ellington, Ella Fitzgerald, Milt Hinton, Big Sid Catlett, Ben Webster, Kenny Burrell, Dizzy Gillespie. Of course, there are so, so many other folks I'd like to play with, but this would be big fun, and I have had dreams where I was playing with many of these folks (only dreams with the exception of Milt Hinton). Another band would have Lester Bowie, Albert Ayler, John Coltrane, Charlie Haden, Elvin Jones, Charlie Parker, Mary Lou Williams and Don Pullen. Not that I think either of these bands would necessarily work well at all. It's really just a partial list of heroes and inspiring folks.

2 When I was 14 or 15 years old, in Chicago, I went to hear Joseph Jarman and Roscoe Mitchell play a duo concert in a Hyde Park church, where I lived. It changed my life!

3 I believe most musicians share in my wish for peace, justice, equality of opportunity, and, perhaps most importantly, that humans learn to live in balance with the ecology of the earth.

Reggie Washington   bass, 1962 USA

1 My "Dream Band" in which I play? It'll have to be big!
This is a complicated one; but the personnel COULD be (in any combination):
Gil Evans and Igor Stravinsky: collaborating composers; saxophones/woodwinds: Dexter Gordon, Sonny Rollins, John Coltrane, Mario Rivera (MD), Harry Carney, Cannonball Adderley, Sidney Bechet; trumpets: Miles Davis, Louis Armstrong, Dizzy Gillespie, Freddie

Hubbard, Roy Hargrove; trombone: J.J. Johnson, Kai Winding, Frank Rosolino; pianos: Phineas Newborn, Kenny Kirkland; guitar: Jimmy Ponder, Jef Lee Johnson; drums: Elvin Jones, Kenny Washington; basses: Ron Carter, Sam Jones, Me.

2 There are so many really memorable moments with the folks I've shared the stage with.

I remember at North Sea Jazz Festival (Den Haag) in 1995, touring with Branford Marsalis and Buckshot LeFonque. We were playing on the Staatenhaal Stages at primetime, 8:30 pm! It was the first time since I had done my first talent show in 1968, when I got stage fright! When the curtain opened up there were over 10,000+ folks standing, cheering with anticipation; plus there were lights and cameras flashing, etc. Once we started, I was cool. But for a moment there I had my mouth WIDE OPEN! I was thinking, "Wow! This is THE FEELING!!" A close second was my very first European tour (2006) as a leader, playing in trio with Ravi Coltrane and Gene Lake, beginning in Vienna at Joe Zawinul's Birdland Jazzklub. What a great feeling of accomplishment to see folks coming to the first gig of my first tour. I got goosebumps . . . and a little nervous too.

3 The Geopolitical climate is a swirling ball of confusion! I think we as musicians/artists can contribute by spreading a POSITIVE message through our music! But first; we desperately need to keep the history of music alive. Never forget the ROOTS of jazz and other musical genres. If we don't know where we came from, we won't know where

we're going! I'm here to share, with whoever will listen, my music and talent that the MOST HIGH has blessed me with. Keep the Bottom!

Regina Carter   violin, 1966 USA

1 That's a very difficult question as I have several dream bands. I love playing in big bands, being a part of the saxophone section so Duke Ellington would be at the top of my list. As for smaller groups, two bands off the top of my head would be: Bass: Jimmy Blanton; Organ: Shirley Scott; violins: Ginger Smock, Stuff Smith; trumpet: Valaida Snow; drums: Roy Haynes; bass: Ray Brown (with whom I was extremely fortunate to work); piano: Shirley Horn; guitar: João Gilberto.

2 Having the opportunity to perform and, later, record on the great Niccolò Paganini's violin "Il Cannone."

3 My wish for myself is to be more mindful and focused; to be a positive influence. For the human race, my wish or dream would be for each of us to look beyond our fears and discrimination, and help to lift each other up.

René Marie   vocal, 1955 USA

1 I have been asked this question before in other interviews and, try as I might, I cannot seem to deviate from this same, steady answer which is this: I do not think in terms of a "dream band." Rather than wish, I could be playing with someone else. What I try to do is appreciate the individual musicality each musician brings to the stage, at any given gig or engagement, with his or her own, unique experiences and personality. My dream gig consists of learning to appreciate them 100 percent, from the first note to the last.

2 So many wonderful events have occurred in my life since I started singing, in 1996! However, if I had to choose just one, I'd say my most memorable musical event was singing with the Lincoln Center Jazz Orchestra. They are such quintessential professionals, extremely kind and considerate. And, the music, of course, is always stellar!

3 It is that someone writes a song that inspires more people to turn away from hatred, and learn how to show more love for each other.

Richard Bona bass and vocal, 1967 Cameroon

1 Joe Zawinul, Miles Davis, James Taylor, Nusrat Ali Fatey Khan, Zakir Hussein.
2 Playing in South Korea for more than 40,000 hot fans …
3 Peace for the world and more Music.

Richard Davis
bass, 1930 USA

1 Duke Ellington, Thelonious Monk, Horace Silver, Eric Dolphy, John Coltrane
2 Working with Eric Dolphy.
3 I will finish this later. I ran out of time! Sorry.

Richard Galliano accordion, 1950 France

1 Grady Tate: drums; Biréli Lagrène: guitar; Ron Carter: double bass.
2 The concert at the Olympia, Paris as a duet with my father Lucien Galliano for his 60th birthday.

3 To return to purely acoustic music. Real music! A worldwide power failure . . . !

Richie Beirach   piano, 1947 USA

1 The dream band (I would have been able to play with) would be: myself on piano, Dave Holland on bass, Jack DeJohnette on drums, John Coltrane and Wayne Shorter on saxes, Miles Davis and Freddie Hubbard on trumpet. That would be a hell of a dream band!!

2 The most memorable concert I ever played was the tribute to John Coltrane, in 1987, live under the sky in Japan, with Dave Liebman, Wayne Shorter on soprano saxes, Eddie Gomez on bass, and Jack DeJohnette on drums. Luckily it was video-taped, recorded and made into a DVD that is available. We played in front of twenty-two thousand Japanese people at Yomuiro land, outside of Tokyo! My first time ever playing with Wayne Shorter, an amazing experience. Dave, Eddie, Jack, of course, my great friends, no rehearsal, just a sound check. We performed these tunes from Trane, "Mr. P.C.," "India," "Naïma" and "Impressions." It was a totally magical, memorable hour of my musical life. Very emotional, tremendous pressure. Live video, no edits possible, documented forever, I was beyond inspired, luckily it came out very well, I think.

3 My wish for the 21st century would be that the music I love so much, and think it is really a perfect combination of intellect intuition and spontaneous creation — that we call, for lack of a better term, jazz — would be better understood and valued, and loved on a much broader scale than it is today. Besides all the pressure on the life of the music itself, in terms of its ability to sell and sustain itself, with the withering winds against it, due to the internet theft of most of our royalties, and the poor, hollowed-out condition of our record companies, now on life support except for a few at the top, truth is jazz, real jazz, was never more than two percent of all sales, in America. It's tragic but true that this incredible music, born in America and grown here, is just not appreciated by the 350 million American people. In comparison, just think how happy Stevie Wonder must feel when he goes to sleep at night. How he is understood, valued, and how many millions love him and his music. And his music is great. And Stevie himself says he loves jazz, and even invited Herbie Hancock to play solos on one of his great albums! But some things are beyond the comprehension of even normal intelligent music lovers. Education might be required, or parents should be playing Miles and Trane and Bill Evans for their young children? Who knows? But, just imagine Charlie Parker and Lester Young, and Bud Powell getting even half of the attention, appreciation and love that Stevie gets; the effect on their lives!! The moral support and feeling of connecting to millions and millions of loving fans, not just thousands, and, of course, the financial rewards! People are people, of course, and it's true that some people even with support and adulation will go down with their own demons, but I just wish that jazz music would be understood, loved and valued in the way other great musics are. That's my hope for this 21st century.

Richie Cole   saxophone, 1948 USA

1. When I finally hit the road with my Dream Band in the Sky, it will consist of: Buddy Rich and Peppe Morola on drums; Marshall Hawkins on bass; Jack Wilson on piano; Bruce Forman and Vic Juris on guitar; Dizzy Gillespie, Chuck Findley, Bobby Shew and Arturo Santavol on trumpet; Sonny Rollins, Sonny Stitt, Turk Mauro, Rudresh Mahanthappa and Nick Brignola on saxophones; Reggie Watkins, Phil Wilson, Al Grey and Tommy Dorsey on trombones; Sammy DeLeon, Jose Pintor, Jeanine Santana and Jose Madera on percussions; and vocals: Eddie Jefferson, Carey Evans and Janis Siegel.

2. I have been so fortunate in my life to have been a part of so many wonderful musical events and to get to know, and many times work with, my heroes. I wouldn't know where to begin. So let's start at the beginning, when I found an old alto sax in the attic of my house in Trenton, New Jersey, when I was 5 years old . . .

3. It is, of course, Peace and also continued development, understanding and appreciation of America's only original art form: JAZZ . . .

Rick Margitza saxophone, 1961 USA

1 My dream band would be to play with John Coltrane's rhythm section: Elvin, McCoy and Jimmy Garrison.

2 The highlight of my musical career so far, is having played with Miles Davis.

3 My wish for the 21st century is that the world doesn't take too long to recover from all the damage that Donald Trump, and the people that he has surrounded himself with, and who support him, are doing.

Rita Marcotulli piano, 1959 Italy

1 This is very difficult to answer. Could it be more than one big band? I love so many different musics!

One band could be: Wayne Shorter, Miles Davis, Jaco Pastorius, Jack DeJohnette. Or an oddity: Charlie Haden with João Gilberto and Paul Motian.

2 Each moment of my career has always been special. Among others, playing with Dewey Redman, for many years, or with Jon Christensen, Palle Danielsson, Pat Metheny, Joe Henderson... or with John Taylor on duo pianos, or with Peter Erskine...

The event where I got the David di Donatello award for the best sound track of a movie, *Basilicata Coast to Coast*.

3 My desire is to live in a more conscious world; to live in peace and harmony, and to share the concept of difference as an enrichment rather than as a menace. Music is the medicine of the soul and an all-inclusive language. It knows no barriers. There is music that touches your purest, most intimate being; a magic that is shared and created together. True music is not competition. It is an exchange of pure love and respect, because, when you listen to me, I imagine

a circle of souls that recognize and embrace one another. Life is a gift destined to end, and so much beauty often escapes. As a wise man once said: we all think that we are different, and even in this we are all similar.

Roberto Fonseca   piano, 1975 Cuba

1 Miles Davis, Cachaito Lopez, Dexter Gordon, Jimi Hendrix, Robert Plant, Jacqueline du Pré, Jack DeJohnette, Joe Zawinul, Freddy Mercury, Bob Marley, Zakir Hussain, Fela Kuti, Miguel "Anga" Diaz, Itzhak Perlman, James Brown, Roberto Fonseca, Mercedes Cortes (my mother).

2 The day I played with Herbie Hancock, Wayne Shorter and Michael Brecker, at the Tokyo Jazz Fest.

3 Art to be the cure for everything in this life.

Roberto Gatto   drums, 1958 Italy

1 It will be: Miles, Trane, Bill Evans, Paul Chambers. I know I'm not the only one, but this still is my dream band.

2 Personally, I had more than one, but if I had the chance to make a choice, I would say it is my first album as a leader, with guest Michael Brecker, called *Notes,* in 1983.

3 For the twenty first century, I wish a better world and much more music on my path.

Roberto Menescal
vocal and guitar, 1937 Brazil

1 Barney Kessel: guitar; Ray Brown: bass; Shelly Manne: drums; Oscar Peterson: piano; Chet Baker: trumpet.

2 Bossa Nova, at Carnegie Hall, in 1962.

3 See the whole world in complete peace; this is a dream . . .

Robin Eubanks   trombone, 1955 USA

1 Clifford Brown, John Coltrane, Charlie Parker, me (?), McCoy Tyner, Elvin Jones, John McLaughlin, Charles Mingus. I've only played with two of them before, and I have no idea what we would play, but it would be amazing to spend time with them, and create music with them.

2 It's impossible to choose one. Playing in the bands of Elvin Jones, Art Blakey and Dave Holland. Getting to play with my band and present my music. Traveling around the world, meeting people and making friends from different cultures, and getting a chance to play my music for them.

3 World Peace. Happiness for people around the world. True equality among all people.

   A focus on the welfare of the masses of people, instead of a few exploiting the many.

Robin McKelle   vocal, 1976 USA

1 Piano: Les McCann; bass: James Jamerson; drums: Bernard Purdie; organ: Jimmy Smith; guitar: Albert King; maybe the JB Horns to top it off! :)

2 One of my favorite moments was opening for B.B. King, at Le Grand Rex, in Paris. Getting the opportunity to meet him, and hang a bit, in the dressing room, was really something I will never forget!

3 My wish is for peace. I wish that we, as a people, could be more accepting and have more compassion towards others. Less violence and hatred. We can teach our children to love unconditionally.

Roger Kellaway   piano, 1939 USA

1 I am honored to be considered part of your book.

   Although my experiences have been quite eclectic, including many years playing Dixieland, with some of the greatest musicians in the world, I've picked a 9-piece band from the last half of the 20th century: piano: Roger Kellaway; bass: Chuck Dominick; guitar: Russell Malone; drums: Philly Joe Jones; trumpet: Clifford Brown; valve trombone: Bob Brookmeyer; alto sax: Cannonball Adderley; tenor sax: Ben Webster; baritone sax: Serge Chaloff — an arranger's dream band, by the way.

2 The creating of my *Cello Quartet,* recorded in 1971 with the addition of chamber Orchestra, which I conducted, for A&M Records (all original music). Also, I must mention touring 55 concerts with Joni Mitchell and Tom Scott, and the L.A. Express (1974). Recording with Sonny Rollins (*Alfie,* 1966), Wes Montgomery (*Bumpin'*, 1965), and Oliver Nelson (*More Blues and the Abstract Truth,* 1964).

3 I would like to see a return to the real craft of songwriting. That is, real singable melody, real harmony, real structure — give me something wonderful to base an improvisation on!

If you like to compose, you must spend a lot of time understanding how to achieve a well-balanced piece. You must study long and hard — that means you have to put down your cell phone, first!

Thank you for this opportunity.

Into the Light.

Romero Lubambo   guitar 1955 Brazil

1 Pixinguinha, Tom Jobim, Wes Montgomery, Hermeto Pascoal, Christian McBride, Michael Brecker, Brian Blade and me!!

2 The show that I was invited to by Pat Metheny, to be his special guest on a show at Disney Hall, in L.A. in April 2010. That year, he was touring the whole year just with the "Orchestrion" — the mechanical orchestra without real musicians on the stage. I was the only one on the stage with Pat that year!!

3 Much better music and good musicians, and not war and hate ...

Ron Carter   bass, 1937 USA

1 Jimmy Blanton: bass; Kenny Clarke: drums; Freddie Green: guitar; Bud Powell: piano.

2 Each night, I look for this moment to appear.

3 That the African-American community in the United States completely and unequivocally endorse and support jazz.

Ron McClure bass, 1941 USA

1 It would be Herbie Hancock, Jack DeJohnette, Rich Perry, and me!

2 The most memorable moment in my career, so far, would have to be replacing Paul Chambers with the Wynton Kelly Trio, featuring Wes Montgomery in 1966, and having *Smokin' at the Penthouse* released on Resonance Records, in 2017, with me in that band — after 50 years of having no idea that the two KING FM Radio broadcasts, in Seattle, had been recorded. Second to that, I think playing with the Charles Lloyd Quartet with Keith Jarrett and Jack DeJohnette, at large venues such as The Fillmore Auditorium, Talin Jazz Festival in Estonia, and college campuses, especially Reed College, in Portland, Oregon.

3 It is for the world to survive the tyranny of Donald J. Trump, the GOP (Republican Party) and corporate greed, so we can get back to making sense and some good music.

Rosa Passos vocal, 1952 Brazil

1 Piano: Bill Evans; bass: Ron Carter; guitar: Wes Montgomery; drums: Arthur Blakey.

2 It was when I sang alone, with my guitar, in a solo concert, at Carnegie Hall, on February 10, 2006.

3 A world where people respect each other more, more understanding, more sincere friendships, with room for quality music and lots of love in the heart of humanity.

Rosario Giuliani saxophone, 1967 Italy

1 I would form a big band to be sure that all musicians I love are part of it. But I would say: me (Rosario Giuliani) on the alto sax, John Coltrane on tenor saxophone, Miles Davis on trumpet, Bill Evans on piano, Paul Chambers on bass, Jimmy Cobb on drums. Finally, K*ind of Blue* sounds, but with me!

2 It's difficult to give only one because there are a few musical events that changed my attitude and relationship to music. But one stands out: in 2005, I had the chance to play some concerts with the Charlie Haden *Land of The Sun* project. This moment was probably the beginning of my artistic growth.

3 I have never spoken before about wish or dreams, but I can say that I have many ideas, and I hope that one will be released. Concerning jazz, I think that, in this time in history, the jazz community is divided into nations. I hope that this can change, in the near future, and it become a unique world community.

Roy McCurdy drums, 1936 USA

1 Sam Jones on bass, and Wynton Kelly, Freddie Hubbard, Cannonball Adderley, Joe Henderson, Roy McCurdy.

2 Playing with Ella Fitzgerald at the 100th Anniversary celebration of the Moulin Rouge, in Paris.

3 It is that our beautiful art form (Jazz) will become bigger than ever, and all the wonderful musicians that play this music will be appreciated for what they do.

Rudresh Mahanthappa   saxophone, 1971 Italy

1 Art Tatum, Clifford Brown, Elvin Jones, Jimmy Garrison.
2 I have three: receiving a standing ovation at the Newport Jazz Festival after playing our first song with my Samdhi project. Playing Jazz Baltica with Bunky Green. Working with Kadri Gopalnath in Chennai, putting the Kinsmen music together. For me, playing with Kadri and Bunky is the living equivalent of playing with Bird or Trane.

3 A world of thinkers and doers, and not a world of followers and consumerism. The minute that we think for ourselves is the same minute that we can relate to our fellow human beings, and feel compassion, love, empathy, and generosity.

Rufus Reid   bass, 1944 USA

1 Don Byas, Sonny Rollins, Clifford Brown, Herbie Hancock, Billy Higgins, Rufus Reid.
2 When I was in Dexter Gordon's band, I had an out-of-body experience during an afternoon concert in Portland, Oregon. The music

became so intense I went out into the audience and watched us. It was an amazing feeling!

3 Our music is still flourishing with great talent emerging all the time. I wish them the greatest success! I hope more of the world finds time for peace and passion, and listens to our music. The world would certainly be a better place.

Russell Malone   guitar, 1963 USA

1 My dream band would be Carmen McRae, Milt Jackson, Ray Brown, Papa Jo Jones, Lester Young, and Roy Eldridge. That would be some great chemistry.

2 One of the most memorable events of my career was the year that I spent playing with saxophone colossus Sonny Rollins. I still get chills when I think of him.

3 My wish for the twenty-first century is to see more love towards our fellow man, no more homelessness, and to see our children and elderly people better taken care of.

Samuel Blaser   trombone, 1981 Switzerland

1 I had the chance to study in my hometown (La Chaux-de-Fonds, Switzerland) conservatory of music. A vibrant music school with open-minded teachers having manifold interests, playing all kinds of music — starting from early music leading to jazz and more. I always learned to remain flexible and try to maintain an interest in as many styles as possible. I honestly have a hard time thinking about a "dream band." I think it would make no sense musically. The bands I am currently building are truly amazing. There's also an aspect of collaboration that is extremely important to me: the relationship I am developing — as everyone does — with musicians I am playing with, is essential. Probably something impossible with a "dream band" from different eras. I have a few rules that I like to keep in mind when performing music: build long-term musical/personal relationships, work with people I can trust, and find people that can be complementary. I have developed some amazing and beautiful relationships with musicians like Pierre Favre or Marc Ducret, and this is a real dream.

2 Of course I have had many memorable musical events during my musical career, but I will always remember when I was finally able to blow into a trombone when I was 7 years old. The legend in the family says that I discovered the trombone when I was 2 years old, while watching some marching bands playing in my hometown. But I had to wait until age 9 to finally start studying the instrument. I remember these years as being endless.

3 I strongly hope the world will wake up, and that we can finally move towards a world in harmony.

Scott Colley bass, 1963 USA

1 So many favorite musicians come to mind, I don't know … John Coltrane, Joni Mitchell, Egbert Gismonti, Lee Morgan, Lester Young, Jimi Hendrix, Jack DeJohnette. Ha, an interesting band!

2 Very difficult to think of one, I've been very blessed to play with many great artists over my lifetime. One particular concert that comes to mind is a concert I did at Aaron Davis Hall, in the early 2000s: Jackie McLean, Bobby Hutcherson, Andrew Hill, and Billy Higgins. It was shortly before Billy died, and his energy, and the spirit of the whole band, was amazing.

3 Any dream I have for the 21st century would have to begin with the removal of those who are currently in power in the United States, and the removal of leaders in other countries with similar ideologies, who put personal ego and power over the good of the people. The tone that has been set by our current government is spreading throughout the world to embolden other leaders who are prone to use racism, sexism, economic power and nationalism to control people and increase their power. This change in direction needs to happen soon, for us to just begin to take care of people in need; to begin to eradicate racism, social injustice, food insecurity, global warming and a general destruction of the planet.

Scott Hamilton   saxophone, 1954 USA

1 It is never possible to imagine what different musicians will sound like together, until you hear them — so, your dream band could easily turn out to be a nightmare. But I always wish I could have had a chance to play with Count Basie on piano.

2 I once played a festival with Illinois Jacquet, Arnett Cobb and Buddy Tate along with John Lewis — very exciting and something like a dream. Once in L.A., Sarah Vaughan came in and sang three tunes with the band I was playing with. Things like this used to happen sometimes if you were lucky.

3 Don't know. It's pretty alarming so far, if you look at it. But I have been very happy in my life the last 18 years. Lots of good gigs and nice audiences. I wish for nothing special.

Seamus Blake   saxophone, 1970 UK

1 Duke on piano, Ray Brown on bass, and Roy Haynes on drums.

2 Playing a tune with Wayne Shorter and Herbie Hancock.

3 I hope that creative improvised music (jazz) continues to flourish and find a home in the hearts of people, everywhere.

Shai Maestro   piano, 1987 Israel

1 John Coltrane, Tony Williams, Ron Carter, Miles Davis.
2 Playing with Jeff Ballard in France.
3 A lot more listening, less ego, and for all of us to understand better that we are in this world together, and should try to live together.

Sheila Jordan   vocal, 1928 USA

1 The musicians I would have as a dream band would be Charlie Parker, Max Roach, Duke Jordan and Tommy Potter. For today it would be Cameron Brown, Billy Drummond, Steve Kuhn and Tom Harrell . . .
2 Hearing Bird in person, at Birdland and other venues, and sitting in, a few times, when he asked me to sing a song.

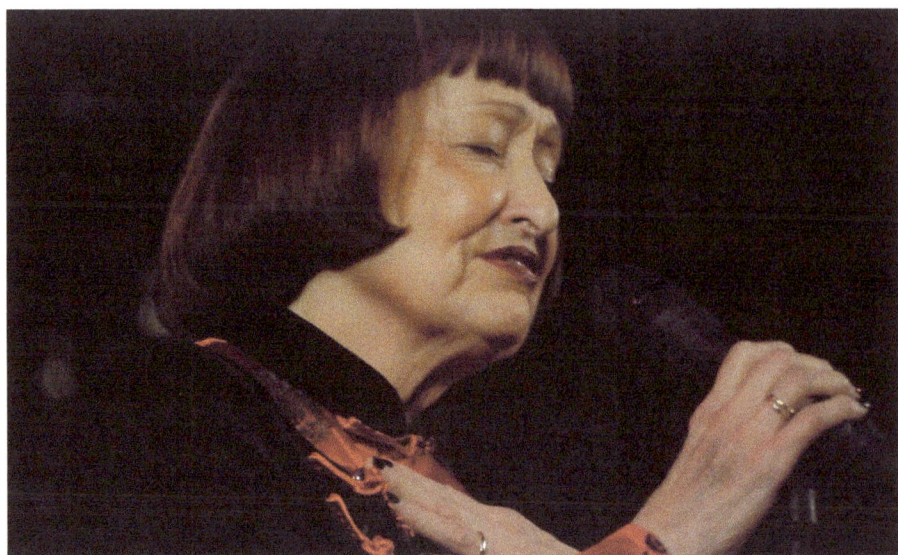

3 That this music will become as popular and as respected as Pop and Rap and R&B, and all the other music. Jazz is like the step child of American music. It's a great music and it should be more respected.

Slide Hampton   trombone, 1932 USA

1 Slide Hampton, Charlie Parker, Dizzy, Bud Powell, Oscar Pettiford, Art Blakey.
2 Paris Reunion Band.
3 Trombone players and horn players to listen to J.J. and Charlie Parker because they made more music than anybody else. You don't have to be the best, just the best you can be.

Sonny Fortune   saxophone, 1939 USA

1 The John Coltrane Quartet.
2 Working with Elvin Jones for as long as I did.
3 For my band to be as great as Coltrane's band. That IS what I got from Coltrane.

Stefano Bollani   piano and vocal, 1972 Italy

1 Louis Armstrong on trumpet. That's it, I'd go for a duo with him!

2 That's always the very last thing I'm doing; that's why I'll say that it's my latest recording *Que bom*.

3 Everybody should be able to follow his own path.

Stéphan Oliva   piano, 1959 France

1 There have been so many dream bands since 1900 ... To take part in one would seem impossible for me since they worked so well thanks to the subtle alchemy between personalities, in ideal symbiosis, at a precise time in history — that which does not last eternally. I had the chance to fulfill this wish by playing with Paul Motian and Bruno Chevillon. Paul was a great musician who found himself at the crossroads of so many sessions and historical encounters, this great poet of the drums, already professionally active before we were born, and who represented, for us, a musical universe in his own right!

2   Perhaps during a solo concert in French Guiana; getting ready to play the first piece of my program with the kind of stage fright that rushes and disturbs the music a little at the beginning of concerts. I took a few seconds to look at the beautiful place where I was performing, feeling the sweetness of the air, perceiving the situation as a whole, realizing the luck of just being there. I then started a completely free improvisation that was only intended to convey all that, and share it immediately. It was like tuning an instrument before playing, but looking for the rightness of the sounds and the music according to time and place, with the strings of the soul.

3   May the earth recover its health, and its inhabitants, finally, live in peace.

Stephanie Richards   trumpet, 1982 Canada

1   There are too many to name. However, a session of two pianos with Ellington and Stravinsky would have been hip. Also, working with Paul Motian and Alice Coltrane simultaneously would be a beautiful experience, no doubt.

2   In the studio with Threadgill, hearing him play the last movement of his latest release (*Dirt . . . And More Dirt*) — when he played, it was a force in the room. That's the best I can describe it. It was as

if a force took over the entire universe for a few timeless minutes. It felt like the ocean.

3   That we keep moving this music forward. Music never stands still, and we need to keep pushing and moving this great Thing forward.

Steve Cardenas   guitar, 1959 USA

1   There are hundreds of great musicians I would've been honored to play with over the last 100 plus years. For me it would be impossible to choose a few from the many. I've been very fortunate, over the years, to have been in bands led by some of the legendary musicians I grew up listening to. So, in that way, I feel like I've already played in some dream bands. I certainly don't ever mean to be evasive, but this sort of exercise doesn't mean much to me. I've played gigs with musicians that weren't well known at all, that were as satisfying as any other gigs. Just to have the opportunity to play creative music is a dream come true, for me.

2   Similar answer to the first question in that I've been fortunate to play in many creative groups. All of these groups, and others, have had very memorable performances. It would be difficult at best to single out any one performance as somehow being most memorable. Lucky for me, there have been many.

3   That somehow, in someway, through some "miracle" of the universe, that all of humanity could come to the true realization that all life on earth is as important as human life. With that realization, a commitment to conservation and aggressive action on climate change would be an obvious pursuit, one would hope.

Steve Davis   trombone, 1967 USA

1   Dream Band . . . (I could have several of these)!
Dexter Gordon: tenor sax; Jackie McLean: alto sax; Freddie Hubbard: trumpet; Curtis Fuller: trombone (and me, too . . . only if you insist); Wes Montgomery: guitar; Bobby Hutcherson: vibes; Hank Jones: piano; Ron Carter: bass; Billy Higgins: drums; Sarah Vaughan: vocals.

2   I've been blessed to have many incredible musical moments during my career this far . . . So here's one: on Oct 21, 2016, playing on Jimmy Heath's 90th Birthday Celebration, at Jazz at Lincoln Center in NYC.

Sonny Rollins and Slide Hampton were in the audience, and spoke about Mr. Heath. Later that night, I proposed to my wife, vocalist/educator Abena Koomson-Davis, who was in attendance, at Smoke Jazz Club in NYC. Pianist, Johnny O'Neal played Stevie Wonder's "Overjoyed" right after I put the ring on Abena's finger. It was her favorite song! That was a good evening "living the jazz life" in NYC!!!

3 I wish that human beings, all over the world, could get along and find their joy in life nearly as well as "Jazz People" do!!!

Steve Kuhn   piano, 1938 USA

1 It is the trio I had with Ron Carter on bass, and Al Foster on drums, in the 80s and 90s.
2 Playing with the great John Coltrane.
3 It would be a better world for everybody. Peace between all human beings.

Steve Laspina   bass, 1954 USA

1 This is a difficult one because there are so many people I would loved to have played with! However, the one band which stands out is the Miles Davis band with Wayne Shorter, Herbie Hancock and Tony Williams. And of course John Coltrane, and Charlie Parker!
2 Playing with Jim Hall.
3 World peace.

Steve Swell   trombone, 1954 USA

1 I would love to have a band with Cecil Taylor, Andrew Cyrille, Fred Hopkins and William Parker (yes, two basses!), altoists Rob Brown and Jemeel Moondoc and Raphe Malik on trumpet. I would have loved to hear Jack Teagarden and Louis Armstrong live. Just hear them, not play with them.

2 I have been lucky to have had the opportunity to play with so many great musicians, and the number of memorable events are many. It's hard to pick just one. I would pick one event that is memorable and important for what I do, and who I am today, that is when I was 15 years old and heard Roswell Rudd for the first time on the radio. I had an immediate connection to what he was doing, and it energized me, and literally woke me up.

For a memorable moment of me playing, I would have to pick a couple or more — sorry. One would be a trip I made, with Roswell, to Mali, Africa, in 2004. Others would be playing at Iridium with Cecil Taylor, or playing with William Parker at Dizzy's Club, and also playing with Bernard Purdie at Joe's Pub, all in NYC.

3 Common sense gun control legislation. No more Trumps. Tolerance and patience with each other. And just a return to common sense in our actions and being. Musically I hope the music I am involved with, becomes more respected, understood and known.

Steve Turre trombone, 1948 USA

1 Because I've had the blessing to play with so many innovators and masters, I will limit this list to people I haven't played with, but always wanted to!

- Early years of the music: Louis Armstrong, Sidney Bechet, Jack Teagarden, Baby Dodds, Fats Waller, Art Tatum, Bessie Smith.
- Middle Years: Earl Hines, Teddy Wilson, Duke Ellington, Count Basie, Roy Eldridge, Tito Rodriguez, Machito, Jimmy Luncford, Ella, Carmen, Billy Holiday, Elis Regina, Billy Eckstein, Illinois Jacquet, Ben Webster, Coleman Hawkins, Lester Young.
- Bop to Modern: Charlie Parker, Monk, John Coltrane, Bud Powell, Miles Davis, Kenny Clark, James Brown, Albert King.

2 Dizzy Gillespie's 70th birthday concert at Wolftrap.

3 My wish for the 21st century is not about music. I wish for an end to the greed and selfishness that is dominating the consciousness of those "in control" at this time. To put people before profits. To put the health of our planet before the shareholder's and boardroom's profits. To finally end racism in ALL its forms and evolve past the US vs THEM mentality. To put proven science before lies. To work together for the betterment of all — rather than the few. This would bring about true World Peace!

Steve Wilson saxophone, 1961 USA

1 Duke Ellington, Roy Haynes, and Paul Chambers.
2 Performing at the White House, for Barack and Michelle Obama, in February 2016.
3 No more war, hate, poverty, and hunger, but the proliferation of love and respect toward one another.

Susanne Abbuehl vocal, 1970 Switzerland

1 I play in, and with, my dream band including some of my very favorite musicians: Matthieu Michel, Wolfert Brederode, Øyvind Hegg-Lunde! But, if the band would time-travel, I'd probably opt for Don Cherry or Miles, Charlie Haden, Paul Bley, Ed Blackwell ... and my late teacher Jeanne Lee.
2 Recording for ECM Records, each time — so special, with Manfred Eicher producing in the studio. Studying, assisting and singing with Jeanne Lee. Doing a three-day residence at the Lyon Opera, in 2018, presenting three groups I work with, including musicians Marilyn Mazur, Stéphan Oliva, Magda Mayas! Being the recipient of the European Jazz Musician 2017 Award by the French Académie du Jazz.
3 That the arts and education be one of our priorities, and contribute substantially to society and its advancement. Jazz and improvised music feed, from the periphery, the center, the mainstream. This has to be recognized and valued.

Tadataka Unno piano, 1980 Japan

1 I wish I could play especially with Art Blakey, Ray Brown, Sonny Rollins, Ernestine Anderson ... this list could go on and on.
2 My mentor, Hank Jones, took my hand while he was passing away, and he said his last words, "Tada, I want to go home and practice."
3 Keep on playing and someday make someone happy.

Taylor Eigsti piano, 1984 USA

1 It might be Eric Harland, Ray Brown, John Coltrane, Wayne Shorter, and Björk. Not quite sure what tunes we would play, but I can only imagine that something cool would happen ...

2 I've been lucky to have many memorable and special musical moments in my career. Near the top of the list are all the opportunities that I had to perform with Dave Brubeck. I learned a lot from him as a musician, and a human being. So I treasure the moments that I was lucky enough to have with him musically. Another great highlight throughout the years was to do a quartet show with Nicholas Payton, with Esperanza Spalding on bass and Karriem Riggins on drums. That was one of the most fun sets of music I've ever been involved in.

3 It is that my fellow musicians will remain unfazed by trying to "save" jazz music and will continue to keep exploring all of the many growing branches and new creative avenues that keep the music expanding. I have a lot of faith in the fact that, despite there being a different economy as it pertains to jazz and improvised music, the creative intent and exciting new sounds will always keep evolving. That is my musical wish. Outside of that, I hope that the world begins to find more ways to celebrate and embrace the diversity and cultural differences that exist throughout the world, and I think music is a big part of that, and always will be.

Terence Blanchard   trumpet, 1962 USA

1 Piano: Herbie Hancock; bass: Ron Carter; drums: Elvin Jones; sax section: Wayne Shorter, John Coltrane, Dexter Gordon, Bird, Ornette; trombone Section: Slide Hampton, Treme Young and J.J. Johnson; trumpet section: Don Cherry, Louis Armstrong, Dizzy Gillespie and Miles Davis.

2 I have a top Three:
- The Kennedy Center Tribute to Herbie Hancock.
- Playing Carnegie Hall with Herbie Hancock, Ron Carter, Jack DeJohnette and Wayne Shorter.
- Playing Carnegie Hall with Sonny Rollins.

3 It is that the government would recognize the importance of Art and Arts education, and make Jazz History a part of American History education, starting from elementary school.

Terri Lyne Carrington   drums, 1965 USA

1 I really cannot answer that question. But, people I would like to have played with would be: Billie Holiday, John Coltrane, Miles Davis, Betty Carter, Ornette Coleman, Don Cherry, Mary Lou Williams, Keith Jarrett, Lee Morgan, Sonny Rollins, Sister Rosetta Tharpe.

2 Playing with Wayne Shorter. Playing with Herbie Hancock. Playing with Aretha Franklin! Doing late night tv shows well as, where I played with many people in pop world: Whitney Houston, Little Richard, James Brown, Rick James and more. But, every 15 years or so, it feels like a new lifetime. A new generational time musically. Right now, I am starting a new Institute at Berklee College of Music. The Berklee Institute of Jazz and Gender Justice; this is a very important new chapter in my life. And it feels like the most, long-lasting part of the work I have done.

3 Gender Justice and Racial Justice, and Environmental Justice. My dream is for all people to be able to truly experience the unalienable rights of life, liberty and the pursuit of happiness as stated in our Declaration of Independence. This is what I would want for all citizens of the world.

Terry Gibbs   vibraphone, 1924 USA

1 Alto saxes: Charlie Parker, Cannonball Adderley; tenor saxes: Al Cohn, Sonny Stitt; baritone sax: Serge Challof; trumpets: Snooky Young, Dizzy Gillespie, Conte Candoli, Clifford Brown; trombone: J.J. Johnson, Frank Rosolino, Carl Fontana, Bill Harris; piano: Bud Powell; bass: Ray Brown; guitar: Charlie Christian; drums: Mel Lewis. These are the musicians in a big band. A small band may have a name or two changed.
2 Playing with Benny Goodman, Charlie Parker and Dizzy Gillespie.
3 World Peace.

Thomas Fonnesbæk   bass, 1977 Denmark

1 This is a hard one — so many fantastic players to choose from! And the variation between all the genres and the nationalities is magnificent. But, vocal-wise, the Brazilian singer and composer, Elis Regina, are still a great influence, and so is the French Pianist, Michel Petrucciani. For this band, Lenny White would be a fantastic cast, and I'm crazy about Wayne Shorter's sound. The last member could be John Scofield; he is still one of the greatest!
2 I can mention many important professional

relationships, but one stands out. I have been very lucky to be a member of Lars Jansson's Trio, a Swedish pianist, who has been a musical mentor. He is, for me, one of the masters of Nordic acoustic jazz, and I believe that we have shared some fantastic moments on stage.

3 I hope that my music, and music in general will continue to make important contributions to the world, and that it will be supported by our politicians. It is easy to take music for granted and not be aware of how difficult it is to make a living being a musician. I wish for more political support so one is able to make this kind of life-choice, so that the cultural nourishment we get from music is not to the detriment of the lives of musicians. Music carries with it great wisdom that we all need.

Till Brönner   trumpet, 1971 Germany

1 Grady Tate: drums; Ray Brown: bass; Shirley Horn: piano and vocals; Wes Montgomery: guitar; Stanley Turrentine: tenor; Till Brönner: trumpet.

2 I still have great memories of the time when I recorded my debut album *Generations of Jazz* in 1993, with the late Ray Brown on bass and Jeff Hamilton on drums. Both were incredibly generous, and the atmosphere was highly creative and inspiring, especially looking back from now. I think of those days, very often, with a smile on my face.

3 To come to a new way of thinking for FUTURE generations would also improve our present situation. Even in democracy, politicians think in election terms — a 4 to 8 year term — and miss to focus on the necessary education programs for the majority of their fellow citizens. Education for everyone, regardless of your social background.

Tim Hagans   trumpet, 1954 USA

1 From the history: John Coltrane, Jimmy Garrison, McCoy Tyner and Elvin Jones.

   My dream band now is: Jon Irabagon, Ravi Coltrane: saxophone; Joe Hertenstein, Jukkis Uotila, Anders Mogensen: drums; Jay Anderson, Rufus Reid, Johnny Åman: bass; Leo Genovese, Luis Perdomo, Carl

Winther: piano; Elliot Mason: trombone. All at the same time!

2 I will list two memorable events of my career (there have been so many!).

The first one I'll list was my first night with the Stan Kenton Orchestra: June 23, 1974, in Zainesville, Ohio. This was my first professional gig. I was 19 years old. In my youth, the historic big bands were still traveling so I heard them all many times. Stan's band was my favorite because of the emphasis on brass and percussion. I was also excited by the extreme dynamics and adventurous compositions. I remember, and can still feel the massive energy of the rhythm section, and the scintillating and triumphant horns, on my first night with the band. And I was now part of this sound. Looking down at Stan at the piano, and conducting in front the band gave me goosebumps. I played with Stan for three years, and developed as a soloist, always experimenting and searching for new melodies. Stan encouraged this exploration by demanding the soloists to play something different every night. His philosophy about innovation and creativity, has guided me through all of my experiences as a musician and composer.

The second event was the recording of *Animation/Imagination* for Blue Note in 1998. This recording was conceived and produced by Bob Belden. Bob and I worked together for 25 years, and I was always astounded, not only by his saxophone playing, but also by his ability to envision and realize amazingly fresh and timely concepts. *Animation/Imagination* was a collaboration between improvising musicians and drum 'n' bass DJs. Bob proposed this wild project after listening to the early Roni Size's drum 'n bass records of Bill Laswell's *Oscillations*, and raw live streaming from underground London.

We recorded for five days in a locked-out Sony Studios. We were able to record around the clock, without interruption, so we could experiment with recording techniques and varied combinations of musicians. Inspired by the Teo Macero/Miles Davis recordings and also the later Beatles' records, Bob was heroically riding on a wave of enlightenment and creative energy. I was given soundscapes and massive grooves to blow over, and offered ideas about form and colors, as well as collaborating with the DJs with melodies and chords. It was a nod to the future and is, perhaps, my favorite recording. I wouldn't change a note or beat.

3 I am inspired and gladdened by the fusion of jazz and world music. Although such collaborations have been realized from the beginning of jazz — jazz is, of course, from its inception a fusion of all the world's music — I am more and more hearing new rhythms and instrumentation being incorporated into the improvised world. This is exciting for both the listener and the musician and will bring a wider audience to improvised music.

I am also encouraged by the combination of jazz and Classical music in regards to composition. This, too, is not new to jazz but this synthesis is new to the Classical world. Many string players and traditional orchestra instrumentalists are now improvising. This enables jazz composers to write for these players and give Classical composers an opportunity to experiment with improvisation. This expands audience interest and also helps obliterate restrictive genre boundaries that, while helping to define music, constrict inquisitiveness before the music is actually heard. I am also encouraged by all of the young musicians I hear. They have a vast knowledge of the first hundred years of jazz, and incredible technique on their instruments. They are constantly searching for new ways to celebrate the past by innovating the future. From the first improvised note, and the first sounded beat, everyone in the jazz tribe has the unbridled desire that this music prosper past infinity. I have complete confidence that the young musicians today not only wish for the same, but will ensure a glorious future of this music.

Tim Warfield   saxophone, 1965 USA

1 I've been fortunate to perform and record with gentlemen of whom I believe to be of kindred spirit. This group includes, Terell Stafford and or Nicholas Payton: trumpet; Stefon Harris: vibraphone; Cyrus Chestnut: piano; Tarus Mateen and or Rodney Whitaker: bass, and Clarence Penn: drums. They are all very distinctive musical personalities not to mention very special people. To play with them is to always invite an excursion in sound and rhythm.

2 For me, no one moment would I consider pinnacles, but I have had important highlights, a pivotal point throughout my career. Yesterday, I performed at the home of jazz legend Louis Armstrong, which is now a tourist attraction. The week before, I was involved in a special recording that included Terell Stafford, Dick Oatts, David Wong and Byron Landham. A few weeks before that I was performing for the Governor of Pennsylvania and his guests at the Governor's Mansion. Every day is a blessing with every moment being memorable.

3 Peace and solidarity amongst nations, in hopes that all people have an opportunity for greater happiness and a higher quality of life.

Tom Harrell   trumpet, 1946 USA

1 Charlie Parker, Dizzy Gillespie, Bud Powell, Charles Mingus, and Max Roach.

2 Playing with Dizzy Gillespie.

3 Peace on earth.

Toninho Horta   guitar, 1948 Brazil

1 I come from a musical family, since my grand father, João Horta, was a composer of sacred and popular music, in the historical cities of Minas Gerais State. I grew up listening to my mother playing bandolim, and to my father on his acoustic guitar (violão). My older brother, Paulo Horta, (a well-known upright bassist, who was highly respected musicians around Belo Horizonte, the Minas Gerais State capital) started to be a musician at the age of 20. He was 15 years older than me, and from his influence, I started to think of being a musician. So, since I was a kid, I have listened to all kinds of music, especially Classical and old popular music from my parents era, and jazz from my brother's collection. I was very lucky, and I want to say "Thank God!" for having all these magical, natural music experiences. The compositions and orchestrations of Classical and jazz masters gave me the power to play and practice my guitar from the age of 9. My first idols were Stan Getz, Art Tatum, Tal Farlow, Frank Sinatra, Ella F., Pat Boone, Oscar Peterson, Bing Crosby, Sammy Davis . . . and all film scores from the 50s. Going straight to your question, I really do not wish for a dream band; I am just thinking at this time to be a musician in any kind of band. My dream really was to be a conductor, but I never liked to concentrate in academic classes, I preferred to hear all kinds of styles and musical conceptions and also to play a lot at home, all the time through my life. To be a maestro, I would have to stop learning all sort of things, but I am kind of a gypsy man: I like to travel, to meet other cultures, musicians, nature, food, arts, to have great memories of my life.

When I started playing with my brother in Belo Horizonte, at parties and weddings and, about two years later, when I started to make recordings, in Rio de Janeiro, with Elis Regina, Milton Nascimento, and Gal Costa, I was sure I would make my own band someday. I started recording my first tracks when I performed in 1973. At that time, I was listening to many bands around Brazil and, of course, to Hendrix, Zappa, Emerson, Lake and Palmer, Jeff Beck, Led Zeppelin. The Brazilians were Tamba trio, Eumir Deodato, Pixinguinha, Luiz Gonzaga . . . That's the time when I really started to get my own band, playing guitar and singing my music. But from the 70s up to this day, I have split my time as musician between collaborating with other singers and bands, and working on my own career. I believe I am a working — operary (operario???) — musician: my great desire is to make everybody happy, and to spread harmony and care to people worldwide.

This month, I just finished the mastering of a new album called *Belo Horizonte*, with my own band ORQUESTRA FANTASMA! YESSSSS! This is my dream band! We have been playing for 37 years, and never did an album together. Those people, after four decades, they really know my music and its contribution; we are all in a real partnership, friendship, familyship. They are truly very important musicians in my career. This album will be released in Brazil in October, with our classic successes, and originals from the band, too. My friends and band members are: Lena Horta on flute, Andre Dequech on piano and keyboards, Iuri Popoff on electric bass, and Esdra Ferreira "Nenem" on drums.

About jazz band influences? I have many: Keith Jarret, Wes Montgomery, Miles Davis, Coltrane. All jazz musicians are my idols. They are an important part of my interest in music. The freedom of improvisation and the discipline to practice and practice and practice is always the best lesson for musicians. But we can't forget all those geniuses in music: they really are the best for making the world a better place, the people gentler, better inspired and holding to their dreams.

Tony Coe
clarinet and saxophone, 1934 UK

1 Johnny Hodges, Paul Gonsalves, Clark Terry, Bob Brookmeyer, Ron Matthewsen: bass; Stan Tracey: piano; Winston Clifford: drums; Ella Fitzgerald: vocals; Alan Paul: singer; Fred Astaire and Cyd Charisse: dancers; Tony Coe: composition and arrangements.
2 Winning the Jazzpar Prize. Being in the Clarke/Boland Band.
3 The end of all weapons of mass destruction, and complete ban on wildlife killing.

Tord Gustavsen piano, 1970 Norway

1 My current band is actually my dream band. There are no other musicians I would rather play with than these fantastic artists. But in case I am forced to put together an imaginary formation, it would be something like Anders Jormin on bass, the young Jon Christensen on drums, Wayne Shorter on saxophones, and myself on piano for an acoustic line-up; or Arve Henriksen on trumpet, Geir Jensen *a.k.a.* Biosphere on electronics, Audun Kleive on drums, and myself on piano and synth bass for an electro-acoustic project.

2 Impossible to choose only one … but here is a small selection: The concert with my first trio at the Oslo Philharmonic Hall, in 2005, was a breakthrough. The music-meditation with saxophonist Trygve Seim last year in Norway, in a small church, was very moving. The concert with my quartet featuring Tore Brunborg, at the Montreal Jazz Festival, stands out as a peak. And the first time I played with vocalist Simin Tander, and started developing the project that became the album *What Was Said* was also very special.

3 That we develop technology for environmentally sustainable air transportation — electric planes, like the electric cars which taking over, now in Norway. That we are able to extinguish extreme poverty worldwide. And that I am allowed to keep making music with the best musicians I know.

Trilok Gurtu percussion, 1951 India

1 Actually there is no such thing because you're dreaming anyway! I'll go for Thelonius Monk, Don Cherry, a great African musician and an Indian sarod player, second, Joe Zawinul, and Shobha Gurtu: vocals.

2 My musical events were: listening to great masters who were teaching my mother, and me talking with, and getting advice from a great musician from India, Mr Palghat Raghu.

3 I've no wish, but if there were one, it would be for musicians to pay less attention to Facebook, Instagram, etc., that is the job of the promoters, and people should get to listen to all kinds of music, not only Jazz.

Trygve Seim   saxophone, 1971 Norway

1 I already have my dream band: my own large ensemble, named Trygve Seim Ensemble, but unfortunately, it seems to be too difficult, economically, nowadays to operate with such a large ensemble (get concerts and do recordings), so we did our last concert in 2012 (at the Oslo Jazz Festival) and our last CD (*Sangam* on ECM Records) was released in 2005. My biggest wish is to get to perform and record with this ensemble again. The ensemble has a line-up with my absolute favorite musicians: Arve Henriksen on trumpet, Øyvind Brække on trombone, Tone Reichelt on French horn, Lars Andreas Haug on tuba, Håvard Lund on clarinet and bass clarinet, Embrik Snerte on bassoon, Nils Jansen and Torben Snekkestad on all saxophones and all clarinets, Svante Henryson on cello, Frode Haltli on accordion, Per Oddvar Johansen on drums and conductor Christian Eggen (plus myself on soprano and tenor saxophones).

2 Every time I'm on stage with my large ensemble (Trygve Seim Ensemble) performing music that I have composed especially for this ensemble and with these specific musicians in mind.

3 No more wars and no more oppression and exploitation of human beings — which we today are seeing done both by many authorities around the world as well as by the rich. Music can be used as a tool in this work.

Ugonna Okegwo   bass, 1962 UK

1 That's an almost impossible question for me to answer thoroughly. There are so many musicians that created this music, that have inspired me, and/or directly influenced me! I'm afraid that I will omit someone that is important to me and my development, even if I tried to list all of them.

There are many bands though that I would love to be part of:
- Charlie Parker, Dizzy Gillespie, Bud Powell and Roy Haynes;
- Sonny Rollins, Thelonius Monk and Art Blakey;
- Miles Davis, Hank Mobley, Red Garland, Philly Joe Jones;
- John Coltrane, McCoy Tyner, Elvin Jones;
- Miles Davis, Wayne Shorter, Herbie Hancock, Tony Williams.

These are just a few off the top of my head, and they are just the tip of the iceberg.

2   When I played my first gig with Tom Harrell, I remember Tom played a solo on a blues which was so powerful that it felt like the whole bandstand was levitating. It was a very deep experience. I was lucky to have had several of those experiences throughout my career, but that is one that always comes to mind.

3   I wish for humanity to keep on evolving into something less greedy, aggressive and war driven. Although we are making steps backwards a lot of the time, I do hope that we'll be able to make leaps forward in the future and become better people eventually.

Victor Lewis   drums, 1950 USA

1   I would like to clarify "me" being a member in my dream band with the fact that I am a composer. That, in itself, gets me past the "me" in the compositional equation. The reason is that I have compositions that I would love to hear what Tane would play or Ralph Peterson or Harvey Mason or Robertino Silva. With that being stated I'll

be brief — the personnel is distributed according to tune: Milton Nascimento, Woody Shaw, Nana Vasconcelos, Don Alias, Women's Choir Of Bulgaria, Wayne Shorter, Ed Howard, Jaco, Seamus Blake, Terell Stafford, Bobby Watson, Hiram Bullock, Stephen Scott, Edward Simon, John Stubblefield, Eddie Henderson, Carmen Lundy, Neil Clarke.

2 Woah, not a simple question for me!!

My most memorable musical events were my early years in New York, being groomed. Not to chump off my track record of the last 44 years, but recognizing what got me here: being tested. Every rookie has to deal with conviction, artistic license, reward, acknowledgment, camaraderie.

3 I wish that producing artistry be not inhibited by money.

Vijay Iyer   piano, 1971 USA

1 Billie Holiday, Alice Coltrane, Amina Claudine Myers, Roy Haynes, Jimmy Garrison, John Gilmore, Wadada Leo Smith, Jimi Hendrix.

2 Open City, my large-ensemble collaboration with Teju Cole, in October 2013 in Montclair, New Jersey, with an incredible lineup: Tyshawn Sorey, Steve Coleman, Mark Shim, Hafez Modirzadeh,

Ambrose Akinmusire, Graham Haynes, Jonathan Finlayson, Adam O'Farrill, Josh Roseman, Rajna Swaminathan, Patricia Brennan, Okkyung Lee, Mat Maneri, Marcus Gilmore, Harish Raghavan, Rafiq Bhatia, Himanshu Suri.

3 Truth, justice, peace, compassion.

Wallace Roney   trumpet, 1960 USA

1 I think I already played with my dream band, beyond reproach, geniuses!!! Wayne Shorter, Tony Williams, Ron Carter, Herbie Hancock!!!

2 And I shared solos with my Idol, Miles Davis! And the greatest moment of my life so far, because I'm looking for more, was SHARING the stage and solos next to my Idol, Miles Davis on that HISTORIC NIGHT he came back to play Straight Ahead Acoustic Jazz!!!!

3 And what do I want for the 21st century? That people support Jazz all over the World!!! And that places to perform your art open all over the world, to sustain all the artists!!!

Walter Smith III   saxophone, 1980 USA

1 The musicians in my dream band. Unfortunately, you said that I must be a part of the band, because I obviously wouldn't have much to play there — maybe I could conduct or something.

Voice: Ray Charles; alto saxophone: Charlie Parker; piano: Andrew Hill; trumpet: Freddie Hubbard; bass: Charles Mingus; drums: Tony Williams.

I have no idea what the music would be, or what this would sound like, but I feel it would be one of the most interesting and unique musical experiences, both as a player and listener.

2 The most memorable musical events of my career, so far, would be the opportunities

I've had to play with some of my biggest living influences. There have been several occasions that I've been lucky enough to do, but one recently was to get the opportunity to record with Joshua Redman on my last album. He is one of the reasons I still play saxophone!

3 My wish for the 21st century — musically speaking, I assume, would be for people to remain open-minded about music, and continue to appreciate all aspects and styles of music, from the old to the new. For musicians, to appreciate each other, and keep building communities, and share ideas in order to continue to advance our art form.

Wayne Escoffery   saxophone, 1975 UK

1 Freddie Hubbard, Herbie Hancock, Ron Carter, Elvin Jones (with Tony Williams as a regular sub for Elvin, and Roy Haynes as a regular sub for Tony).

2 My 10-year tenure as a member of the Tom Harrell Quintet. That's one of the most memorable.

3 I'm saddened to say that, given the current state of affairs globally and particularly in the US, I have very little confidence in humanity and our mutual desire, or effort towards peace and healthy lives for all. Therefore, I won't waste a wish on that. My concern, at this point, is for the survival and prosperity of my son and close family. So, for the twenty-first century, I selfishly wish for my own financial security and independence. With that security and independence, I hope to ensure my well being and that of my son and close family.

William Parker bass, 1952 USA

1 Hamid Drake, Cooper Moore, Rob Brown, Billy Bang, Roy Campbell.

2 A concert I did a few days ago with Hamid Drake on drums, Steve Swell on trombone, Rob Brown on alto sax, James Brandon Lewis on tenor sax, Dave Sewelson on baritone sax, and Elleb Christi, Lisa Sokolov, AnneMarie Sandy, Raina Sokolov Gonzalez, and Noa Fort, voices. It was revolutionary.

3 The same wish that I have had since I was 10 years old: Peace, ending of all war.

Wolfgang Muthspiel guitar, 1965 Austria

1 Honestly, many bands I play with are dream bands to me, but in the spirit of this game, why not Paul Motian on drums; Charlie Haden: bass; Keith Jarrett: piano; Billie Holiday: vocals; Miles Davis: trumpet; Wayne Shorter: tenor and soprano saxophone.

2 Very hard to choose only one, but I will say: listening to Pat Metheny, in my hometown, at the age of 16.

3 That we all develop our higher self and realize our potential.

Youn Sun Nah   vocal, 1969 South Korea

1 It would be made out of all the musicians I have sung with until now. Of course, I'm hoping to meet other musicians in the future, so the dream team can expand.

2 It was during the summer of 2018, I had the honor to be on the same stage as Norma Winstone, my favorite singer for 25 years. I was so touched to meet her.

3 That the future generations do not repeat the same mistakes we made.

Yuri Goloubev   bass, 1972 Russia

1 This boils down to "who are your favorite musicians?" or "which 10 albums you'd take with you on a desert island" type of questions :). I am not sure how fair this is, as there is a multitude of great artists, and picking just a few is not really possible. I can "form" a variety of potentially great bands out of those artists I did work with, and I did not, and — in the latter case — even if the individual musicians can be amazing, you never know whether this would work as a band. However, OK — let's put it like this: with Michael Brecker on sax, Eddie Daniels on clarinet, Alan Pasqua on piano, and Tony Williams on drums. But, once again, this is just one of a great many options.

2 Like with the previous question, there isn't just one. I can say, though, that what always gives me a nice satisfaction is performing in jazz line-ups, at the same venues and festivals where I still used to perform as a classical player, many years ago. I can, for example, mention the Perth Festival, Köln Philharmonie, Sala Verdi in Milan, and many more.

3 I wish that more and more "normal" people that do care about others (like the new Prime Minister of Armenia, the President of Croatia, etc.) were elected to govern nations.

PHOTO CREDITS

Antonio Porcar Cano, p.1; Janis Wilkins, p.1; Tony Kellers, p.4; Weimen Huang, p.5; Diana Acuña, p.6; Patricia Huchot Boissier, p.7; Glen Di Crocco, p.8; Caterinas foto, p.9; Marcin Kydrynski, p.13; Sylvie Da Costa, p.14; Lonnie Timmons, p.19; Sam Harfouche, p.22; Alan Messer, p.24; Pierre Darmon, p.24; Douwe Dijkstra, p.26; Monica Jane Frisell, p.30; Judy Kirtley, p.31 Paul Bevan, p.32; Roberto Cifarelli, p.33; Alberto Reina, p.35; Todd Winters, p.39; Bernard Vidal, p.40; Lafiya Watson Ramirez, p.42; Egil Hansen, p.42; Kaká B.M & Café Braga, p.43; Jens Bangsbo, p.47; Jean-Baptiste Millot, p.48; R. Andrew Lepley, p.49; Alfred Bailey, p.54; Paolo Soriani, p.55; Debra Scherre, p.57; Stephanie Ahn-Weiss, p.58; Me Whale China Shirt, p.63; Jimmy Katz, p.65; Josephine Zeitlin, p.71; Christopher Drukker, p.81; Liza McCarthy, p.83; SOUKIZY.COM, p.84; Patricia Watts, p.85; Caroline Forbes, p.88; Richard Koek, p.89; Martin Zeman, p.94; Brad Bruckman, p.96; Nina Simone Bentley, p.97; Kate Elliot, p.98; Giulio Carmassi, p.100; Mitch Haddad, p.101; Manfred Pollert, p.102; David Forman, p.103; Martine Thomas, p.104; Duda Lins, p.109; Samuele Romano, p.110; Vincent Soyez, p.114; Janis Wilkins, p.117; Stéphane Barthod, p.118; Conor Nickerson, p.120; Emilano Neri, p.123 Ssirius Pakzhad, p.125; Jamey Moncreif, p.126; Richard Conde, p.128; Judi Silvano, p.129; Robert Frahm, p.129; Michael Sheerer, p.130; Peter Freed, p.132; Emra Islek, p.132; Dragan Tasic, p.136; Myriam Vilas Boas, p.137; John Surman, p.139; Rolf Schoellkopf, p.140; Anna Webber, p.140; Renato Nunes, p.142; Elizabeth Leitzell, p.143; Erol Gurian, p.144; Juan Hitters, p.145; Bob Barry, p.146; Chico Rasta Brandão, p.148; Jean-Baptiste Millot, p.148; Caterina Di Perri, p.149; KIM FOX, p.153; Coutouzis, p.153; Torben Christensen, p.155; Kentaro Hisadomi, p.155; Fabrizio Sodani, p.156; Sauvage, p.157; Claire Stefani, p.158; K-Rade, p.159; Anna Yatskevich, p.160; D. Matvejev, p.161; Olff Appold, p.163; Michiko Morell, p.164; Claus Peuckert, p.165; Chris Drukker, p.166; David Redfern, p.169; L. Szelag, p.170; Jean-Baptiste Millot, p.171; Frankie Celenza, p.171; Chris Drucker, p.173; Melanie Baker-Futorian, p.175; Lieve Boussauw, p.176; Mireya Acierto, p.177; Jacky Lepage, p.178; Rob Shanahan, p.179; André Gustafson, p.181; Lande, p.182; Column-Ricardo-Rios, p.185; Ibrahim Elkest, p.187; John Rogers, p.191; Ravinia Festival, p.193; Rob Shanahan, p.194; Lorenzo de Simone, p.196; Erika Kapin, p.197; Roberto Russo, p.198; Carl Stormer, p.203; Luciano Viti, p.204; Washington Possato, p.205; Jacob Blickenstaff, p.206; Jorjana Kellaway, p.207; Andrea Nestreaj, p.207; Fortuna Sung, p.208; Mirna Modolo, p.210; Aleksey Shkoldin, p.211; Ethan Levitas, p.212; Pete Coco, p.213; Remi Angeli, p.214; Frank Woeste, p.215; Hardy Klink, p.216; Gabriel Baharlia, 217; Ed Ianni, p.218; Valentina Cenni, p.219; Chris Weiss, p.220; John Abbott, p.222; Simon Thomas, p.222; Ziga Koritnik, p.223; Aragon Outlook, p.226; Gorm Valentin, p.228; Peter Josyph, p.231; Angela Harrell, p.233; Barka Fabiánová, p.237; Antonio Armenta, p.238; Philip Stark, p.239; Lynne Harty, p.240; Jati Lindsay, p.241; Kasia Idzkowaska, p.242; Ken Weiss, p.243; Laura Pleifer, p.243.

Three Questions

Lilian Dericq with Enrico Pieranunzi

INDEX

Aaron Parks, ♫ 1
Aaron Diehl, 50
Abbey Lincoln, 193
Adam Cruz, ♫ 1, 59
Adam Holzman, ♫ 2
Adam Nussbaum, ♫ 2, 168
Adam O'Farrill, 241
Adam Rogers, 127
Airto Moreira, ♫ 3, 60, 90, 189
Al Cohn, 41, 129, 131, 228
Al Foster, 66, 77, 78, 134, 222
Al Green, 122, 193
Al Grey, 58, 134, 202
Alain Perez, 59
Alan Broadbent, ♫ 4
Alan Dawson, 170
Alan Holdsworth, 62
Alan Pasqua ♫ 5, 244
Alan Paul, 235
Albert Ayler, 23, 40
Albert Dailey, 2
Albert King, 206, 224
Albert Stinson, 154
Aldo Romano, ♫ 6
Alex Acuña, ♫ 6
Alex Taylor, 183
Ali Jackson, ♫ 7
Alice Coltrane, 1, 154, 220, 240
Allan Holdsworth, 2, 62, 69, 96, 134, 141
Allen Toussaint, 77
Alphonse Mouzon, 18
Alphonso Johnson, 65, 138

Ambrose Akinmusire, 62, 120, 241
Amina Claudine Myers, 240
Amir ElSaffar, 114
Anat Fort, ♫ 8
Anders Jormin, ♫ 9, 236
André Ceccarelli, ♫ 10, 189
Andreas Schaerer, ♫ 10
Andrew Cyrille, ♫ 11, 223
Andrew Hill, 215, 241
Andy Gonzalez, 53
Andy Laverne, ♫ 12
Andy Narell, 153
Angélica Negrón, 153
Angélique Kidjo, 117
Angelo Comisso, 161
Angus Young, 117
Anja Lechner, 92
Anna Maria Jopek, ♫ 12
Anthony Jackson, 70, 138
Antonio Carlos Jobim, 110, 155
Antonio Farao, ♫ 14
Antonio Hart, ♫ 15, 112
Antonio Sanchez, ♫ 16, 31
Aphex Twin, 117
Aretha Franklin, 54, 117, 121, 133, 157, 227
Ari Hoenig, ♫ 16, 111
Arild Andersen, ♫ 18, 161
Armando Marçal, 45
Arnett Cobb, 216
Arsenio Rodriguez, 117
Art Blakey, 26, 27, 35, 39, 41, 53, 54, 69, 75, 76, 77, 82, 86, 87, 131, 138, 152, 171, 175, 188, 205, 209, 218, 225, 239
Art Farmer, 26, 174, 175
Art Tatum, 26, 39, 84, 102, 134, 157, 193, 212, 224, 234
Arturo Sandoval, ♫ 19, 172
Arve Henriksen, 69, 236, 238
Arvell Show, 92
Astor Piazzolla, 60, 155
Audun Kleive, 133, 236
Avishai Cohen (trumpet), 67, 79, 180
Aydin Esen, ♫ 19

B.B. King, 133
Baby Dodds, 69, 76, 224
Baden Powell, 102, 189
Baptiste Trotignon, ♫ 21
Barack Obama, 42, 149, 179, 225
Barney Bigard, 92
Barney Kessel, 137, 205
Barre Phillips, ♫ 22
Barry Altschul, ♫ 23
Beatles, 230
Béla Bartók, 14
Béla Fleck, ♫ 23
Belton Evans, 134
Ben Sidran, ♫ 24
Ben Street, 59
Ben Webster, 34, 72, 116, 127, 197, 206, 224
Benjamin Koppel, ♫ 25
Benjamin Wendel, ♫ 25

♫ *Indicates musicians who answered the three questions.*

Benny Carter, 133
Benny Golson, ♪ viii, 2, **26**, 138, 163, 187
Benny Goodman, 23, 43, 72, 138, 228
Benny Green, ♪ **27**, 150, 169
Benny Powell, 134
Benoît Delbecq, ♪ **28**
Bernard Purdie, 206, 223
Bernie Worrell, 91
Bessie Smith, 224
Betty Carter, 67, 69, 88, 186, 227
Beyoncé, 147
Bhapuji Tisziji Munoz, 36-37
BHB (D.J.), 91
Big Sid Catlett, 104, 197
Bill Carrothers, ♪ **28**
Bill Cunliffe, 164
Bill Evans (piano), 18, 26, 29, 43, 51, 64, 65, 70, 78, 80, 82, 98, 102, 106, 109, 110, 116, 118, 127, 137, 146, 155, 162, 163, 164, 165, 174, 175, 179, 184, 188, 192, 195, 202, 205, 209, 211
Bill Evans (sax), ♪ **29**
Bill Frisell, ♪ 1, 8, 18, **29**, 121, 124, 138, 158, 169
Bill Harris, 228
Bill Mays, ♪ **31**
Bill McElhiney, 34
Bill Summers, 77
Bill Watrous, 4, 72
Bill Wither, 100
Billie Holiday, 25, 53, 69, 99, 102, 116, 121, 133, 165, 227, 240, 243
Billy Bang, 243
Billy Child, ♪ **31**, 129
Billy Cobham, 76
Billy Drummond, ♪ **32**, 139, 217
Billy Eckstein, 224
Billy Higgins, 36, 39, 50, 66, 101, 129, 173, 195, 212, 215, 221
Billy Kyle, 92
Billy Strayhorn, 134, 150
Bing Crosby, 234
Biréli Lagrène, 200

Bix Beiderbecke, 9, 72
Bjarte Eike, 133
Björk, 147, 225
Blue Mitchell, 24, 150,
Bob Berg, 2
Bob Brookmeyer, 2, 4, 26, 59, 60, 88, 109, 124, 174, 206, 235
Bob Cranshaw, 121, 173-174, 195
Bob Franceschini, 70
Bob Gordon, 134
Bob James, ♪ **34**
Bob Mann, 195
Bob Marley, 204
Bob Mintzer, ♪ **35**, 46
Bob Moses, ♪ 19, **36**, 104
Bob Sheppard, ♪ 31, **37**
Bob Stewart, 67, 133
Bobby Battles, 44
Bobby Broom, ♪ **39**
Bobby Few, ♪ **39**
Bobby Hutchinson, 141
Bobby LaVell, 112
Bobby McFerrin, 10, 25
Bobby Pring, 134
Bobby Shew ♪ **41**, 202
Bobby Timmons, 26
Bobby Watson, ♪ **41**, 240
Bola de Nieve, 183
Booker Little, 53, 138
Brad Mehldau, 45, 121, 129
Brad Shepik, 114
Branford Marsalis, 15, 69, 75, 82, 138, 183, 198
Brian Blade, 8, 18, 25, 31, 45, 59, 62, 67, 79, 83, 103, 146, 176, 207
Brian Bromberg, 12
Bruce Cox, 95
Bruce Forman, 202
Bruno Chevillon, 219
Bud Freeman, 92
Bud Powell, 2, 4, 23, 26, 39, 44, 68, 76, 95, 105, 141, 202, 207, 218, 224, 228, 232, 239
Buddy Montgomery, 66
Buddy Rich, 19, 35, 36, 41, 55, 72, 85, 155, 202

Buddy Tate, 113, 216
Bugge Wesseltoft, ♪ **42**
Bunky Green, 212
Buster Williams, 70, 75, 181
Butch Warren, 138
Byron Landham, 232
Byron Wallen, 138

Cachaito López, 204
Caetano Veloso, 102
Cameron Brown, 217
Cannonball Adderley, 41, 58, 73, 75, 87, 119, 131, 157, 171, 174, 179, 188, 196, 197, 206, 211, 228
Carey Evans, 202
Carl Fontana, 41, 228
Carl Winther, 229
Carlos Enrique, 43
Carlos Lyra, ♪ **43**
Carlos "Patato" Valdes, 183
Carmen Lundy, 240
Carmen McRae, 131, 160, 167, 213
Carol Fredette, 2
Caroline Shaw, 153
Carter Beaufort, 23
Cartola, 102
Cary Grant, 34
Catherine Leech, 32
Cecil Brooks III, 73
Cecil McBee, 64, 125
Cecil Taylor, 11, 39, 56, 88, 127, 158, 223
Cécile McLorin Salvant, 50
Cedar Walton, 66, 125, 154
Chaka Khan, 2
Chano Dominguez, ♪ **43**
Chano Pozo, 115
Charles Davis, 69
Charles Ives, 62
Charles Lloyd, 94, 188, 209
Charles McPherson, ♪ viii, **44**
Charles Mingus, 23, 44, 49, 69, 113, 115, 121, 135, 144, 175, 181, 183, 193, 205, 232, 241
Charlie Christian, 67, 87, 101, 104, 228

Charlie Haden, 1, 4, 36, 42, 52, 69, 78, 85, 92, 99, 101, 110, 115, 116, 129, 140, 141, 146, 167, 178, 183, 190, 191, 197, 203, 211, 225, 243

Charlie Mariano, 169

Charlie Parker, 2, 7, 11, 15, 23, 25, 26, 34, 45, 50, 53, 59, 69, 72, 76, 83, 85, 86, 95, 96, 105, 113, 115, 130, 124, 133, 136, 138, 141, 144, 150, 171, 173, 174, 179, 188, 197, 202, 205, 217, 218, 222, 224, 228, 232, 239, 241,

Charlie Porter, 50

Chet Baker, 4, 43, 55, 105, 175, 179, 205

Chick Corea, 18, 24, 35, 43, 93, 107, 112, 155, 157, 174, 179, 184

Chico Freeman, ♪ **44**

Chico Pinheiro, ♪ **45**

Chippie Hill, 113

Chris Cheek, 121

Chris Connor, 193

Chris Daddy Dave, 98

Chris Hunter, 61

Chris Komer, 114

Chris Minh Doky, ♪ **46**

Chris Parker, 195

Chris Potter, ♪ 16, 31, **48**, 77, 176

Chris Speed, 124

Christian Escoudé ♪ **48**

Christian Fennez, 182

Christian McBride ♪ **49**, 67, 77, 112, 125 138, 187, 207

Christian Scott, ♪ **49**, 77

Christian Thome, 161

Christine Jensen, ♪ **49**

Chucho Valdés, 111, 153, 172

Chuck Dominick, 206

Chuck Findley, 202

Chuck Israels, ♪ **50**

Chuck Loeb, 100

Chuck Rainey, 69

Clara Rockmore, 2

Clarence "C" Sharpe, 117

Clarence Penn, ♪ **52**, 232

Clark Terry, 7, 41, 55, 107, 133, 143, 153, 235

Clark Tracey, ♪ **52**

Claude Debussy, 14

Claudio Roditi, ♪ **53**, 59

Claus Ogerman, 137

Claus Stötter, 169

Clifford Brown, 27, 31, 38, 45, 50, 61, 86, 102, 133, 134, 138, 150, 171, 188, 205, 206, 121, 228

Clint Houston, 125

Clive Davis, 195

Clyde Stubblefield, 117

Coleman Hawkins, 23, 26, 69, 72, 113, 139, 167, 170, 193, 224

Collin Walcott, 191

Conte Candoli, 228

Cooper Moore, 243

Cootie Williams, 138

Count Basie, 14, 26, 56, 58, 67, 69, 76, 113, 131, 175, 188, 216, 224

Courtney Pine, ♪ **53**

Craig Street, 67

Craig Taborn, 62

Cuong Vu, 169

Curtis Fowlkes, 4

Curtis Fuller, 7, 26, 41, 45, 120, 125, 131, 150, 173, 221

Cyd Charisse, 235

Cyrus Chestnut, ♪ **54**, 77, 232

D'Angelo, 111, 124

Dado Moroni, ♪ **55**

Dan Tepfer, ♪ **57**

Dan Weiss, ♪ **58**, 62

Daniel Humair, ♪ **58**

Daniel Lanois, 182

Danilo Perez, ♪ **59**

Danny Gottlieb ♪ **60**

Darrell Grant, 73

Darryl Jones, 2

Dave Bargeron, 41, 61

Dave Brubeck, 175, 226

Dave Douglas, 124

Dave Holland, 5, 12, 21,49, 72, 109, 129, 130, 134, 148, 176, 177, 182, 201, 205

Dave Liebman, ♪ 3, 19, **61**, 123, 124, 188, 201

Dave Samuels, 184

Dave Steinmeyer, 61

Dave Taylor, 124

Dave Valentin, 53

David Binney, ♪ **62**

David Budway, 107

David Friesen, ♪ **64**

David Gilmore ♪ **65**

David Hazeltime, ♪ **66**

David Linx, ♪ **66**, 73

David Sanborn, 61

David Taylor, 124, 133

David Williams, ♪ **68**

David Wong, 113, 232

Dayna Stephens, ♪ **69**

Dean Brown, 34, 70

Delfeayo Marsalis, ♪ **69**, 82

Dennis Chambers, ♪ 2, 53, **70**, 157

Dennis Irwin, 134

Dennis Rollins, 138

Denny Zeitlin, ♪ **71**

Derya Turkan, 133

Dewey Redman, 115, 140, 165, 167, 203

Dexter Gordon, 26, 27, 39, 56, 87, 88, 97, 141, 150, 155, 197, 204, 212, 221, 227

Diane Schuur, ♪ **72**

Dianne Reeves, 60, 153

Dick Hyman, ♪ 43, **72**

Dick Oatts, 31, 232

Dicky Wells, 69, 113

Diederik Wissels ♪ 67-68, **73**

Diego Urcola, ♪ 43, **73**, 112

Dinah Washington, 133

Dizzy Gillespie, 2, 11, 15, 19, 23, 25, 26, 27, 41, 45, 53, 58, 59, 69, 76, 87, 90, 115, 124, 133, 147, 171, 172, 175, 188, 193, 197, 202, 224, 227, 228, 232, 239

DJ Olive, 191

Django Reinhardt, 25, 83, 137, 147

Djavan, 62, 102

Doc Cheatham, 134

Dominguinhos, 147
Dominique Pifarély, ♪ 73
Don Braden, ♪ 73
Don Byas, 113, 212
Don Cherry, 2, 36, 69, 92, 129, 183, 195, 225, 227, 236
Don Ellis, 22, 139
Don Grolnick, 195
Don Pullen, 44, 113, 115, 197
Donald Bailey, 50
Donald Brown, ♪ 75
Donald Edwards, ♪ 75
Donald Harrison, ♪ 49, **76**, 186
Donald Trump, 4, 27, 125, 175, 203, 209
Donny Hathaway, 176
Doris Day, 167
Dorothy Ashby, 189
Doudou N' Diaye, 117
Doug Weiss, ♪ 77
Douglas Purviance, 113, 133
Dr. John, 77
Dr. Lonnie Smith, ♪ 78
Dré Pallemaerts, ♪ 78
Drew Gress, 156
Duduka Da Fonseca, 31
Duke Ellington, 7, 11, 25, 26, 48, 76, 95, 101, 102, 121, 136, 144, 150, 165, 167, 175, 181, 188, 192, 197, 199, 200, 224, 225
Duke Jordan, 217
Dwayne Burno, 73
Dwayne Dolphin, 73

Earl Bostic, 25, 72
Earl Hines, 23, 105, 224
Ed Blackwell, 116, 168, 225
Ed Cherry, 56
Ed Neumeister, 117
Eddie Arkin, 150
Eddie Bert, 134
Eddie Chamblee, 134
Eddie Daniels, ♪ **78**, 244
Eddie Gomez, 2, 62, 99, 125, 188, 189, 201

Eddie Harris, 176
Eddie Henderson, 240
Eddie Jefferson, 25, 202
Eddie Locke, 134
Eddie "Lockjaw" Davis, 113, 150
Eddie Palmieri, 76
Eden Ladin, 16
Edgar Bateman, 38
Edward Simon, ♪ **79**, 240
Egberto Gismonti, 66, 115, 155
EIC (Ensemble intercontemporain), 19
Eivind Aarset, 171
Eivind Opsvik, 62
Eli Degibri, ♪ **79**
Eliane Elias, ♪ 2, **80**
Eliot Zigmund, ♪ **81**
Elis Regina, 9, 60, 224, 228, 234
Elisabeth Kontomanou, ♪ **82**
Ella Fitzgerald, 14, 53, 55, 69, 102, 133, 179, 197, 211, 235
Elliot Mason, 138, 230
Ellis Marsalis, ♪ **82**
Elmo Tanner, 34
Elvin Jones, 1, 12, 25, 26, 29, 36, 38, 39, 41, 44, 48, 59, 62, 64, 65, 69-70, 73, 76, 84, 85, 87, 88, 89, 93, 96, 99, 105, 115, 129, 130, 132, 133, 138, 140, 141, 144, 160, 168, 174-175, 179, 181, 183, 185, 187, 197, 198, 205, 212, 218, 227, 229, 239, 242
Emiliano Salvador, 183
Emma Dayhuff, 185
Ernestine Anderson, 225
Ennio Morricone, 106
Eno, 182
Enrico Pieranunzi, ♪ **83**, 105, 246
Enrico Rava, ♪ **84**
Eric Clapton, 141
Eric Dolphy, 23, 34, 36, 61, 124, 138, 165, 200
Eric Gravatt, ♪ **85**
Eric Harland, 31, 73, 79, 138, 225
Eric Reed, ♪ **85**
Eric Revis, 138, 183

Ernesto Nazareth, 102
Ernie Hayes, 134
Ernie Watts, ♪ **85**
Erroll Garner, 56, 113, 155
Esbjörn Svensson, 181
Esperanza Spalding, 9, 34, 77, 102, 158, 189, 226
Essiet Essiet, ♪ **86**, 97
Etta Jones, 174
Eumir Deodato, ♪ **87**, 234
Evan Parker, ♪ **88**
Evan Sherman, 113

Fatima Guedes, 102
Fats Navarro, 85, 120, 133, 144
Fats Waller, 39, 133, 150, 224
Fay Classen, ♪ **88**
Fay Victor, ♪ **89**
Fela Kuti, 204
Ferenc Nemeth, ♪ **90**
Ferenc Snétberger, 161
Flip Phillips, 129
Flora Purim, ♪ 3, 61, **90**, 189
Florian Weber, 161
Foley, ♪ **91**
Franco D'Andrea, ♪ **92**
François Couturier, ♪ **92**
François Moutin, 16
Frank Foster, 67
Frank Gambale, ♪ **93**
Frank Greene, 61, 112
Frank Rosolino, 120, 133, 138, 198, 228
Frank Sinatra, 38, 61, 80, 133, 179, 190, 234
Frank Tiberi, 129
Frank Woeste, 52
Frank Zappa, 110, 234
Fred Hersch, ♪ **94**
Fred Hopkins, 44, 223
Fred Wesley, ♪ 76, 91, **95**, 143
Freddie Green, 34, 207
Freddie Hendrix, 112
Freddie Hubbard, 4, 26, 38, 41, 49, 53, 59, 65, 66, 68, 73, 75, 76, 85, 87, 97, 125, 129, 131, 141, 143,

150, 157, 160, 173, 174, 181, 187, 196, 201, 211, 221, 241, 242
Freddy Cole, ♪ **95**
Freddy Mercury, 204
Freddy Stone, 91

Gal Costa, 234
Gary Bartz, 5, 55
Gary Burton, 43, 155
Gary Grainger, 70
Gary King, 34
Gary Peacock, 156, 191
Gary Smulyan, ♪ **95**, 112, 133
Gary Thomas, 15
Gary Valente, 99
Gary Versace, 3
Gary Winters, 95
Gautier Garrigue, 106
Geir Jensen, 236
Gene Ammons, 131, 150
Gene Krupa, 26
Gene Lake, 198
Gene Perla, 3
Gene Taylor, 24
Geoffrey Keezer, ♪ **96**
George Benson, 72, 87, 138, 157, 170, 172, 181, 187
George Bohanon, 69
George Cables, ♪ **97**
George Coleman, 31, 41, 66, 77, 125, 138
George Duke, 70, 157
George Gershwin, 144, 172
George Gruntz, 61
George Lewis, 23, 69
George Mraz, 106
George Russell, 5, 71, 176
George Shearing, 39, 72
Gerald Cleaver, 28
Geri Allen, 82, 101, 107, 167
Gerry Mulligan, 26, 138, 171
Gianni Basso, 55
Gil Evans, 2, 35, 60, 61, 66, 78, 90, 98-99, 110, 134, 175, 197
Gil Goldstein, ♪ 61, **98**, 259

Gilad Hekselman, ♪ 16, **99**
Ginger Smock, 199
Giovanni Hidalgo, 1, 60, 184
Giulio Carmassi, ♪ **99**
Glauco Venier, 183
Glenn Miller, 192
Gonzalo Rubalcaba, 67, 172, 185
Gracham Moncur III, 39
Graham Haynes, 241
Grant Gershon, 32
Grant Green, 153
Greg Gisbert, 112
Greg Osby, ♪ **101**
Gregoire Maret, ♪ **101**
Gregory Hines, 7
Gretchen Parlato, 101
Guinga, ♪ **102**
Gwilym Simcock, ♪ **103**

Hafez Modirzadeh, 240
Hal Galper, ♪ **104**
Hal Singer, ♪ **104**
Hamid Drake, 243
Hamilton de Holanda, ♪ **105**
Hampton Hawes, 139
Hank Jones, 48, 50, 134, 154, 163, 221, 225
Hank Mobley, 26, 39, 50, 54, 82, 239
Harish Raghavan, 149, 241
Harold "Shorty" Baker, 69
Harold Danko, ♪ **105**
Harold Marbern, 125, 154
Harpo Marx, 135
Harry "Sweets" Edison, 113, 131, 133
Harry Carney, 4, 72, 113, 150, 197
Harry Swift, 39
Harvey Mason, 34, 138, 195, 239
Hayden Powell, 108
Hazel Scott, 25
Hein Van de Geyn, ♪ **105**
Heitor Villa-Lobos, 102, 147
Helen Merrill, ♪ **106**
Helge Norbakken, 133

Hélio Delmiro, 102
Henri Texier, ♪ **106**
Henry Mancini, 155, 175
Herb Ellis, 27, 187
Herb Pomeroy, 170
Herbert Von Karajan, 19
Herbie Hancock, 14, 15, 16, 32, 35, 46, 49, 52, 53, 62, 64, 69, 70, 73, 76, 79, 87, 90, 91, 101, 107, 114, 116, 121, 125, 141, 148, 152, 155, 157, 167, 170, 172, 174, 180, 182, 186, 202, 205, 209, 212, 216, 222, 227, 239, 241, 242
Herman Foster, 150
Hermeto Pascoal, 1, 3, 90, 101, 105, 110, 154, 207
Hilton Ruiz, 53
Hiram Bullock, 240
Hiromi, 172
Holger Czukay, 182
Horace Silver, 24, 26, 31, 41, 168, 175, 200
Horacio Hernandez, 59
Howard Alden, 72
Howard Johnson, 41
Howard McGhee, 113
Hubert Laws, ♪ **107**, 109, 175

Ichiro Onoe, 39
Idris Muhammad, 150
Ignacio Berroa, 53, 56
Igor Stravinsky 10, 34, 117, 197
Ike Sturm, 176
Illinois Jacquet, 216, 224
Ingrid Jensen, ♪ **107**
Iro Haarla, ♪ **108**
Israel Lopez "Cachao" 153
Itzhak Perlman, 204
Ivan Lins, ♪ 62, **109**, 116

J.J. Johnson, 4, 7, 26, 34, 41, 49, 50, 53, 59, 68, 69, 73, 76, 83, 86, 120, 124, 131, 133, 138, 150, 168, 171, 174, 196, 198, 227, 228
Jaap Blonk, 133
Jabbo Smith, 113

Jack DeJohnette, 9, 12, 18, 36, 43, 49, 62, 69, 101, 114, 125, 135, 154, 157, 174-175, 180, 181, 182, 191, 196, 201, 203, 204, 209, 215, 227
Jack Teagarden, 69, 223, 224
Jack Wilson, 202
Jackie McLean, 125, 215, 221
Jackson Mathod, 138
Jaco Pastorius, 1, 2, 25, 35, 45, 59, 65, 67, 88, 93, 96, 103, 107, 138, 172, 175, 203
Jacqueline du Pré, 204
Jacques Demierre, 22
Jacques Morelenbaum, ♪ **110**
Jacques Schwarz-Bart, ♪ **110**
Jaki Byard, 89, 168
Jaleel Shaw, ♪ **112**
James Baldwin, 67
James Brown, 49, 204, 224, 227
James Carter, ♪ 7, **112**
James "Diamond" Williams, 91
James Francies, 125
James Gadson, 176
James "Jimmy" Heath, ♪ x, 26, **113**, 133, 173, 221
James Hurt, 111
James Jamerson, 122, 206
James Lewis, 39
James Moody, 3, 25, 133
James P. Johnson, 28
James Shipp, 176
James Taylor, 200
James-Allen Ford, 85
Jamie Baum, ♪ **114**
Jan Garbarek, 42, 46, 99, 108, 158
Jan Hammer, 93
Jane Bunnett, ♪ **115**
Jane Ira Bloom, ♪ **116**, 117
Jane Monheit, ♪ **116**
Janis Siegel, 202
Jason Horowitz, 193
Jason Jackson, 113
Jason Lindner, ♪ **117**
Jason Moran, 149

Jay Anderson, 2, 229
Jay Clayton, ♪ **117**
Jayne Cortez, 89
Jaz Sawyer, 147
Jean Barraqué, 19
Jean Toussaint, 138
Jean-François Jenny-Clark, 58
Jean-Luc Ponty, ♪ **118**
Jean-Michel Pilc, ♪ 16, **119**
Jean-Paul Céléa, 92
Jean-Pierre Rampal, 107
Jeanine Santana, 202
Jeanne Lee, 225
Jeb Patton, 113
Jef Lee Johnson, 91, 198
Jeff Ballard, ♪ **120**, 217
Jeff Beck, 2, 186, 234
Jeff Hamilton, 229
Jeff Hirshfield, 114,
Jeff "Tain" Watts, ♪ 69, 73, 107, **121**, 138, 183
Jelly Roll Morton, 76
Jemeel Moondoc, 223
Jeremy Pelt, ♪ **121**
Jerome Harris, 115
Jerome Richardson, 69
Jerry Bergonzi, 2
Jerry Granelli, 117
Jesse Lewis, 176
Jessé Sadoc, 102
Jessica Williams, ♪ **121**
Jessie Powell, 113
Jim Beard, ♪ 65, 70, **122**
Jim Black, ♪ 8, **123**
Jim McNeely, ♪ 3, **124**
Jim Rotondi, ♪ **125**
Jimi Hendrix, 1, 2, 25, 29, 49, 59, 121, 144, 154, 204, 215, 240
Jimmy Blanton, 23, 69, 84, 121, 199, 207
Jimmy Garrison, 2, 48, 59, 64, 130, 147, 195, 203, 212, 229, 240
Jimmy Giuffre, 92, 129, 167
Jimmy Johnson, 31
Jimmy Knepper, 50, 115, 174, 193

Jimmy Lewis, 134
Jimmy Luncford, 224
Jimmy Lyons, 11
Jimmy Ponder, 198
Jimmy Slyde, 23
Jimmy Smith, 78, 131, 133, 157, 175, 206
Joanne Brackeen, ♪ **125**
João Gilberto, 43, 110, 190, 199, 203
João Horta, 234
Joe Chambers, ♪ **126**, 138
Joe Cucuso, 22
Joe Farrell, 90, 99
Joe Henderson, 2, 12, 31, 39, 41, 64, 73, 77, 85, 87, 125, 132, 134, 138, 141, 144, 174, 175, 203, 211
Joe Jones, 4, 76, 157,
Joe LaBarbera, ♪ 80, **127**, 164
Joe Locke, ♪ 96, **127**, 188
Joe Lovano, ♪ 3, 6, **129**, 134, 157
Joe Pass, 26
Joe Sanders, 73
Joe Temperley, 50
Joe Venuti, 34
Joe Williams, 50, 61
Joel Frahm, ♪ **129**
Joey Alexander, 43
Joey Baron, ♪ **130**, 156, 191
Joey Calderazzo, ♪ 2, **130**, 183
Johannes Weidenmüller, 16
John Abercrombie, 2, 105, 156, 174, 175, 191
John Bonham, 147
John Clark, 61
John Clayton, ♪ **131**
John Collins, 113
John Coltrane, 1, 2, 4, 9, 11, 12, 23, 25, 26-27, 32, 36, 39, 41, 45, 48, 49, 51, 52, 53, 58, 59, 61, 62, 64, 67, 68, 69, 76, 83, 86, 90, 92, 93, 99, 102, 105, 109, 110, 121, 124, 130, 131, 132, 133, 135, 138, 141, 143, 148, 154, 160, 171, 173, 174, 175, 183, 184, 185, 188, 191, 193, 196, 197-198, 200, 201, 203,

205, 211, 215, 217, 218, 222, 224, 225, 227, 229, 235, 239
John Engels, 105
John Escreet, 114
John Gilmore, 240
John Guerin, 99
John Hébert, 94
John Lee, 56,
John Lee Hooker, 140
John Lewis, 113, 173, 216
John McLaughlin, 60, 61, 70, 138, 169, 205
John Mosca, 113
John Patitucci, ♪ 59, 90, **132**, 184
John Scofield, 2, 3, 16, 70, 99, 103, 134, 138, 169, 174, 228
John Stubblefield, 240
John Taylor, 18, 177, 182
John Zorn, 67
Johnathan Blake, ♪ **132**, 177
Johnny Aman, 229
Johnny Coles, 120
Johnny Griffin, 55, 138, 187
Johnny Hartman, 133
Johnny Hodges, 26, 41, 69, 72, 77, 133, 150, 193, 235
Johnny Mandel, 137
Jøkleba, 133
Jon Balke, ♪ **133**
Jon Christensen, 42, 105, 178, 182, 203, 236
Jon Faddis, ♪ 26, 61, **133**, 173
Jon Gordon, ♪ **134**
Jon Hendricks, 7, 25
Jonas Burgwinkel, 169
Jonathan Batiste, 77
Jonathan Finlayson, 241
Jonathan Kreisberg, ♪ **134**
Joni Mitchell, 38, 107, 188, 207, 215
Jörg Brinkmann, 161
Jorge "El Niño" Alfonso, 154
Jorge Rossy, ♪ **135**
Jose Madera, 202
Jose Pintor, 202

Joseph Jarman, 197
Joseph Magnarelli, ♪ **136**
Joshua Redman, 67, 242
Joyce Moreno, ♪ **137**
Julian Joseph, ♪ **138**
Julian Priester, 117
Julian Sanchez, 169
Junior Cook, 24
Junior Mance, 154
Justin Brown, 62
Justin Faulkner, ♪ **138**, 139

Kadri Gopalnath, 212
Kai Winding, 34, 198
Karaikudi Mani, 115
Karin Krog, ♪ **139**
Karlheinz Stockhausen, 117
Karriem Riggins, 226
Keith Emerson, 155
Keith Jarrett, 6, 58, 62, 78, 85, 146, 176, 183, 191, 209, 227, 243
Keith Richards, 98
Ken Filiano, 118
Ken Peplowski, 72
Kendrick Lamar, 53
Kenny Barron, 154, 174
Kenny Burrell, 26, 197
Kenny Clarke, 41, 113, 134, 135, 207
Kenny Dorham, 7, 26, 95, 135, 138, 173
Kenny Garrett, 59, 87, 121, 170
Kenny John, 92
Kenny Kirkland, 3, 39, 69, 73, 87, 121, 127, 198
Kenny "Pancho" Hagood, 113
Kenny Washington, 48, 50, 198
Kenny Werner, ♪ **140**
Kenny Wessel, 115
Kenny Wheeler, 3, 88, 105, 146, 169, 174, 176, 182
Kent Carter, 23
Kevin Eubanks, ♪ **140**
Kevin Hays, ♪ **141**
Kevin Oliver, 70

Khalil Madhi, 134
Kid Ory, 69
Kip Hanrahan, 67
Kirk Whalum, 34
Kit Downes, ♪ **141**
Klaus Gesing, 183
Kurt Elling, ♪ **141**
Kurt Rosenwinkel, ♪ 43, 124, **141**, 142

Lakecia Benjamin, ♪ **143**
Lalo Schifrin, 134
Langston Hughes, 25
Larry Bunker, 50
Larry Coryell, ♪ **144**
Larry Grenadier, ♪ 121, **144**
Larry Koonse, ♪ 146
Larry McKenna, 41
Larry Young, 5, 140
Lars Danielsson, 181
Laurie Antonioli, ♪ **146**
Led Zeppelin, 234
Lee Konitz, 4, 57, 168, 175
Lee Morgan, 26, 27, 39, 41, 45, 82, 131, 138, 139, 167, 175, 185, 215, 227
LeeAnn Ledgerwood, ♪ **147**
Leila Pinheiro, 102
Lenine, ♪ **147**
Lennie Tristano, 67, 93, 134
Lenny White, 77, 91, 170, 228
Leo Genovese, 229
Leo Nocentelli, 76
Leo Taylor, 183
Leonard Bernstein, 22, 46, 102, 155
Leonard Slatkin, 172
Leroy "Sugarfoot" Bonner, 91
Les McCann, 143, 206
Lester Bowie, 113, 197
Lester Young, 2, 4, 7, 18, 69, 104, 105, 106, 113, 127, 133, 135, 168, 188, 202, 213, 215, 224
Lew Soloff, 61, 99
Lew Tabackin, 41

Lewis Nash, 27, 31, 113
Linda Oh, 125
Lionel Hampton, 12, 26, 69
Lionel Loueke, ♪ 59, 90, **148**, 152
Lisa Fischer, 127
Little Richard, 227
Logan Richardson, ♪ **149**
Lorraine Feather, ♪ **150**
Lou Donaldson, ♪ **150**
Lou Rawls, 61
Louis Armstrong, 2, 4, 7, 23, 26, 44, 56, 58, 61, 67, 69, 72, 76, 82, 92, 95, 105, 113, 120, 131, 133, 157, 176, 192, 193, 197, 218, 223, 224, 227, 232
Louis Hayes, ♪ ix, **152**
Louis Jordan, 195
Louis Moutin, ♪ **152**
Louis Sclavis, 8
Luciana Souza, ♪ 32, **152**
Luciano Perrone, 105
Lucky Thompson, 50
Luis Conte, ♪ **153**
Luis Perdomo, ♪ **154**, 229
Luiz Gonzaga, 234
Lula Galvao, 102
Luther Vandross, 157
Lyle Mays, 31, 99
Lynne Arriale, ♪ **154**

Maceo Parker, 53
Machito, 224
Mads Vinding, ♪ **155**
Maeve Gilchrist, 176
Magda Mayas, 225
Mahalia Jackson, 193
Makoto Ozone, ♪ **155**
Manfred Eicher, 92, 109, 171, 225
Manu Codjia, 106
Manu Katché, ♪ **156**
Marc Copland, ♪ 146, **156**
Marc Johnson, 3, 80, 84, 127
Marcin Wasilewski, ♪ **157**
Marcus Miller, ♪ 15, 70, 138, 143, 147, **157**, 170, 186

Marcus Robert, 7
Marcus Tardelli, 102
Maria Callas, 144
Maria João, 73
Maria Schneider, 9, 66, 177, 178
Marian McPartland, 185
Marilyn Crispell, ♪ **158**
Marilyn Mazur, ♪ **158**, 159, 225
Mario Rivera, 53, 197
Mark Egan, 60
Mark Gross, 112
Mark Levinson, 23
Mark Shim, 240
Mark Turner, 79, 121
Mark Walker, 184
Mark Whitfield, ♪ 77, 138, **160**
Markku Ounaskari, 108
Markus Stockhausen, ♪ **161**
Marshall Hawkins, 202
Martial Solal, 14, 120
Martin Taylor, ♪ **162**
Martin Wind, ♪ **163**
Marty Morrell, ♪ **164**
Marvin Gaye, 25
Mary Lou Williams, 7, 193, 197, 227
Mathias Eick, 73
Mathias Rüegg, ♪ **165**
Matt Brewer, 16, 62
Matt Mitchell, ♪ 62, **165**
Matt Penman, ♪ 16, 79, 147, **165**
Matt Wilson, ♪ **167**
Matthieu Michel, 171, 225
Maurice Ravel, 80
Maurice White, 93
Mavis Staples, 91
Max Roach, 39, 49, 50, 68, 104, 138, 162, 188, 193, 217, 232
Maynard Ferguson, 69
McCoy Tyner, 3, 41, 44, 49, 64, 76, 85, 86, 105, 112, 121, 132, 143, 160, 174, 205, 229, 239
Mel Lewis, 35, 124, 133, 175, 188, 228
Melissa Aldana, ♪ **167**

Mercedes Cortes, 204
Merle Haggard, 62
Meshell Ndegeocello, 59, 140
Michael Baker, 31
Michael Brecker, 19, 45, 46, 88, 98, 103, 125, 146, 163, 175, 181, 187, 188, 205, 207, 244
Michael Clarke, 186
Michael Formanek, ♪ **168**
Michael Gibbs, ♪ **168**
Michael Jackson, 179
Michal Urbaniak, ♪ **170**
Michel Benita, ♪ **171**
Michel Camilo, ♪ **171**
Michel Legrand, 175
Michel Petrucciani, 99, 228
Michele Hendricks, 118
Michelle Obama, 42, 225
Mick Goodrick, 19
Mickey Roker, 173-174
Mieko Miyazaki, 171
Miguel "Anga" Diaz, 59, 204
Miguel Zenón, ♪ 79, 154, **172**
Mike Clark, 77
Mike LeDonne, ♪ **173**
Mike Manieri, 35
Mike Mossman, 112
Mike Richmond, ♪ **174**
Mike Stern, ♪ **175**
Mike Walker, ♪ **176**, 182
Mildred Falls, 193
Miles Black, 50
Miles Davis, 1, 2, 3, 10, 14, 15, 16, 18, 21, 23, 25, 26, 28, 32, 44, 45, 46, 50, 52, 53, 59, 62, 64, 67, 71, 76, 79, 90, 91, 92, 94, 98, 102, 104, 109, 110, 114, 116, 120, 130, 132, 133, 140, 141, 154, 157, 158, 160, 163, 167, 169, 170, 172, 174, 175, 181, 183, 184, 188, 191, 194, 197, 200, 201, 203, 204, 211, 217, 222, 224, 227, 230, 235, 239, 241, 243
Miles Evans, 61
Milt Hinton, 72, 197

Milt Jackson, 26, 58, 69, 75, 87, 109, 131, 133, 173, 175, 213
Milton Nascimento, 60, 102, 152, 189, 234, 240
Mino Cinelu, 2
Miroslav Vitous, 19
Mitch Mitchell, 93
Mona Boutchebak, 133
Mongo Santamaria, 53, 172
Monica Salmaso, 102
Monica Zetterlund, 51
Monty Alexander, ♪ 131, 154, **176**
Morton Feldman, 66
Morton Schmidt, 146
Mtume, 170
Muhal Richard Abrams, 23, 117
Mulgrew Miller, 15, 26, 87, 121, 134
Murray McEachern, 131

Nadje Noordhuis, ♪ **176**
Nailor Proveta, 102
Nana Vasconcelos, 105, 137, 147, 182, 240
Nancy Wilson, 38, 131
Nasheet Waits, 149
Nat Adderley, 39, 174
Nat King Cole, 56, 127, 135, 192
Nate Radley, 3
Nate Wood, 62
Nathalie Loriers, ♪ **178**
Nathan East, ♪ **179**
Neil Clarke, 240
Niels-Henning Ørsted Pedersen, 19, 48, 58
Nguyên Lê, ♪ 146, **180**
Niccolo Paganini, 199
Nicholas Payton, 226, 232
Nick Brignola, 34, 202
Nick Smith, 70
Nico Assumpçao, 105
Nicolaï Rimsky-Korsakov, 87
Niels Lan Doky, ♪ **181**
Nikhil Banerjee, 58
Nils Landgren, ♪ **181**

Nils Petter Molvaer, ♪ **182**
Nina Simone, 147
Nitai Hershkovits, 16
Norma Winstone, ♪ 99, 118, **182**, 244
Notorious B.I.G., 117
Nusrat Ali Fatey Khan, 200

Ohad Talmor, 3
Olga Guillot, 60
Oliver Nelson, 76, 207
Olivier Messiaen, 135
Omar Hakim, 134
Omar Sosa, ♪ **183**
Orestes Vilató, 1
Orlando le Fleming, ♪ 16, **183**
Ornette Coleman, 1, 23, 28, 36, 69, 138, 139, 158, 167, 191, 227
Oscar Peterson, 19, 20, 23, 26, 27, 48, 56, 58, 102, 104, 131, 155, 187, 205, 234
Oscar Pettiford, 11, 25, 39, 44, 144, 167, 218
Osie Johnson, 72
Oteil Burbridge, 101
Oyvind Hegg-Lunde, 225
Oz Noy, 3

Paco Sery, ♪ **184**
Palghat Raghu, 236
Palle Danielson, 178
Paolo Fresu, ♪ **184**
Papa Jo Jones, 69, 157, 167, 213
Paquito D'Rivera, ♪ 53, 153, 172, **184**
Pat Boone, ,234
Pat Martino, ♪ 87, 138, **185**
Pat Metheny, 8, 16, 60, 73, 98, 99-100, 109, 135, 138, 149, 163, 174-175, 179, 181, 203, 207, 244
Patricia Barber, ♪ **185**
Patti Lupone, 34
Paul Bley, 23, 115, 191, 225
Paul Chambers, 1, 7, 27, 32, 41, 44, 52, 54, 68, 76, 85, 95, 121, 136, 141, 160, 173, 187,195, 196, 205, 209, 211, 225
Paul Desmond, 23, 185
Paul Gonsalves, 5, 50, 169, 235
Paul Jackson, ♪ 138, **186**
Paul McCandless, 191
Paul Motian, 5, 8, 57, 64, 84, 92, 129, 140, 146, 203, 219, 220, 243
Paulinho Da Costa, ♪ 109, **186**, 189
Paulinho da Viola, 102
Paulo Horta, 234
Paulo Sérgio Santos, 102
Pedram Khavarzamini, 133
Pee Wee Ellis, ♪ **187**
Peppe Morola, 202
Pepper Adams, 7, 41, 95, 124, 131, 133, 138, 173
Per Jørgensen, 133
Percy Heath, 113
Percy Pursglove, 169
Pete La Roca, 36
Peter Erskine ♪ 35, 129, **188**, 203
Peter Gabriel, 2, 52
Peter Madsen, 95
Peter Sprague, 31
Petter Eldh, 28
Pharoah Sanders, 36, 158
Phil Markowitz, ♪ **188**
Phil Wilson, 85, 113, 202
Phil Woods, 3, 31, 41, 50, 134, 174-175
Philip Glass, 66
Philippe Baden Powell, ♪ **189**
Philippe Le Baraillec, ♪ **190**
Philippe Garcia, 171
Phillip Whack, 95
Philly Joe Jones, 4, 26, 48, 55, 95, 121, 125, 133, 157, 163, 206, 239
Phineas Newborn, 87, 155, 198
Pierre Michelot, 48
Pierre Van Dormael, 67
Pino Palladino, 127
Pixinguinha, 102, 105, 147, 207, 234

Questlove, 165
Quincy Jones, 34, 69, 98, 155, 179

Rahsaan Roland Kirk, 113
Ralph Alessi, ♪ **191**
Ralph MacDonald, 195
Ralph Penland, 107
Ralph Peterson, 239
Ralph Towner, ♪ **191**
Ramsey Lewis ♪ ix, **193**
Ran Blake, ♪ **193**
Rance Allen, 91
Randy Brecker, ♪ 35, 61, 104, 154, 163, 175, **194**
Randy Weston, 89
Raphael Rabello, 102
Raphe Malik, 223
Rashied Ali, 36, 44
Raul De Souza, ♪ 147, **196**
Ravi Coltrane, 125, 154, 198, 229
Ravi Shankar, 147, 175
Ray Anderson, ♪ **197**
Ray Barretto, 136, 154
Ray Brown, 23, 27, 39, 55, 58, 69, 76, 116, 131, 133, 138, 141, 162, 171, 193, 199, 205, 213, 216, 225, 228, 229
Ray Bryant, 26, 154
Ray Charles, 67, 121, 193, 241
Ray Nance, 167
Ray Santisi, 170
Red Garland, 75, 87, 172, 196, 239
Red Mitchell, 31, 139
Red Rodney, 53
Reggie Washington, ♪ **197**
Reggie Watkins, 202
Regina Carter, ♪ **199**
Reginald Veal, 82, 138
Reginald Ward, 95
Renaud Garcia-Fons, 146
René Marie, ♪ **199**
Renee Rosnes, 3
Return to Forever, 93
Rich Perry, 209
Richard Allen, 122

Richard Bona, ♪ **200**
Richard B. Boone, 120
Richard Davis ♪ ix, 165, 185, **200**
Richard Egües, 183
Richard Galliano, ♪ **200**
Richie Beirach, ♪ 2, 62, 115, 146, 201, 259
Richie Cole, ♪ 25, **202**
Rick James, 227
Rick Margitza, ♪ 52, **203**
Rick Wakeman, 155
Rita Marcotulli, ♪ **203**
Rob Brown, 223, 243
Robert Hurst, 31
Robert Pete Williams, 193
Robert Plant, 204
Robert Rockwell, 85
Roberta Flack, 69
Roberta Gambarini, 113
Robertino Silva, 239
Roberto Fonseca, ♪ **204**
Roberto Gatto, ♪ **205**
Roberto Menescal, ♪ **205**
Robin Eubanks, ♪ 79, **205**
Robin McKelle, ♪ **206**
Roby Lakatos, 172
Rodney Holmes, 65
Rodney Skeet Curtis, 70
Rodney Whitaker, 15, 138, 232
Rodolfo Stroeter, 137
Roger Kellaway, ♪ 154, **206**
Roland Kirk, 113, 175
Roman Diaz, 59
Romero Lubambo, ♪ 184, 207
Ron Carter ♪ ix, 3, 14, 26, 32, 43, 49, 55, 59, 66, 69, 70, 71, 73, 75, 76, 77, 79, 84, 90, 107, 112, 113, 114, 116, 125, 132, 138, 167, 198, 200, **207**, 209, 217, 221, 222, 227, 241, 242
Ron Evaniuk, 85
Ron Matthewsen, 235
Ron McClure, ♪ 3, **209**
Ronnie Cuber, 50
Rosa Passos, ♪ **209**

Rosario Giuliani, ♪ **211**
Roscoe Mitchell, 197
Roswell Rudd, 39, 92, 223
Roy Brooks, 24
Roy Campbell, 243
Roy Eldridge, 5, 53, 89, 134, 213, 224
Roy Hargrove, 111, 198
Roy Haynes, 15, 26, 36, 43, 50, 64, 76, 112, 121, 136, 138, 141, 143, 175, 199, 216, 225, 239, 240, 242
Roy McCurdy, ♪ **211**
Rudresh Mahanthappa, ♪ 202, **212**
Rudy Royston, 125
Rufus Reid, ♪ 124, **212**, 229
Russell Bennett, 138
Russell Ferrante, 150
Russell Malone, ♪ **213**, 296
Ryan Kisor, 7
Rza, 53

Sal Nistico, 50
Sam Dillon, 112
Sam Jones, 66, 82, 167, 198, 211
Sam Rivers, 11, 23, 56, 65, 165, 170
Sam Sadigursky, 114
Sammy Davis, 34, 179, 234
Sammy DeLeon, 202
Samuel Blaser, ♪ **214**
Sandman Sims, 7
Sarah Kirkland Snyder, 153
Sarah Vaughan, 7, 60, 61, 131, 133, 216, 221
Scott Colley, ♪ 16, 25, 31, 52, 79, 129, 152, **215**
Scott Hamilton, ♪ **216**
Scott LaFaro, 53, 64, 78, 83, 105, 157, 164, 191
Scott Robinson, 164
Seamus Blake, ♪ 2, **216**, 240
Sébastien Texier, 106
Serge Chaloff, 193, 206
Sergei Prokofiev, 155

Shai Maestro, ♪ **217**
Shara Nova, 153
Sheila Jordan, ♪ 3, 5, 118, **217**
Shelly Berg, 150
Shirley Horn, 139, 199, 229
Shirley Scott, 199
Shobha Gurtu, 236
Shorty Trombone, 153
Sibongile Khumalo, 60
Sidney Bechet, 69, 76, 89, 138, 197, 224
Sister Rosetta Tharpe, 227
Slam Stewart, 76, 104, 113
Slide Hampton, ♪ 41, 53, 55, 66, 67, 124, 133, 173, 174, **218**, 222, 227
Slim Gaillard, 115
Sly Stone, 91
Smitty Smith, 31
Snooky Young, 124, 131, 133, 228
Sonny Clark, 27,
Sonny Fortune, ♪ **218**
Sonny Rollins, 3, 11, 26, 39, 55, 58, 59, 94, 97, 124, 133, 134, 141, 167, 187, 195, 197, 202, 207, 212, 213, 222, 225, 227, 239
Sonny Stitt, 91, 150, 202, 228
Specs Wright, 113
Spike Jones, 34
Squarepusher, 62
Stan Getz, 2, 28, 43, 50, 125, 129, 155, 175, 234
Stan Kenton, 95, 230
Stan Tracey, 52, 235
Stanley Clarke, 23, 53, 70, 93
Stanley Turrentine, 39, 170, 174, 229
Steely Dan, 38, 70
Stefano Bollani, ♪ **218**
Stefon Harris, 79, 232
Stéphan Oliva, ♪ **219**, 225
Stéphane Grappelli, 162
Stephanie Richards, ♪ **220**
Stephen Scott, 240
Steve Cardenas, ♪ 2, **221**

Steve Coleman, 67, 124, 191, 240
Steve Davis, ♪ 113, **221**
Steve Gadd, 2, 100, 153
Steve Grossman, 147
Steve Khan, 195
Steve Kuhn, ♪ 36, 217, **222**
Steve Laspina, ♪ **222**
Steve Lawrence, 61
Steve Martin, 34
Steve Swallow, 3, 43, 169
Steve Swell, ♪ **223**, 243
Steve Thornton, 91
Steve Turre, ♪ **224**
Steve Wilson, ♪ 31, **225**
Stevie Wonder, 1, 21, 72, 143, 179, 191, 193, 201-202, 222
Sting, 8, 61, 98,
Sullivan Fortner, 43
Susanne Abbuehl, ♪ **225**

Tadataka Unno, ♪ **225**
Tal Farlow, 234
Tara Bouman, 161
Tarus Mateen, 232
Tata Güines, 19
Taylor Eigsti, ♪ **225**
Ted Dunbar, 113
Ted Nash, 7
Teddy Wilson, 106, 224
Teju Cole, 240
Teo Macero, 230
Terell Stafford, 232, 240
Terence Blanchard, ♪ 23, **227**
Terreon Gully, 127
Terri Lyne Carrington, ♪ 59, 125, **227**
Terry Gibbs, ♪ ix, **228**
Terumasa Hino, 2
Thad Jones, 35, 38, 41, 55, 95, 124, 134, 155, 175, 181, 188
The Funky Meters, 76
The Headhunters, 76
The Manhattan Transfer, 25
Thelonius Monk, 53, 77, 236, 239
Thomas Fonnesbæk, ♪ **228**

Thomas Lehn, 22
TIG, 3
Tigran Hamasyan, 16
Till Brönner, ♪ **229**
Tim Hagans, ♪ **229**
Tim Hauser, 25
Tim Warfield, ♪ **232**
Tina Turner, 147
Tineke Postma, 178
Tito Puente, 35, 53, 172
Tito Rodriguez, 224
Tivon Pennicott, 16
Todd Coolman, 2
Tom Harrell, ♪ 41, 55, 134, 154, 217, **232**, 239, 242, 260
Tom Malone, 61
Tom Scott, 207
Tommy Dorsey, 202
Tommy Flanagan, 50, 95, 116, 154, 168, 175
Tommy Potter, 217
Toninho Horta, ♪ **234**
Tony Allen, 117
Tony Coe, ♪ **235**
Tony Kofi, 138
Tony Scott, 92
Tony Williams, 5, 14, 25, 46, 49, 59, 64, 67, 71, 76, 84, 85, 86, 110, 114, 121, 120, 138, 148, 165, 167, 188, 191, 217, 222, 239, 241, 242, 244
Toots Thielemans, 3, 67, 69, 80, 88, 103, 109, 123, 147, 175
Tord Gustavsen, ♪ **236**
Torrie Zito, 106
Toshiko Akiyoshi, 41
Treme Young, 227
Tracey Coryell, 144
Tricky Sam Nanton, 7, 133
Trilok Gurtu, ♪ **236**
Trummy Young, 92
Trygve Seim, ♪ 108, 236, **238**
Turk Mauro, 202
Tutty Moreno, 137
Tyshawn Sorey, 240

Ugonna Okegwo, ♪ 125, **238**
Ulf Krokfors, 108
Urbie Green, 69, 72
Urs Leimgruber, 22
Ursula Dudziak, 118

Vernon Biddle, 113
Vic Dickenson, 69
Vic Juris, 3, 202
Victor Borge, 34
Victor Feldman, 53, 192
Victor Lewis, ♪ 97, 185, **239**
Victor Provost, 184
Vijay Iyer, ♪ **240**
Vince Mendoza, 5, 35, 46, 163
Vincent Gardner, 7
Vincent Le Quang, 106
Vinnie Colaiuta, 3, 31, 109, 152
Wadada Leo Smith, 240
Wallace Roney, ♪ **241**
Walter Smith III, ♪ **241**

Warne Marsh, 1
Wayne Bergeron, 61
Wayne Dockery, 39, 104
Wayne Escoffery, ♪ **242**
Wayne Shorter, 1, 2, 14, 16, 26, 31, 46, 49, 59, 62, 64, 65, 71, 73, 78, 79, 87, 90, 92, 99, 101, 105, 107, 109, 114, 116, 121, 132, 148, 152, 157, 163, 166, 180, 183, 189, 201, 203, 205, 216, 222, 225, 227, 228, 236, 239, 240, 241, 243
Weather Report, 6, 123
Wes Montgomery, 4, 7, 41, 48, 55, 86, 131, 132, 133, 138, 173, 174, 179, 207, 209, 221, 229, 235
Whitney Houston, 227
Wilbur Ware, 89, 135
Will Lee, 100, 195
William Parker, ♪ **223**, 243
Willie Weeks, 176
Winston Clifford, 235
Witold Lutoslawski, 62

Wolfert Brederode, 225
Wolfgang Amadeus Mozart, 20, 184
Wolfgang Haffner, 181
Wolfgang Muthspiel, ♪ **243**
Woody Allen, 34
Woody Herman, 129
Woody Shaw, 12, 15, 19, 41, 87, 115, 132, 138, 240
Wycliffe Gordon, 138
Wynton Kelly, 41, 82, 87, 174, 195, 209, 211
Wynton Marsalis, 26, 138, 184

Yellowjackets, 35, 36
Youn Sun Nah, ♪ **244**
Yuri Goloubev, ♪ **244**
Yusef Lateef, 78

Zack Lober, 114
Zakir Hussein, 59, 200
Zoot Sims, 50, 55, 129

ACKNOWLEDGMENTS

Thank you Richie Beirach and Gil Goldstein for your help and support from the very beginning of this book.

Thank you Ruben Greenberg for your rigorous proofreading and translations.

Lydie and Jim Haenlin, thank you for the realization of this exciting project.

ABOUT THE AUTHOR

Lilian Dericq, PhD in Musicology, has been teaching Jazz Harmony at the University of Paris-8 for more than twenty years. He also teaches piano at the Bill Evans Piano Academy, a music school founded in Paris in 1996 by Bernard Maury and Samy Abenaïn. Lilian has been heading this well renowned, highly regarded school since 2005.

A passionate lover of music, and jazz in particular, Lilian has published several books on Harmony and Jazz theory (Hal Leonard, Outre-Mesure). However, he sees this book not as a scholastic endeavor, but an homage to the great musicians he met or talks about in his classes and conferences. Those many men and women have been, and still are inspiring him and his students deeply.

Lilian Dericq with Tom Harrell

www.ingramcontent.com/pod-product-compliance
Lightning Source LLC
Chambersburg PA
CBHW041410300426
44114CB00028B/2968